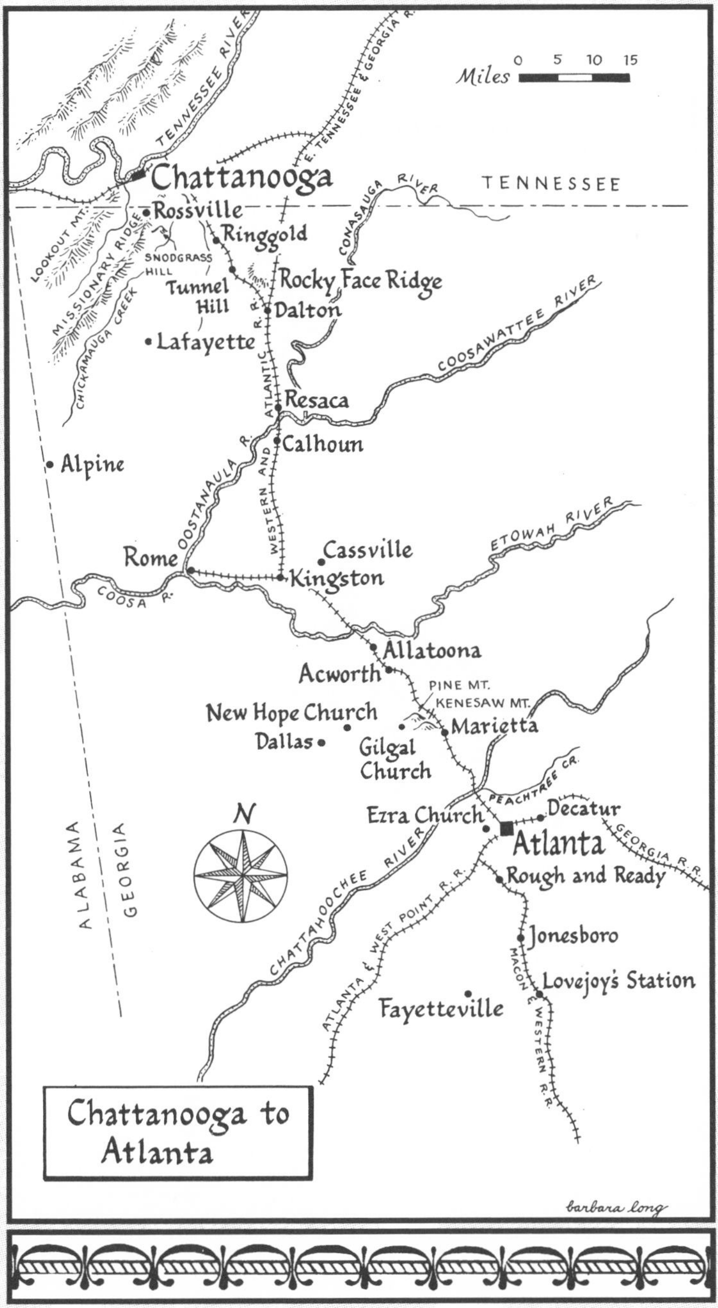

TENNESSEE RIVER

E. TENNESSEE & GEORGIA R.R.

CONASAUGA RIVER

TENNESSEE

Miles 0 5 10 15

Chattanooga

Rossville

Ringgold

LOOKOUT MT.

MISSIONARY RIDGE

SNODGRASS HILL

Rocky Face Ridge

Tunnel Hill

Dalton

CHICKAMAUGA CREEK

Lafayette

COOSAWATTEE RIVER

Resaca

Calhoun

WESTERN AND ATLANTIC R.R.

OOSTANAULA

Alpine

ETOWAH RIVER

Rome

Cassville

Kingston

COOSA R.

Allatoona

Acworth

PINE MT.
KENESAW MT.

New Hope Church

Dallas

Marietta

Gilgal Church

PEACHTREE CR.

N

Ezra Church

Decatur

CHATTAHOOCHEE RIVER

Atlanta

GEORGIA R.R.

Rough and Ready

ALABAMA

GEORGIA

ATLANTA & WEST POINT R.R.

Jonesboro

Lovejoy's Station

MACON & WESTERN R.R.

Fayetteville

Chattanooga to Atlanta

barbara long

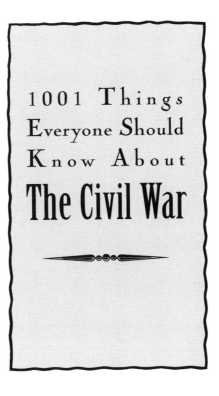

1001 Things
Everyone Should
Know About

The Civil War

Doubleday

New York   Toronto

London   Sydney   Auckland

1001 Things Everyone Should Know About The Civil War

FRANK E. VANDIVER

PUBLISHED BY DOUBLEDAY
a division of Random House, Inc.
1540 Broadway, New York, New York 10036

DOUBLEDAY and the portrayal of an anchor with a dolphin are
trademarks of Doubleday, a division of Random House, Inc.

Book design by Donna Sinisgalli

Library of Congress Cataloging-in-Publication Data
Vandiver, Frank Everson, 1925–
1001 things everyone should know about the Civil War / Frank E.
Vandiver.—1st ed.
p.   cm.
1. United States—History—Civil War, 1861–1865—Miscellanea.
I. Title.
E468.V35   1999
973.7—dc21   98-22084
CIP
ISBN 0-385-47385-0

To the Blue
and the Gray

❖

Contents

FOREWORD

At the start, let me confess that the length, breadth, cost, and anguish of the American Civil War cannot be encompassed in 1001 entries. The war stretched over nearly half a continent, flared on the high seas, had diplomatic repercussions from Mexico to Europe, Great Britain, and Russia, sustained more than 10,500 combats and more than a million casualties. Facing the impossible, then, I offer here a highly personal selection of some things that make the war, for me, endlessly interesting. I include some things the war caused or modified, some people who were important to it or in it, some odd things that happened in the conflict, along with some obvious changes wrought by the Civil War. I offer some things that strike me as important to know, some things unimportant but interesting, some unusual, and some simply funny.

Certainly, these choices are not Everyman's; some readers will be irked by what's in, others by what's out (the Rebel Yell, for instance), still others will find more about one side or the other than they want. Again, the selection is a personal one—and probably not the same one I would make if I did the book again.

A caveat: there are several versions of some of my topics—if mine is not the one you know, remember, what you're reading are my selections.

I am indebted to several people for excellent help in compiling the list of topics. Professor Todd Brereton, the University of Louisville, suggested several and did drafts for me, as did Ms. Edith Anderson Wakefield, College Station, who also did her customary splendid service in selecting pictures and doing captions—all the pictures are from Francis T. Miller's *Photographic History of the Civil War* (1911). Shannon Maxwell, my secretary at Texas A&M University, did repeated drafts of the manuscript with skill and ease.

Frances Jones, my editor at Doubleday, deserves special thanks for good ideas and for understanding the need of shifts and changes. To Frances Apt, copyeditor at Doubleday, I offer warm appreciation for her lively and humorous comments and for making this a much better book. Thanks also to my agent, John Hawkins, who smoothed the way with customary ease and toleration. I owe a huge debt of gratitude to the staff of the Sterling C. Evans Library of Texas A&M University for letting me keep books beyond time and for endless patience with Interlibrary Loans.

My wife, Renée, listened to long reaches of the book with unfeigned enthusiasm, suffered long isolations, ran over the manuscript with her shrewd and critical eye, offered encouragement and creative suggestions for improvement. This book is for her—love and thank you, ma'am.

Finally, to good friend Herman Gollob, former editor at Doubleday, who started this, to Doubleday's Pat Mulcahy, Michael Palgon, Jennifer Griffin, and Katie Burns Howard, who nurtured it along, my admiring thanks—I am permanently indebted.

Frank E. Vandiver
College Station, Texas
November 1998

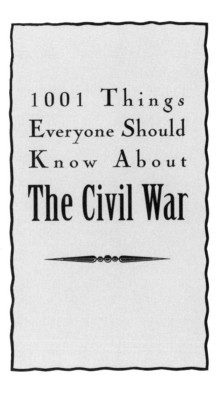

1001 Things
Everyone Should
Know About
The Civil War

INTRODUCTION

No war is simple or uncomplicated, certainly not the American Civil War of 1861 to 1865. There were encounters involving hundreds of thousands of soldiers and irregulars, and the war spread across the American continent from Maine to California, Florida to Wyoming, even into Canada. More than a million men were killed or wounded or died of disease. More than 25 percent of the manpower available in the North and South became casualties. Costs went far beyond battles, treasure beyond belief poured into the war, and a terrible process of change created a different Union from the wreckage of the old.

How can such a maelstrom be encompassed in a mere 1001 entries? The best way is to discuss the physical and human geography of the sides that faced each other in 1861, see how the governments were organized, and indicate the people, events, and items that came to the fore during each year of the war. Some extras will still have to be tucked in here and there when the complexities of war defy logical presentation.

1 **The election of Abraham Lincoln of Illinois, a "Black" Republican, to the presidency presented the possibility of fundamental changes in Southern rights and causes.** Lincoln's party threatened the continuation of slavery, but that alone did not lead to secession. Setting the slaves free was the real threat. What would happen if slaves were loosed across the South, and the time-honored system of social control were to vanish? And if slaves as private property could be confiscated, where would Federal dictatorship stop? Lincoln's election, in November 1860, led not only to the secession from the Union of South Carolina but, within a few weeks, to that of Mississippi, Florida, Alabama, Georgia, Louisiana, and Texas. Some of the border states leaned toward the South but waited on events.

2 **In the Institute Hall of Charleston, South Carolina, on Thursday, December 20, 1860, the delegates to the South Carolina Convention, having listened to fiery rhetoric for several days, made their declaration.** "The Ordinance adopted by us in Convention on the

The ruins of Institute or Secession Hall, Charleston, 1865.

twenty-third day of May, in the year of our Lord one thousand seven hundred and eight-eight, whereby the Constitution of the United States of America was ratified, and also all Acts, and parts of Acts, of the General Assembly of this State, ratifying amendments of the said Constitution are hereby repealed; and that the union now subsisting between South Carolina and other States, under the name of 'The United States of America' is hereby dissolved." Ayes, 169; nays, 0.

3 **Did secession mean war?** To some, yes. Others hoped for a different and better

Union; a few, for quick return to what had been.

4 **Secession came despite the harried efforts to save the Union.** The Senate Committee of Thirteen, charged with preserving the country, had put forth, on December 18, 1861, the "Crittenden Compromise." John J. Crittenden (1787–1863) of Kentucky, a strong Union man, proposed to the new committee several constitutional amendments. They would prohibit slavery in territories north of 36° 30′; Congress would not interfere with the system below that line. States

were to be admitted to the Union with or without slavery, according to each state's constitution. Congress could not abolish slavery in places it controlled, including the District of Columbia. Congress would have no power to inhibit interstate slave transportation, and it was to compensate owners for slaves lost to lax law enforcement. No future amendments could change these provisions nor abolish slavery where it existed. Crittenden thought that reviving the old Missouri Compromise line would restrict slavery expansion, just what Southerners could not accept.

5 On December 4, 1860, the House of Representatives created the Committee of Thirty-three (each state had a member) to study the nation's condition.

6 Other efforts to avoid war included the Peace Convention (sometimes known as the "Old Man's Convention" because of the venerability of its members) called by Virginia and chaired by a highly respected former President, John Tyler (1790–1862). With only twenty-one states represented and with secession already taking place, the convention never was accorded the respect its deliberations deserved.

7 At 8 P.M. on December 26, 1860, Major Robert Anderson (1805–1871), commanding U.S. forces in Charleston Harbor, transferred his garrison from Fort Moultrie, on South Carolina land, to Fort Sumter, in the city's harbor. Outraged cries greeted the move, but Anderson said, "The step which I have taken was, in my opinion, necessary to prevent the effusion of blood." President Buchanan deplored the move as likely to spread secession.

8 Forts Moultrie and Sumter were not vital installations—they were remnants of an earlier age—but they, along with Fort Pickens in Pensacola Harbor, were symbols charged with emotion.

9 Secession caused deep rifts of opinion in both the North and South. Most

Fort Sumter, South Carolina, April 16, 1861.

Southerners wanted secession, but among these were some who hoped (as did some in the North) for a new arrangement of the Union, with slavery guarantees and with concessions to the North's economic needs.

10 **One Southern group advised delay.** The "cooperationists" wanted South Carolina and other states to wait until a large groundswell in favor of secession would guarantee enough states for success. But this group, an offshoot of the Unionist camp in the South, lacked cohesion and force.

11 **Unionists existed in the North and the South.** Many Southern Unionists were respected men. Alexander H. Stephens, a United States representative from Georgia, embraced the Union longer than did most Georgians. His influence troubled many Georgian consciences for a time.

12 **In Texas, General Sam Houston, hero of the Texas Revolution, held the governor's chair in 1860 and resisted disunion.** Because he spoke against it, he had to be removed from office before Texas could call a secession convention.

13 **Unionist sentiments were evident at** most state secession conventions but, like the "cooperationists," Unionists largely adjusted to secession. Those who did not were the "Tories" of the South and would suffer like their namesakes.

14 **In "the Great Secession Winter," many Southern states saw the rise of voluntary groups that preached a new patriotism.** The most representative, and probably the best organized, was South Carolina's Winyah Association of 1860. Its members urged secession across the Palmetto State, worked to influence election of delegates to a secession convention, and inflamed the public mind through newspaper editorials, broadsides, speeches, and even through appearances at churches.

15 **Southern newspapers were nearly unanimous in urging separation.** Under the editorship of Robert Barnwell Rhett, Charleston's *News and Courier* was among the most fiery of all. The *Examiner* in Richmond, Virginia, stirred the cauldron, as did most of the other papers in the city. In Alabama, the Montgomery *Advertiser* called for swift disunion and a new nation built to suit Southern needs. Newspaper propaganda fanned a good deal of Southern ardor.

1861

THE FIRST
YEAR OF
THE WAR

16 **New Year's Day of 1861 began the most violent year of change in American memory.** Foreboding shaded all celebrations as strong emotions seemed to point everyone toward a dreaded future. Sometimes rumors of war created the kind of thrill that pulls people along with it. So it was in 1861. The rumors overshadowed the peacemakers, weakened bonds of friendship, and, for the first time, made a broken union a possibility.

17 **In February 1861, delegates from six seceded states (Texas was coming) gathered in Montgomery, Alabama, to form a new Confederacy.** That action, in addition to the divided Northern opinion, trapped the luckless President of the United States.

18 **The early days of the Confederate government in Montgomery were hectic.** William Howard Russell, a correspondent for the London *Times* who published in 1861 *The Civil War in America,* visited President Jefferson Davis in the makeshift capitol building and reported on the hasty preparations for government. His sharp descriptions of the new administration are among the best available.

19 **First sentiments were important.** Some Northerners wanted to keep the South in the Union; some thought its departure would cleanse the country; a few were ambivalent. Southerners had strong feelings, because war would burden them heavily. Fears of being consumed by Northern commercialism and crassness were real, as a Georgia poem of April 1861 shows:

> *Yankee Doodle is a knave,*
> *And everybody knows it,*
> *And swindling is his natural trade,*
> *For by his tricks he shows it.*
>
> *He'll go to church and sing and pray,*
> *Be full of grace on Sunday,*
> *With wooden hams and paper shoes,*
> *He'll cheat you on a Monday.*

THE PRESIDENTS

20 **James Buchanan (1791–1868), a Democrat, came to the presidency in**

1856 as a compromise candidate to ease the ferment of the slavery issue. He watched in growing dismay as calamities gathered around him, like the bloodshed in Kansas as slaveholders and Free Staters took up arms against one another. And with Abraham Lincoln's election, Buchanan faced the actuality of secession in the remaining months of his term.

21 Many hoped the President would take steps to save the Union, but his principles shackled his freedom of action. Although he thought secession unconstitutional and inveighed against it, he believed he had no power to stop it. The country disintegrated before his eyes. For the President-elect, Buchanan's inaction had some merit: it left all options open.

22 Abraham Lincoln (1809–1865) became the sixteenth President of the United States at the country's most chaotic moment. He knew it, and, in mid-February 1861, said that he came as the humblest of his predecessors, with "a more difficult task to perform than any one of them."

Born in Illinois, a lawyer in Springfield with experience as a United States congressman, Lincoln made a political ascent that matched the quick rise of the Republican Party. His careful reticence in the weeks following his election blurred his image just when Northerners wanted guidance as the South drifted away.

23 Uncertain about the best ways to save the Union, Lincoln crafted his Inaugural Address with great care. As he spoke, on a gray March 4, he began to reveal himself. Despite the uncomplimentary talk about him—that he was a rustic from the Illinois backcountry, a gangling, gawky man whose main claim to fame was telling jokes and arguing with Stephen A. Douglas—it became clear as he spoke that this plain man would strive to save the crumbling country.

24 Southerners need not fear Federal interference with their social institutions, he said, but because the Union was perpetual, secession was impossible, and any act of violence against United States authority would be considered revolutionary. Lincoln said he would enforce the laws but do nothing to provoke violence. "In *your* hands, my dissatisfied fellow countrymen, and not in *mine,* is the momentous issue of civil war. The government will not assail *you.* You can have no conflict without being yourselves the aggressors. *You* have no oath registered in Heaven to destroy the government, while *I* have the most solemn one to 'preserve, protect, and defend' it." A poetic peroration closed on a hopeful note: "The mystic chords of memory, streching [sic] from every battlefield and patriot grave to every living heart and hearthstone, all over this broad land, will yet swell the chorus of the Union when again touched, as surely they will be, by the better angels of our nature."

25 Reaction ran according to passions: Southerners mostly heard war in Lincoln's declaration of perpetual Union, while some Northerners felt Lincoln had sounded all the right notes. The address rewards careful reading. In it he proclaimed a policy of preserving the Union, focused on slavery as the evil that was in dispute, and fixed any guilt for war on the South.

26 To many, though, Lincoln's words were anticlimactic. The new Confederacy had probably picked the best man available to fashion a country and a cause. Mississippi-born Jefferson Davis, a graduate of West Point, a hero of the

Inauguration of Jefferson Davis, State House, Montgomery, Alabama, February 18, 1861.

Mexican War, a long-time United States senator, a Southern moderate with many Northern admirers, and now President of the new Confederate States of America, had already set a tone of moderation in his Inaugural Address, delivered in Montgomery, Alabama, on February 18, 1861.

27 Tall, distinguished-looking, devoted to his new country, Davis proclaimed that evolution, not revolution, had brought the new nation into existence. "We have changed the constituent parts, but not the system of our government, [a government born of] the American idea that governments rest on the consent of the governed, and that it is the right of the people to alter or abolish governments whenever they become destructive of the ends for which they were established." Since the Union no longer served its original purpose, the South had seceded in order to preserve the government of the founders. "Actuated solely by the desire to preserve our own rights and promote our own welfare, the separation of the Confederate States has been marked by no aggression upon others and followed by no domestic convulsion." He hoped for peaceful separation but stressed preparation for war to a people still thrilled with independence. If war did come, he said, "we must prepare to meet the emergency and maintain, by the final arbitrament of the sword, the position which we have assumed among the nations of the earth.

We have entered upon the career of independence, and it must be inflexibly pursued."

28 Davis's brave words cloaked much discomfort. In a letter to his wife, written on February 20, he described the inaugural and his feelings: "I saw troubles and thorns innumerable. We are without machinery, without means, and threatened by powerful opposition, but I do not despond and will not shrink from the task imposed upon me."

THE VICE PRESIDENTS

29 Maine's Hannibal Hamlin, once a Democrat, balanced the 1860 Re- publican ticket as vice president. Usually forgotten by history, Hamlin worked loyally for Lincoln and in 1864 worked to elect his replacement, Andrew Johnson (q.v.). His loyalty brought him the post of Collector of the Port of Boston.

30 While the Montgomery Convention worked at forming a government, writing a constitution, and making laws, it also had to fill executive positions. After choosing Davis to be President, the Convention called United States Representative Alexander Hamilton Stephens of Georgia to be vice president. Stephens possessed a brilliant legal mind trapped in a wizened, pain-racked body, but his political skills

Hannibal Hamlin, Lincoln's first Vice President.

Alexander H. Stephens, Vice President of the Confederacy.

and eloquence commanded wide respect. Long a Union man, and only lately a supporter of secession, Stephens represented the possibility of cooperation. Fearful of secession, certain that a war would be ruinous, he nonetheless worked hard at Montgomery to fashion both the Provisional and Permanent Constitutions. His presence conferred on the convention a staid and solid history. He was sworn in as vice president even before Davis reached Montgomery, but he soon lapsed into curmudgeonly opposition.

31 **Shortly after the formation of the new government,** Stephens embarrassed the Confederacy by announcing that its "cornerstone rests upon the great truth that the Negro is not equal to the white man." He came to oppose most of Davis's programs, sulked much of the time in Georgia, joined with other dissidents, and nearly courted treason. 32 Stephens's shenanigans showed the weakness of Confederate politics. The one-party oligarchy found no way to chastise this churl in their midst.

33 **After the war Stephens wrote a lengthy treatise titled** *A Constitutional View of the Late War Between the States: Its Causes, Character, Conduct, and Results* (2 volumes, 1868–1870), in which he wrote harshly of Davis, whom he had never liked.

CABINETS

As the two countries girded for war, politicians, would-be contractors, office seekers, enthusiastic patriots, and military men jockeyed for notice. Cabinet positions were eagerly sought and handed out with special care.

34 **Lincoln tried to reward the party faithful, nod toward the old Democratic wing of his party, fulfill campaign promises, and assuage disappointed rivals.** Results were uneven, sometimes awkward, but the President's iron fist in a velvet glove, and his persistent humor, brought together an odd mix of men into a Cabinet. One of his best appointments seemed a mistake in the beginning.

35 **The New Yorker William H. Seward, former Whig, accepted the position of Secretary of State from varying motives.** He had hoped to be President (and had contended for the Republican nomination in 1856 and in 1860), and now sought to be the unofficial "prime minister" to the inept President. Behind his ambition lay much ability. Earnest, energetic, patriotic, innovative, Seward blinked at nothing to save the Union. Lincoln came to rely on his strengths while curbing his ambitions, no easy task.

36 **Among Seward's suggestions was involvement in a foreign war to end the**

William H. Seward, U.S. Secretary of State.

secession crisis. Failing that, he urged the abandonment of Fort Sumter, because it was a symbol of slavery, but the defense of all other forts, and an enforced blockade. These things he thought essential, and said that somebody must energetically "pursue and direct" them; he offered to do so himself. Lincoln parried this attempt as executive pre-emption. Seward further complicated things after Queen Victoria granted belligerent rights to the Confederacy. He sent a "Bold Remonstrance," ordering U.S. Ambassador Charles Francis Adams (q.v.) to have no dealings with the British government as long as it interfered with the American scene.

37 **Although Seward's diplomatic skills were questionable, he had his virtues:** determination, devotion to the Union, fearless candor, and energy. Gideon Welles (q.v.) tagged him aptly as a man who "liked to be called premier." He kept his post throughout the war, and Lincoln often called on him for unofficial tasks.

38 **Salmon P. Chase, a former Free Soiler and radical antislavery man, was chosen to head the Treasury, not because of his financial acumen but for his political influence.** Emergencies brought out the best in Chase, and he became the right man to support such experiments in public funding as an income tax, "greenback" currency, a national banking system, and wide use of loans and bonding. He shrewdly brought

Salmon P. Chase, U.S. Secretary of the Treasury.

Jay Cooke's banking house into the loan-selling business, and the Union, which had nearly suffered monetary collapse, became soundly funded as the economy shifted into high gear. The gross national product not only sustained the huge war effort; it also effected westward expansion.

39 But Chase became a burden to Lincoln. His good work at the Treasury was offset by his contentiousness and his unconcealed ambition to be President. One senator, in fact, said that Chase thought himself the fourth member of the Trinity. He formed a cabal in his department to work for him in the election of 1864, and he connived with anti-Lincoln Republicans. When he left the Cabinet, in 1864, Lincoln appointed him Chief Justice of the Supreme Court.

40 **Lincoln named Simon Cameron to be Secretary of War.** A Pennsylvanian with slippery integrity, Cameron had at one time or another embraced almost all the political parties. His appointment resulted from a deal, made without Lincoln's prior knowledge, during the election campaign, and Lincoln resented the obligation. Inept, incompetent, and overwhelmed by the deluge of men, Cameron was blamed for fraudulent war contracts, and allowed chaos to send his department tottering toward collapse. Lincoln replaced him in January 1862.

41 **Edwin M. Stanton took Cameron's**

place. An Ohioan who had moved to Pittsburgh and become a great success at the bar, Stanton, a Democrat, opposed slavery but defended the constitutional rights of slaveholders. Although he had opposed Lincoln, the President called him to the War Department because of his brilliance, energy, and rigid honesty. Stern-faced, his receding hairline accentuated by small rimmed glasses and a flowing beard, Stanton proved effective, vigorous, and occasionally harsh. He cleaned up the contract mess, pushed lagging generals (of whom he found many!), supplied the swelling legions, and handled, with aplomb, the difficult demobilization problems at war's end. Turned Republican, he became, next to Chase, the most radical Cabinet member.

Edwin M. Stanton, U.S. Secretary of War.

42 Lincoln could hardly have picked a more unlikely Secretary of the Navy. Gideon Welles of Connecticut, former Democrat and New England newspaper publisher, had a mordant wit best seen in his *Diary.* About ships and sailors he had little knowledge, but of people and their ways he knew much. Lincoln liked the cheeky candor of his "Father Neptune" and correctly assessed him to be a fine organizer and administrator. Welles, aided by able senior naval officers and skilled marine engineers and architects, built a powerful Union Navy that blockaded an enemy shoreline of 3000 miles and coped with daring Confederate cruisers, privateers, and blockade runners.

Gideon Welles, U.S. Secretary of the Navy.

43 For Attorney General, Lincoln picked Missourian Edward Bates, a former Whig with weak Republican presidential ambitions. A good lawyer, he followed Lincoln's extra-constitutional actions with later justifications (some of them strained to threads), and proved loyal and helpful in councils.

44 Beyond these key appointments, Lincoln filled the Cabinet with representatives of every Republican hue. Historians generally consider the Union Cabinet members able and conscientious men, better, on paper, than the Confederate Cabinet members.

45 Jefferson Davis had special problems in filling his Cabinet posts. Like Lincoln, he had to soothe ruffled political feathers, appease different states, and, rummaging among an uncertain list, put together a working group. Like Lincoln, Davis did reasonably well, although men of real Southern influence were lacking, and some of the first appointees soon departed.

46 Fiery Robert Toombs of Georgia became Davis's Secretary of State, doubtless because of his prestige and stalwart support of secession. He had the juggler's job of dealing with the United States on issues of separation and with foreign nations on the matter of recognition of the new nation. Hopes ran high for recognition of the

Confederacy when both Britain and France acknowledged Confederate belligerency, but Queen Victoria's proclamation of neutrality, and her acceptance of the Union blockade, dampened foreign prospects. Toombs was prepared to take on these tasks, but found his freedom of action curtailed by the President and by circumstances. Finding the job unchallenging, he resigned in July 1861 and became an army general. Virginia's Robert M.T. Hunter (q.v.) became the first of Toombs's two successors.

47 **Alabama's Leroy Pope Walker took charge of the War Department.** Walker, who had considerable influence on the secession movement, had led Alabama's delegation at the Charleston Convention. His military qualifications were confined to a stint as a militia general. Like Simon Cameron (q.v.), he confronted confusing needs in trying to create the department and to coordinate military activities. He did focus on procuring arms, and he encouraged ordnance purchases abroad so that he could equip the early groups of volunteers. He and his four successors, however, were unable to influence strategy, which remained the President's domain.

48 **Stephen R. Mallory, born in Trinidad, served as one of Florida's senators when that state seceded.** He then became Secretary of the Navy and, against overwhelming odds (few naval engine

Stephen Russell Mallory, Secretary of the Confederate Navy.

shops, scarcity of iron and steel, competition with the army for ordnance and manpower), built a respectable force, saw the value of the ironclads, and made a small fleet of raiders the terror of Union merchant shipping; the *Sumter* (q.v.) and the *Alabama* (q.v.) earned world renown. An able administrator and naval theorist, he held office throughout the war and enjoyed the full support of the President, who never meddled in Navy Department activities.

49 A steadying influence at Confederate Cabinet meetings, Mallory, like his Union counterpart, kept a highly informative diary. His successes in building and buying warships, in riverine warfare, and his emphasis on modern ironclads rank him among the best Navy Secretaries in American history.

50 Christopher G. Memminger of South Carolina, who was born in Germany, took over the difficult Treasury. His political career in the state legislature had given him some financial background, but Confederate monetary problems overwhelmed his experience. Memminger, somewhat like Albert Gallatin in the War of 1812, had no expectation of the magnitude of war needs. He suggested some minor taxes, a small bond issue, and urged a uniform currency, but soon the Confederacy became nearly inundated in a flood of paper money. Although he thought that Confederate cotton should be purchased by the government and shipped abroad to sustain the national credit, he realized that shortages of the commodity and of shipping made this impossible.

51 Memminger flirted with foreign loans. In February 1864, he came up with an ingenious method of refunding the currency (two new dollars for three old) to stabilize the situation. But all his efforts were undercut by state and local bank currencies, by the Confederacy's inability to reach foreign markets, by military reverses, and by a critical shortage of specie in the country (only $27 million). Popular outcry forced Memminger to resign in the summer of 1864.

52 Memminger's personality also

Christopher G. Memminger, Secretary of the Treasury of the Confederacy.

worked against him. Direct, blunt, businesslike, he wasted no time on charm, but he faced a Congress that rarely listened to any of his proposals, and he usually found himself administering financial policies of which he disapproved.

53 **Confederate finances were shaken by various ills.** Inflation, of course, sapped monetary strength, as did the misfortunes of battle. Perhaps the most constant threat came from Northern printing presses. The Federal Treasury aimed a deliberate counterfeiting campaign against the Rebels, and although the South did good engraving, copying Southern paper money proved a fairly easy challenge. Part of the ruinous inflation stemmed from bogus bills.

54 **The Confederacy created a Justice Department and assigned to it many former functions of the Interior Department.** The Attorney General ran this new branch of government, and the first incumbent of five was, arguably, Davis's best Cabinet member. Judah P. Benjamin was born on the island of St. Croix in the British West Indies in 1811, moved to Charleston, then to New Orleans. A lawyer, Benjamin was serving as a Louisiana U.S. senator when that state left the Union. He joined the Confederacy and became one of Jefferson Davis's closest confidants. Unlike Davis in many ways—their personalities were chasms apart—they shared a love of the South that welded an odd and lasting friendship.

55 Trusted fully, Benjamin worked better with Davis than did any other Cabinet member. He served as Attorney General, Secretary of War, and finally as Secretary of State. Behind his smiling countenance was a brilliant, ingenious mind, one that nearly succeeded in winning foreign recognition for the Confederate States.

56 Benjamin often served as a lightning rod for criticism directed at Davis. Confederate congressmen came to see some kind of evil, Sephardic genius as the cause of Southern failures. Those who hated Benjamin could never quite reach him, however. Each time they closed in on him, Davis promoted him to another, higher post. Benjamin's loyalty stood above question, and he stuck to his cause and chieftain with a deep sense of honor.

57 **Historians have tended to see the Confederate Cabinet as a kind of middling collection dominated by Jefferson Davis.** This was true to an extent, but Benjamin, Mallory, and 58 **John Reagan,** the Texan who served as Postmaster General, were men of substance, as were at least two of the Secretaries of War, George W. Randolph (q.v.) and James A. Seddon (q.v.). Most of them were good administrators, honest, hardworking, and swamped.

ARMY LEADERS, 1861

59 **Both sides began in hope of peace but expectation of war.** Consequently, both Presidents looked for military men who could carry the burden of a brother's war.

60 **Lincoln doubted that his limited experience in the Black Hawk War gave him much knowledge of modern combat.** He realized the country's woeful unreadiness for war (16,000 men scattered far and wide in small units, a third of the officers joining the Confederacy, old bureau chiefs entrenched in red tape, a Navy with only forty-two ships in commission), and turned to the senior general of the United States Army for advice.

61 **Lieutenant General Winfield Scott,**

"Old Fuss and Feathers," Lieutenant General Winfield Scott, seated, Lincoln's first General-in-Chief of the Army.

General-in-Chief of the Army, had America's best military reputation. His brilliant record stretched from Lundy's Lane, in the War of 1812, through his splendid campaign to capture Mexico City in the Mexican War. His ideas and his people were the mainstays of the U.S. Army in 1861. Old Fuss and Feathers—the nickname stemming from his fondness for detail and for elaborate uniforms—had presided over the army since 1841, and the memory of man ran not to the contrary. Seventy-four years old in 1861, Scott, a Virginian, did not follow his state into the Confederacy. He begged Robert E. Lee (q.v.) to stay and take command of the expanding United States Army.

62 Scott tried valiantly to help organize for the war, but he was grossly overweight, unable to sit a horse, suffered from dropsy, and often slept through meetings. As younger officers appeared on the scene—usually men he knew—his days were numbered. Lincoln consulted him on early strategy and nearly adopted Scott's Anaconda Plan. He did, in fact, return to its outline later in the war. Scott voluntarily retired on November 1, 1862, and lived to see victory.

63 Irvin McDowell was given command of the volunteers clustering around Washington and had the unenviable task of molding raw recruits into a semblance of an army and moving against the Rebels under General P.G.T. Beauregard (q.v.) in northern Virginia. A plodder, somewhat aloof, described as "inattentive, and unable to remember names," McDowell finally moved his army to the attack. He had a sound plan for defeating the Rebels, but its execution at the First Battle of Bull Run (known to the Confederates as First Manassas) was spoiled by his inexperienced and distrustful soldiers. Unexpected Confederate reinforcements cost him the battle.

64 In the aftermath of First Bull Run, Lincoln turned to a younger general who had ridden into prominence in 1861, during a campaign in what is now West Virginia. As a major general of Ohio volunteers, he had defeated inferior Con-

Union Generals Irvin McDowell (left) and
George Brinton McClellan (right), who
succeeded Scott as General-in-Chief of the
Army.

federate forces. George Brinton McClellan
(alias the Young Napoleon or Little Mac),
a Pennsylvanian, took Scott's post as General-in-Chief of the Army as well as command of the defeated Army of the
Potomac. Dashing, well mounted on a
prancer, McClellan proved the man for the
moment. Overwhelmingly self-confident
(he wrote to his wife, "By some strange
operation of magic I have become the
power of the land . . . God has placed a

great work in my hands . . . I was called to
it; my previous life seems to have been
unwittingly directed to this great end"),
McClellan swept aside Lincoln's worry
that he might be wearing too many hats. "I
can do it all," he said.

65 Bombast and spit-and-polish organizing brought some pride back to the
Army of the Potomac, and it grew into
a burnished instrument in McClellan's
hands. McClellan was surely one of the
most controversial generals of the Civil
War. He had all the trappings of military
greatness—West Point training, administrative experience in civilian life, early victory, organizing ability, rapport with his
men—but he lacked the essential ingredi-
ent for success: audacity. He could not
bring himself to take his splendid army
into battle.

66 As the army grew, so did Lincoln's
impatience. When would McClellan
advance? Finally, early in 1862, the President asked whether he might use the army,
since the general apparently had no plans
for it! When McClellan did make plans,
they were on a scale to rival those of
Xerxes and Napoleon: he proposed an
amphibious turning movement that would
land his army on the York Peninsula below
Richmond. From there, the men would
march on the Confederate capital and end
the war in a single blow.

67 The plan might have worked had a
more resolute general carried it out. Once
on enemy territory, McClellan convinced
himself that the Rebels had assembled a

vast and growing army to oppose him, so he moved his army toward Richmond at glacial speed. His creeping advance allowed General Robert E. Lee (q.v.) to assemble sufficient strength to launch a pre-emptive attack.

68 **In the Seven Days' Battles that followed, McClellan retreated ahead of a weaker foe to the James River** and the protection of Union gunboats. Lincoln removed him from command, turned the

army over to John Pope (q.v.), who blundered into defeat at the Second Battle of Bull Run. Reluctantly, Lincoln restored McClellan to command on hearing reports that Lee was marching north.

69 At the Battle of Antietam, McClellan had a chance to destroy Lee's army and possibly win the war, but his attacks were piecemeal, hesitant, and narrowly repulsed. He then allowed Lee's battered legions to retire unmolested across the Potomac. When McClellan ignored Lincoln's pleas

Lincoln visiting General-in-Chief McClellan in his headquarters two weeks after Antietam, shortly before relieving him of command.

to pursue Lee, the President permanently relieved him of command.

70 In 1864, McClellan, as the Democratic candidate for President, had the chance for revenge, but he lost badly, because he could not reconcile his determination to prosecute the war with his party's compromise program. He served as governor of New Jersey from 1878 to 1881, and died in 1885.

71 Though McClellan lacked audacity, he had some inexplicable magnetism, as seen in the following testimonial from E. J. Warner's *Generals in Blue:* "The effect of this man's presence upon the Army of the Potomac—in sunshine or in rain, in darkness or in daylight, in victory or defeat—was electrical, and too wonderful to make it worthwhile attempting to give a reason for it."

72 **Jefferson Davis's military experience from West Point through the Black Hawk and Mexican Wars made him careful about military appointments.** Some Northern officers he sought directly; others he selected from those who "went South." He had good men to choose from. For the Confederacy's first general, Davis and Leroy Walker picked a man who had all the trappings of success.

73 **Pierre Gustave Toutant Beauregard, a native of Louisiana known as the Great Creole, became the Confederacy's first field commander.** Beauregard had served with distinction in the Mexican War, and,

for a few days on the eve of the Civil War, had been Superintendent of the Military Academy at West Point. Relieved because of his well-known Southern sympathies, he became a brigadier general in the Provisional Army of the Confederacy on March 1, 1861, and was assigned to Charleston Harbor. When the Confederate government decided to capture Charleston's Fort Sumter, in April 1861, the task fell to Beauregard. With scrupulous attention to military etiquette, he opened fire

"The Great Creole," Confederate General Pierre Gustave Toutant Beauregard, 1862.

on the fort on April 12. The next day, when it was surrendered, Beauregard became the first martial hero of the new nation.

74 He ought to have been one of the South's greatest generals, and despite his poor relations with President Davis, he did perform outstanding service. Like McClellan, he devised grandiose battle orders, but unlike McClellan, his true military talents emerged in battle. When he was given command of Southern forces gathering in northern Virginia in mid-1861, he organized an army along Bull Run Creek, near Manassas Junction, Virginia. Aware that his forces would be outnumbered when McDowell finally advanced, Beauregard called for help from Confederate forces in the Shenandoah Valley of Virginia. Reinforcements arrived in time to ensure Beauregard's victory at First Manassas (the Southern name for First Bull Run).

75 Subsequent arguments about strategy, rank, and position (he became a full general in the Regular Army to rank from July 21, 1861) soured Beauregard's relations with Jefferson Davis. He was sent west to serve as Albert Sidney Johnston's (q.v.) second in command at Shiloh, where he found it necessary to retreat on the second day, after Johnston's death. He was supplanted in the West but later did invaluable service defending Charleston Harbor and aiding Lee's defense of Petersburg, Virginia, in 1864.

76 Having been given theater command after the fall of Atlanta, Beauregard tried to help General John Bell Hood (q.v.) in his Tennessee campaign, and in the last months aided Joseph E. Johnston's efforts to stem Sherman's march through the Carolinas.

77 Beauregard was too flamboyant for Jefferson Davis's stern personality, too grandiose in battle plans, yet had great ability as a tactician. He probably saved Richmond during Grant's summer campaign in 1864 because he grasped the tactical situation more quickly than Lee did. His understanding of the strategic situation of the Confederacy, combined with his logistical knowledge and his familiarity with Southern soldiers, might have made him an ideal chief of staff to the President— had they been friends.

78 **Albert Sidney Johnston was President Davis's favorite general early in the war.** Born in Kentucky in February 1803 and raised in Louisiana, Johnston befriended Davis at Transylvania University; he graduated from the U.S. Military Academy in 1826.

79 In May 1861 he resigned from a distinguished career in the armies of the United States and of the Texas Republic and joined the Confederacy. On being appointed full general in the Regular Army in August 1861, he took command of all Southern troops west of the Alleghenies. By failing to concentrate, however, he lost Forts Henry and Donelson (q.v.). Then, goaded by General Beauregard (q.v.), his second in command,

General Albert Sidney Johnston, C.S.A.

sas, Joseph E. Johnston, ranks with McClellan and Braxton Bragg (q.v.) as one of the most complicated personalities of the Civil War. Born at Farmville, Virginia, in February 1807, he was a classmate of Robert E. Lee (q.v.) at the United States Military Academy. Unusual stints of combat service in the Seminole and Mexican Wars brought him repeated wounds and brevet promotions. By 1860 he had become Quartermaster General of the U.S. Army with the staff rank of brigadier general. He joined the Confederacy in April 1861 as a brigadier general in the Regular Army and was assigned to the Shenandoah Valley, where he eluded a Union force and marched to General

Johnston finally concentrated and surprised General U. S. Grant's (q.v.) army at Shiloh (q.v.) on April 6, 1862. During the successful first day, he was mortally wounded and died on the field.

80 The arguments about Johnston's abilities persist. Davis rebutted critics by saying that "if Sidney Johnston is not a general . . . we have no general," which may have been the most sweeping condemnation ever uttered about Confederate military leadership. Grant thought Johnston vacillating. Johnston made no great contribution to the Southern cause and probably died at the right moment for his reputation.

81 Beauregard's superior at First Manas-

Confederate Generals Joseph E. Johnston (left) and Robert E. Lee after the war, 1869.

Beauregard's assistance at First Manassas. There, his service won him appointment as a full general in the Regular Army to rank from July 4, 1861. His complaints about date of rank (he stood below three others) broke his friendship with President Davis. On taking command of the Confederate forces at Manassas, he moved south to the York Peninsula, where he opposed McClellan's advance toward Richmond. He was wounded at the Battle of Seven Pines, in May 1862, and yielded command to Robert E. Lee.

82 In November 1862, Davis, overcoming his doubts, gave Joe Johnston one of the great opportunities of the war: he appointed him commander of the Department of the West. Failing to understand this unique experiment in theater command, Johnston missed the chance to combine several armies under his command and lapsed into the role of an army commander as he tried unsuccessfully to relieve Vicksburg.

83 In November 1863, Johnston took command of the Army of Tennessee after the loss of Chattanooga, Tennessee. His cautious withdrawal ahead of the Army of General William T. Sherman (q.v.), going from Dalton to Atlanta, Georgia, was one of the masterly retreats in military history. The outcome, though, displeased President Davis, and General John Bell Hood (q.v.) replaced Johnston in July 1864. When Robert E. Lee became General-in-Chief of the Confederate Armies in 1865, he recalled Johnston to

duty with the Army of Tennessee. Johnston's efforts to stall Sherman were valiant but hopeless, and he surrendered his army at Durham Station, North Carolina, on April 26, 1865. He died in Washington on March 21, 1891, supposedly from a cold contracted while marching bareheaded in Sherman's funeral procession.

84 Was Johnston a genius or a bungler? The question still sounds in the corridors of history. His Atlanta campaign marked him a defensive tactician of the highest order. Critics, though, argue that he lacked aggressiveness; they brand him Retreating Joe. He represented an alternative strategy. Audacity is often urged on the weaker side, but Johnston's method of fighting retreats, which inflicted more casualties on his foes than on his men, might have prolonged the war.

85 Probably the most noted hero of First Manassas was Thomas Jonathan Jackson, whose decisive stand on the Confederate left flank during the Battle of First Manassas labeled him as "Stonewall" Jackson.

Born in Clarksburg, in what is now West Virginia, in January 1824, Jackson graduated from the U.S. Military Academy in 1846. Distinguished service in the Mexican War brought him recognition and a brevet majority. After routine assignments and a luckless stint in Florida, he resigned from the army to accept a teaching position at the Virginia Military Institute, where he earned a reputation as a mar-

Confederate Major General Thomas Jonathan (Stonewall) Jackson at Winchester, Virginia, during the Valley campaign of 1862.

tinet, though some cadets in each class thought him a military genius. As a colonel of Virginia militia at the start of the Civil War, Jackson took command at Harpers Ferry. After General J. E. Johnston replaced him, Jackson became a Confederate brigadier general.

86 **In August 1861, Jackson was promoted to major general and went to the Shenandoah Valley,** where, in 1862, he waged one of the great campaigns of American military history against three Union armies threatening to join McClellan's advance on Richmond. Jackson attacked and defeated General John C. Frémont's (q.v.) army near Staunton, Virginia, then turned northward to strike General N. P. Banks's (q.v.) army advancing southward in the Valley. Hitting Banks at Front Royal and Winchester, on May 23 to 25, Jackson drove him across the Potomac. Jackson's position posed a threat to Washington itself, and an army under General James Shields was sent to trap the audacious Stonewall. In a brilliant series of actions at Cross Keys and Port Republic, on June 8 and 9, 87 Jackson defeated both Frémont and Shields and soon moved to Lee's aid in the Seven Days' Battles against McClellan.

88 Early in that campaign, Jackson gave confused orders, suffered from fatigue, and displayed none of his vaunted speed. As the battles continued, however, he did well, and Lee, recognizing Jackson's brilliance in independent command, detached him with half the army to meet General John Pope's (q.v.) new invasion of Virginia. A lightning campaign in August 1862 turned Pope's right and set the stage for Lee's great victory at Second Manassas (the Confederate name for Second Bull Run). In September, Jackson joined Lee at Sharpsburg and saved the Army of Northern Virginia; he was promoted to lieutenant general.

Jackson commanded the right wing in Lee's victory at Fredericksburg in December. 89 In the spring of the following year, 1863, Lee sent Jackson to meet General Joseph Hooker's army at Chancellorsville, Virginia. The battle there broke out on May 1, and Jackson, at the height of success, was wounded by his own men on

May 2. His left arm was amputated. Lee wrote, "He has lost his left arm; but I have lost my right arm." Jackson died of pneumonia on May 10, 1863. He ranks with the Great Captains in applying the basic maxims of war—and in exemplifying daring and grace.

90 **David Emanuel Twiggs, born in Georgia in 1790, distinguished himself in the War of 1812.** In the Mexican War, he was promoted to brigadier and, for service at Monterey, brevetted major general. One of the four line generals in the army in 1860, he commanded the Department of Texas. When he was cashiered for surrendering the department to Texas forces, Twiggs became a Confederate brigadier, in May 1861, with assignment in Louisiana. Virtually retired by age and illness, Twiggs died on July 15, 1862.

STAFF OFFICERS

91 **Supporting the growing field armies in the North and the South required knowledge of an arcane subject, little discussed in 1860, called logistics.** The art of procurement, collection, and distribution of supplies was among the most important and oldest areas of military competence, but it had, in the past, been part of general preparations. By the time the Civil War began, logistics, blessed by Lazare Carnot's contributions to the French Revolution, was recognized as the science of supply—without which armies could not operate.

92 Both the North and the South boasted logistical expertise at the beginning, although the North had to unseat some entrenched bureau chiefs who had dominated army supply through many years and many small wars.

93 **Fortunately for the North, Montgomery C. Meigs became Quartermaster General of the Union Army in May 1861.** Born in Georgia, he grew up in his mother's home town, Philadelphia,

Montgomery C. Meigs, U.S. Army Quartermaster General.

attended the University of Pennsylvania, entered West Point in 1836, and served in a variety of engineering assignments until he became brigadier general and Quartermaster General.

94 Throughout the war, Meigs did an outstanding job of supplying Union forces with equipment. Outstandingly honest, he presided over the swift expansion of the Union armies with skill and wisdom. Not bound by old ideas, he supported innovation and expended more than a billion and a half dollars over his signature without raising a question about misappropriation.

95 There were, of course, speculators who profited from Union needs, but Meigs's accounts were scrupulously audited, and he gave no grounds for criticism. Indeed, it was his probity and open-mindedness that made the Union armies the best equipped and supplied in military history. After his retirement, Meigs helped build the Pension Office Building in Washington. He died in Washington in January 1892.

96 **Josiah Gorgas, an authentic genius of American logistics, served the Confederacy as chief of ordnance throughout the war.** Born in Pennsylvania in July 1818, Gorgas graduated from West Point in 1841 as sixth in a class of fifty-two. He joined the ordnance corps and did distinguished service at Vera Cruz during the Mexican War. While doing service in Alabama, he mar-

ried Amelia Gayle, daughter of a former governor; one of their six children, William Crawford Gorgas, became U.S. Surgeon General and led the team that conquered yellow fever.

97 Jefferson Davis had offered Captain Gorgas a job fraught with difficulty. The South, having manufactured almost no munitions before 1861, lacked foundries and rolling mills; all the state arsenals contained a total of only 159,010 small arms. Gorgas picked able subordinates, organized his department, built arsenals and armories, bought blockade runners, and for four years provided arms, ammunition, and other necessary accou-

Josiah Gorgas, the Confederacy's Chief of Ordnance throughout the war.

terments to Confederate forces. In one of his first moves, he sent **98** Major Caleb Huse to buy arms and ammunition in Europe, where Huse proved remarkably effective. Innovative, Gorgas created the **99** Bureau of Foreign Supplies, which did much to coordinate the blockade-running efforts, and also created the **100** Nitre and Mining Bureau, which found or produced the basics of gunpowder, along with copper, brass, iron, and essential chemicals.

101 Ordnance supplies sometimes ran short because of the lack of transportation, but Gorgas's department largely succeeded, and he was promoted to brigadier general in November 1864. After the war he managed an ironworks in Alabama,

served as vice chancellor of the University of the South, at Sewanee, Tennessee (1866–1877), and as president of the University of Alabama (1877–1878), where he stayed until his death, in May 1883.

MEDICINE, SUCH AS IT WAS

102 **The wounded of both sides tried to stay out of hospitals, since medical service seemed almost an extension of battlefield killing, although it was often more brutal.** Antiseptic surgery had not been adopted, medicines were crude, chloroform was widely used (but ran short in the blockaded Confederacy), instruments

The *Red Rover,* Union hospital ship of the Mississippi Squadron, commanded by Lieutenant W. R. Wells.

U.S. Sanitary Commission nurse and patients at Fredericksburg, Virginia, May 1864.

had progressed little from the saws and claws of the Revolutionary War, amputation remained the primary treatment for shattered limbs, and the closed, fetid conditions of many hospitals made postsurgical gangrene nearly a certainty.

103 The conditions in Northern camps and hospitals were ameliorated by nurses and by the United States Sanitary Commission. With Frederick Law Olm-sted at the helm, the commission sent workers into the field, aided by members of the 104 U.S. Christian Commission, to nurse and feed the wounded and to provide personal services to the rank and file. Sanitary Commission "homes," much like present-day USOs, fed and helped recruits, disabled soldiers, and those on leave. By the end of the war the Sanitary Commission had raised and spent over $15 million.

Dr. Jonathan Letterman, Medical Director of the Army of the Potomac, and his staff, November 1862.

Both Blue and Gray benefited from the skills of excellent surgeons general. 105 William Alexander Hammond, born in Maryland in August 1828, took charge of the Union Army's Medical Department in April 1862. By that time, the department had become a slough of disease and despond, but Hammond swept through it like a whirlwind. Bypassing the seniority system, under which he had suffered, he brought younger doctors into responsible jobs, began keeping records, cut red tape, organized an ambulance corps with specially trained men, produced manuals on hygiene and sanitation, even opposed the heavy use of calomel, a cathartic, and tartar emetic, an expectorant and emetic, against prevalent medical opinion.

106 **Hammond's appointment of Jonathan Letterman as medical director of the Army of the Potomac proved Hammond's most important contribution.** Letterman's treatment system for that army became the basis for present-day "field medicine."

107 **Hammond, in his rush for improvement, was often brusque.** Among the people he offended was Secretary of War Edwin M. Stanton (q.v.). Trumped-up charges resulted in Hammond's dismissal from the service in August 1864, but about a dozen years later, when he was an outstanding neurosurgeon, Hammond was restored to the rank of brigadier general.

108 The Confederacy's surgeon general, Samuel Preston Moore, was born in Charleston in 1813 and received his M.D. from the Medical College of South Carolina in 1834. He joined the Confederacy in June 1861, where he applied his administrative genius. Almost single-handed, he constructed a medical service for the Confederate Army that ranks him among the best American surgeons general. Beginning with no organization at all, without medicines and ambulances, with fewer than fifty doctors, he recruited "contract surgeons," established field depots, sent medical purveyors

Samuel Preston Moore, Surgeon General of the Confederacy.

to administer them, worked tirelessly to build and support hospitals, and to find effective medicines from home nostrums, Southern flora and fauna, and Indian remedies.

109 Not only did he build a functioning Medical Department and advance professional standards; he also founded the Confederate States *Medical and Surgical Journal,* established the Association of Army and Navy Surgeons of the Confederacy, pioneered in pharmaceuticals, and, in a major step forward, stressed one-story wards. He instituted training programs, directed relief associations, and created the Reserve Surgical Corps.

110 Moore worked with Confederate Chief of Ordnance Josiah Gorgas (q.v.) in purchasing blockade runners to bring in supplies of medicine and equipment. Despite the acute shortages it had to deal with, the Medical Department was a success. After the war Moore practiced in Richmond, where he died, in May 1889.

111 Horrors of Civil War medicine are described graphically in newspapers, military medical journals, soldiers' and nurses' diaries, letters, and in the brutal scene of an Atlanta hospital in the movie version of *Gone With the Wind*.

112 Walt Whitman's war memoranda transmit much of the hideousness. He was a nurse in Northern hospitals and wrote: "These hospitals, so different from all others—these thousands and tens and twenties of thousands of American young men, badly wounded, all sorts of wounds, operated on, pallid with diarrhoea, languishing, dying with fever, pneumonia . . . open a new world somehow to me, giving closer insights . . . than any yet, showing our humanity (I sometimes put myself in fancy in the cot, with typhoid, or under the knife), tried by terrible, fearfullest tests, probed deepest, the living soul's, the body's tragedies, bursting the petty bonds of art."

113 **Louisa May Alcott, who would later write *Little Women,* went to help at a Union hospital in December 1862.** Fresh from a sheltered life, she was horrified by what she saw. "The first

Louisa May Alcott, a nurse in 1862, wrote wartime newspaper letters, "Hospital Sketches," and later won renown as author of *Little Women.*

thing I met was a regiment of the vilest odors that ever assailed the human nose." Armed with a vial of lavender water as her defense, she tended many of the wounded from Fredericksburg. Her worst duty was scrubbing the maimed with cakes of brown soap.

114 **Moore and the other Confederate medical administrators had to contend with the dislocation caused by the North's push into Southern territory.** All logistics were thrown off when the hospitals had to pick up and move suddenly and yet continue to treat the wounded. 115 A special case was the Army of Tennessee, which backed and filled, advanced and retreated, on a wide scale. The medical officers of the Army of Tennessee became adept at moving, establishing new hospitals, and transferring or acquiring new supplies. From these emergencies came the useful idea of open-air hospitals.

Navy Leaders

116 **Captain Charles Wilkes, U.S.N., competent but eager for glory, nearly involved the United States in a war with England.** Born in New York City in April 1798, Wilkes combined a naval career with his interest in exploring, and part of Antarctica is named for him: Wilkes Land.

On November 8, 1861, the U.S.S. *San*

Rear Admiral Charles Wilkes, U.S.N.

Jacinto, with Wilkes in command, intercepted the Royal Mail packet *Trent,* one day out of Havana. Wilkes removed two passengers, James M. Mason (q.v.) and John Slidell (q.v.), who had just been designated Confederate Commissioners to England and France, and transported them to prison in Boston.

117 Northern jubilation greeted Wilkes's action. He received a special medal from the House of Representatives, and Secretary Gideon Welles (q.v.) applauded a brave act at a time of sparse Union successes. The Confederates were hopeful that the insult would bring them swift recognition from London. England's reaction was anger, and neutrality teetered. Prime Minister Palmerston told a worried

Cabinet, "You may stand for this, but damned if I will!"

118 British reinforcements were sent to Canada, warships were alerted, and munitions shipments to the United States were prohibited. A stinging demand for release of the prisoners, softened in tone by Prince Albert and Queen Victoria, tweaked Seward's Anglophobia, but reason finally prevailed on both sides. Mason and Slidell were released and reached England late in January 1862. The **119** *Trent* Affair ended without war.

Wilkes's fame encouraged his buccaneering. In 1864, he was court-martialed for continued neutrality violations and was suspended. Later granted a commission as a rear admiral, he retired in 1866 and died in February 1877.

120 All that some men need to achieve greatness is a chance. Raphael Semmes was such a man. He looked like a rascal, with a high forehead framed by long hair, with eyes deep-set below fierce brows, with his nose accented by a stiff and twisted mustache. He had a gentleman's manners but a corsair's heart, and he became one of history's great sea raiders. Semmes, born in Maryland in September 1809, attended the U.S. Military Academy, studied law, and accepted a lieutenant's commission in the U.S. Navy in 1826. He saw active service in the Mexican War, and in 1861, as a commander, was put in charge of the Lighthouse Bureau. He resigned that position to join the Confederacy (he had adopted Alabama as home in 1849), and President Davis sent him on a successful mission to buy munitions in the North.

121 On Sunday, June 8, 1861, Semmes's chance came. He took the Confederacy's first warship, **122** the C.S.S. *Sumter,* through the New Orleans blockade, cruised the Caribbean and Atlantic for six months, was welcomed in several neutral ports, captured eighteen vessels, and at last was trapped at Gibraltar. Semmes paid off his crew and made his way back to the Confederacy.

123 On August 24, 1862, off the island of Terceria, he took command of a powerful 1000-ton, 220-foot-long steam-and-sailing ship that had been built in Liverpool, commissioned her the C.S.S. *Alabama,* and began a legend. For two years the *Alabama* was the scourge of Yankee commerce, from the Newfoundland Banks to the Caribbean to Galveston Bay, where she sank the larger U.S.S. *Hatteras.* From there she sailed to the Cape of Good Hope, to Singapore, to Cape Town, to the Azores, and on to Cherbourg, France.

EASTERN LAND BATTLES

124 **Many skirmishes took place in 1861.** Some were bloody, like Big Bethel, a victory that helped briefly preserve that part of Virginia for the Union. It all started at **125** Fort Sumter on April 12, 1861, when, after much agonizing about sovereignty and the onus of starting a war, the Confederate Cabinet ordered General Beauregard to fire on the fort sitting in Charleston Harbor.

126 After the attack on Fort Sumter, Lincoln issued a call for 75,000 men to put down the insurrection. Shortly after, Davis called for 100,000. Diplomacy (q.v.) had failed to keep the peace.

127 **Big Bethel, Virginia, is often named as the site of the Civil War's first battle, a distinction it shares with Phillipi, in what is now West Virginia.** Because more troops were engaged at Big Bethel, it is considered the more important of the two, even though it was not decisive. On June 10, 1861, General Benjamin Butler (q.v.), commanding a division at Fort Monroe, ordered a poorly conceived surprise attack against a Rebel outpost at Big Bethel. The troops were repulsed, with heavy losses. Butler's immediate subordinate, E. W. Pierce, bungled the advance by warning the Confederates and dooming the attack. But First Bull Run **128** ranks as the major action of the year.

129 **As Irvin McDowell (q.v.) prepared to move his large army southward on July 16, 1861,** Confederate forces continued to concentrate around Manassas Junction, an important rail hub with westward connections, toward the Shenandoah Valley. Near Manassas, Beauregard's numbers grew to 20,000, with another 3000 on the way. If McDowell's army attacked Confederate positions scattered along Bull Run Creek, Beauregard would need help from the Shenandoah Valley. There, General Joseph E. Johnston's (q.v.) force of about 12,000 faced an 18,000-man Union force under General Robert Patterson, whose job was to pin Johnston in place.

130 Beauregard, learning of McDowell's march, called for help. Oddly, that first help came from the Union Army. Because of terrible marching discipline, disorganization, and mixed orders, the march was delayed. Not until July 18 did McDowell's men, exhausted, hungry, dispirited, reach Centreville. McDowell thought Beauregard's force equal to his own 35,000 and intended to turn the Confederate right. A reconnaissance toward Bull Run late in the day convinced him otherwise, and he shifted to turn the Rebel left. Beauregard had developed much the same plan; he was to turn McDowell's left.

131 McDowell's reconnaissance on July 18 led the Confederate War Department to call for Johnston's aid. General Patterson unwittingly cooperated. Instead of pressing Johnston, he fell back, baffled by conflicting orders and confused by Colonel J.E.B. Stuart's cavalry. Johnston slipped away and marched to Piedmont Station on the Manassas Gap railroad, where he entrained his infantry. He ordered his artillery and cavalry to ride horses for Manassas, about thirty miles eastward.

132 The battle turned bad for Beauregard early on July 21. His Byzantine orders had been misinterpreted, confusing some recipients, and the enemy had turned his left flank. As fighting raged on the left,

Johnston, who had left the battle to his junior, went northwest to the sound of firing, collecting bits and pieces of units and artillery batteries as he went.

133 **General Thomas J. Jackson** (q.v.), **whose brigade was part of the strategic reserve on the right, received orders early on July 21 to reinforce the left.** About 11:30 in the morning he selected strong ground on the Henry House Hill and waited for the retreating Confederate forces to reach him. With a good artilleryman's sense of ground, Jackson selected the military crest of the Henry House Hill, put his artillery slightly in front of his

General Barnard E. Bee, C.S.A.

Stonewall Jackson at Winchester, Virginia, in February 1862.

infantry, recruited all the stray guns he could find along with infantry, and strengthened his line.

Not long after, 134 General Barnard E. Bee, whose men had faced heavy odds all morning, rode back to rally his men. When he saw Jackson, he said, "General, they are beating us back." Jackson fixed him with cold blue eyes and said, "Sir, we'll give them the bayonet." Excited, Bee directed his men to the shelter of Jackson's line and shouted, "There is Jackson, standing like a stone wall. Let us determine to die here, and we will conquer. Follow me." Bee soon fell, but his words lived after him, and Jackson was forever known as Stonewall.

135 **Beauregard, understanding tactics, took charge on his threatened flank as**

Johnston fed reinforcements to the left. By one o'clock Beauregard could sense some stability in his command, but suddenly two Union batteries careened up the Henry House Hill, took position some three hundred yards from Jackson's line, and began firing. Chaos reigned until the Thirty-third Virginia of Jackson's brigade dashed forward in their pale blue garb. The Blue cannoneers, thinking they were friends, halted and were swept away by a sudden volley. Charge and countercharge continued.

136 By midafternoon, there was a standoff, neither side having prevailed. The Confederates did finally grip all of the Henry House Hill, and as both sides prepared for a final rush, more of Johnston's men arrived on Beauregard's left. If one more brigade showed up, the Blue flankers would be flanked. In the shimmering distance Beauregard noted a long column of dust. Raising his field glasses, he looked anxiously to his left and saw a flag, but it drooped around the pole and could not be read.

137 Beauregard knew that if McDowell, who had commanded personally on his right, brought in more men, the battle was lost and the Rebels would have to retreat. The hero of Fort Sumter watched—a puff of wind, the flag unfurled. Confederate! Jubal Early's (q.v.) brigade had turned the Union right, and the Federals began to retreat, broken, and finally disintegrated across Bull Run. On they hurried toward Centreville and into Washington, sweeping

up guns, men, congressmen, and ladies as they went.

138 Although it was a smashing Confederate victory, First Manassas revealed that both sides were amateurs. The battle, the biggest on the American continent, had exacted a heavy price. The Union's killed, wounded, and captured came to 2896; the Confederacy's, 1982. For the South it was a Pyrrhic victory, for it tended to prove that one Rebel could whip ten Yankees and shocked the North with the realization that it was in for a long war.

WESTERN LAND BATTLES

139 On August 10, 1861, there was a bloody battle in southwestern Missouri that illustrated the discord in that slave state. Some Missourians wanted a Kentucky kind of neutrality; others wanted adherence to the Union; fewer sided with the Confederacy.

140 One man probably saved Missouri for the Union: Captain Nathaniel Lyon. He was a tough Connecticut Yankee in command of the important St. Louis Arsenal, which contained 50,000 muskets and other equipment. Pro-Southerners, including **141** Governor Claiborne Jackson, wanted the arsenal. Lyon, aided by Representative Francis P. Blair, Jr., brother of Lincoln's postmaster general, moved most of the arms into Illinois and

equipped pro-Union Germans in St. Louis. Jackson called out the militia, but Lyon surrounded their camp with his "Hessians" and forced surrender. St. Louis erupted into a small Civil War, and many pro-Union people defected to the Confederate camp, among them the former governor **142** Sterling Price. Boasting of his service in the Mexican War, Price took command of pro-Confederate troops.

143 Lincoln, worried about Missouri, quickly promoted Lyon to brigadier general and put him in charge of 10,000 Union troops. Lyon and Price met to talk of keeping the peace, but their meeting resulted in Lyon's declaring personal war on the Missouri Rebels and moving to capture the capital, Jefferson City. Price's force retreated, and Lyon pursued them to the southwestern corner of the state.

144 While the military maneuvered, the state convention declared the governorship vacant and appointed a new governor. Claiborne Jackson reacted by forming a rump Confederate government, which the Confederacy recognized in November. Lyon continued pressing Price with 6000 men, but his problems mounted as he moved farther from his base and his ninety-day enlistment men got ready to go home.

145 By August, Price's army had been reinforced by General Ben McCulloch's army from Arkansas, which included some Cherokee regiments and outnumbered Lyon's force nearly two to one. Lyon attacked Price at Wilson's Creek, about ten miles from Springfield, on August 10, 1861, audaciously splitting his force in two and surprising the Rebels. One of Lyon's columns mistook a blue-clad Louisiana force for Yankees, failed to fire, and was decimated. Lyon's remaining force, now outnumbered three to one, fought fiercely, ran short of ammunition, and retreated after Lyon was killed.

146 Wilson's Creek (also known as Springfield and as Oak Hills) hardly ranks as one of the great battles of the Civil War, but it was vicious. Of 5400 Federals engaged, 1317 were casualties: 258 killed,

Brigadier General Benjamin McCulloch, C.S.A.

873 wounded, 186 missing. Of 11,000 engaged, Confederate losses totaled 1230: 279 killed, 951 wounded. Wilson's Creek had some important effects; it opened nearly half of Missouri to the Rebels, ignited raider activities, and forced a new Northern start in the West.

ODDITIES

147 General Beauregard entertained many visitors after Manassas, among them the beautiful Cary sisters of Baltimore and their fetching cousin Constance. At a mock ceremony, the ever gallant Great Creole, as Beauregard was known, commissioned them into the "Cary Invincibles." He was much moved by hearing their musical version of James Ryder Randall's fiery "Maryland, My Maryland," which Jennie Cary had set to the tune of "Lauriger Horatius" (and was later adapted to "O Tannenbaum").

148 Not long afterward, these patriotic belles were asked by the Confederate Congress to design a new flag. The Stars and Bars—three bars, red, white, red, and a variable circle of stars held in a blue union—looked too much like the Stars and Stripes in battle, so they devised the Southern Cross, which was adopted in October 1861 and was known always as the Battle Flag.

149 When possible, Confederates named battles for the nearest town or community; the Union, for the nearest body of water—hence Bull Run and Manassas; Antietam (Creek) and Sharpsburg; Wilson's Creek and Oak Hills or Springfield; Stone's River and Murfreesboro; Ocean Pond and Olustee.

150 Kentucky declared itself neutral at the beginning of the war, hoping to profit from both sides. **151** Governor Beriah Magoffin, pro-Confederate, and the legislature, pro-Union, declared that Kentucky would defend its border against all comers. This anomalous situation had won agreement from both Lincoln and Davis; each coveted Kentucky and sought to win it by cajolery. By the end of the year neutrality ended in favor of the North, but only after a good deal of bumbling by both Southern and Northern sympathizers and soldiers. **152** Missouri, Kentucky, and Tennessee had both Union and Confederate governments, because their people were heavily divided. A question lingers about whether there were eleven or thirteen Confederate States. Tennessee authentically seceded, so it is counted among the eleven. The not quite legitimate governments in Missouri and Kentucky were recognized by the Confederacy and had representatives sitting in the Confederate Congress.

153 Beauregard knew of McDowell's advance toward Manassas almost the moment he started because of the effective spying by Rose O'Neal Greenhow, who was one of Washington's most influential and popular hostesses. The great and near-great accepted her invitations, and she listened carefully as they talked. A fervid Southern sympathizer, she set up a system to transmit intelligence to the Confederates across the Potomac. She was caught and placed under house arrest, but in May 1862 was sent through the lines. The next year she went abroad as a courier for the Confederacy. She was returning to the South, in 1864, aboard a blockade runner that was chased by the U.S.S. *Niphon*. She escaped in a small boat, but it was swamped by the surf, and she drowned off the North Carolina coast.

154 Robert Selden Garnett, a West Point graduate of 1841, was the first general killed on either side. He had been appointed a Confederate brigadier general on June 6, 1861, and on July 13, while operating in northwestern Virginia, he fell near Corrick's Ford on Cheat River.

155 Each side had two armies, one regular and one volunteer. It was possible for men to hold commissions, of different ranks, in both services, not unlike the United States Army in the Second World War, when the U.S. Army denoted the regular service and Army of the United States referred to the temporary service. **156** Although the Confederate Regular Army remained small, there were officers who held regular commissions as well as commissions in the Provisional Army of the Confederate States. Ezra J. Warner, in *Generals in Blue,* described the Union situation: "It was possible to hold four separate and distinct ranks at one and the same time. Many officers of the Regular Army, who held substantive and brevet rank [conferred for distinction], obtained leaves in order to accept commissions in the volunteer service, where substantive and brevet rank also existed. Ranald S. Mackenzie at the end of the war was a full-rank brigadier general of U.S. volunteers, a major general of volunteers by brevet, and a brigadier general by brevet in the Regular Army, although his substantive rank in the Regulars was captain of engineers."

157 **Lincoln's own house was divided.** Four brothers-in-law wore Gray: Mrs. Lincoln's brother, Dr. George R. C. Todd, was a Confederate surgeon; one of Mrs. Lincoln's sisters was married to Confederate General Ben Hardin Helm, who rejected a commission from Lincoln. Frequently, men from divided families met on the battlefield or in the hospital.

158 **Lincoln proclaimed a blockade of the 3000 miles of Southern coast on April 19, 1861.** This had an important effect on neutral nations, most of which decided to honor the blockade, even though the 1856 Declaration of Paris had

announced that a blockade must be effective to be honored. During the first year of the war, the Union squadrons caught only one out of ten ships running the blockade.

159 **The Confederate Provisional Constitution, in effect for a year, provided for a unicameral legislature** and election of the President and vice president by the states, each with one vote. The supreme court would consist of the judges of the district courts, and an amendment could be made by a two-thirds vote of Congress.

160 **The permanent Constitution of the Confederacy contained important clarifications of the Federal Constitution.** The Bill of Rights was worked into the text; "Almighty God" appeared in the preamble; the President and vice president each was to serve for six years and the President could not succeed himself; the President had the item veto; he had to report reasons to the Senate for removal of all officers except Cabinet members and diplomats. With congressional consent, Cabinet members might sit on the floor of either house to discuss their departments. No bounties would be granted, no protective tariff passed or export tax levied without a two-thirds majority, unless it was requested in the President's budget. Each law was to have one title and was to focus on one subject. No general welfare

Federal naval blockade of Southern coast.

clause appeared in the document. Slavery was recognized in the territories, but the slave trade was strictly prohibited. Sundry phrases paid homage to the state-rights nature of the government. Amendments would be difficult to achieve. Generally, though, the Confederate Constitution copied much of the Federal document.

161 Some things are hard to kill, even in war. Audacity, for instance. In mid-November 1861, a Wisconsin volunteer fifer challenged—in the columns of the Louisville *Journal*—any Confederate fifer to compete with him for $500. The program would be "Yankee Doodle" and "The Star-Spangled Banner," and the match was to come off when Confederate General Simon B. Buckner and his army had been taken prisoner.

162 On December 30, 1861, the U.S. government and banks in leading cities suspended specie payment, a harsh indication of the rising costs of war.

163 Late in 1861 the Confederate medical service began building the largest military hospital on the continent, an 8000-bed complex above the James River. Opened early in 1862, Chimborazo Hospital treated more than 76,000 men during the war and pioneered in layout, administration, and service.

164 Colonel Ephraim Elmer Ellsworth was the first Union casualty of McDowell's advance toward Richmond. Only twenty-four, Ellsworth had organized the famed 11th New York Fire Zouave drill team. As they were marching through Alexandria on May 24, 1861, he and some others spotted a secession flag over the Marshall House and rushed to tear it down. On his way downstairs, carrying the flag, Ellsworth was shot by the hotel keeper, **165** James Jackson, who was shot in retaliation. Ellsworth, a friend of Lincoln, became a martyr, and many babies received "Colonel Ellsworth" as a given name. James Jackson became a Confederate martyr.

166 Both armies studied tactics from a Rebel general's book, General W. J. Hardee's *Tactics.*

167 Radical labor theories by Karl Marx (probably written by his friend Friedrich Engels) were followed in Northern newspapers. A few continued early in the war. Marx's treatise on labor, *Das Kapital,* was relatively unknown.

168 Marx wrote the International Workingmen's Association's address to Lincoln in January 1865: "The workingmen of Europe feel sure that, as the American War of Independence initiated a new era of ascendency for the middle class, so the American anti-slavery war will do for the working classes. They consider it an earnest of the epoch to come that it fell to the lot of Abraham Lincoln, the single-minded son of the working class, to lead the country through the matchless struggle for the rescue of an enchained race and the reconstruction of a social world."

169 Hugh McVey, 4th Kentucky Cavalry, fell at Shiloh. A veteran of Waterloo, McVey was more than seventy years old.

170 An eleven-year-old in the Orphan Brigade spurred a charge at Shiloh. A bugler, known as Little Oirish, picked up the brigade flag, rushed a captured gun, and led a charge.

171 Sutlers, who sold personal items, including food, to the camps, were notorious profiteers. Rumor had it that, after Shiloh, Union troops paid fifteen cents for a lemon, forty cents for a pound of cheese, and a dollar for a pint of whiskey. Confederate sutlers were equally adept at fleecing the poorer Rebs, since they usually offered such scarce items as clothing, scrawny chickens, and sometimes candy.

172 The differences in diet could be noted in the slain. The thinner Rebel dead decayed more slowly than the fatter Yankee bodies.

173 One Union officer was shocked as he looked through a dead Rebel boy's haversack. The day's rations: "A handful of black beans, a few pieces of sorghum, and a half-dozen roasted acorns."

174 When Stonewall Jackson's men took the huge Union supply depot at Manassas, during the August 1862 campaign against General Pope, the vast riches were beyond Confederate imagination. The Rebs nearly immobilized themselves by gorging, and it was only Stonewall's harsh discipline that induced them to destroy what was left.

175 Rebel rations became tragically scant during the final stages of the Siege of Petersburg. Interrupted communications cut the daily issue to a handful of parched corn and a spoonful of brown sugar.

176 Many officers and men in the war sported sideburns, hair grown down the cheeks. This tonsorial innovation got its name from U.S. General Ambrose Burnside, who proudly wore the brush.

DIPLOMACY

177 Jefferson Davis and his Cabinet hoped for a negotiated secession, al-

Manassas Junction after Confederate attack of August 26, 1862.

Ambrose Everett Burnside, Commander of the Army of the Potomac during the Fredericksburg campaign, 1862–1863.

though after reading Lincoln's Inaugural Address, Davis doubted there was any chance for one. Davis's earlier career had not prepared him for the arcane area of diplomacy. It was not that he subscribed to the idea that diplomats are paid to "go abroad and lie for their countries"; he did not realize that diplomacy is a subtlety best understood by veteran knaves and venerable nations.

178 Still, with some hope, he sent a three-man delegation to discuss separation, and introduced them to Lincoln with a conciliatory letter. He had picked his men with care, showing a firm faith in old verities at a time when verities were shifting with reality. The delegation, thought Davis, "should have conciliated the sympathy and cooperation of every element of conservatism with which they might . . . deal."

179 Former Governor Alfred Roman of Louisiana went because he was an old-line Whig who had shifted to the Constitutional Union party in 1860.

180 Georgia's Martin Crawford, a state-rights Democrat, had supported Breckinridge in 1860.

181 John Forsyth of Alabama had forcefully supported Douglas in 1860.

182 Once in Washington, the three men were given a run-around. Lincoln avoided them and left them to the subtle mercies of Seward, who dealt with them through intermediaries, tantalized them with hints of surrendering Fort Sumter, professed all kinds of good will, and eventually duped them. Davis doubted much that Seward said, but he could hardly have guessed the depths of his duplicity. The result of the mission was dashed hopes and angered honor, with Lincoln's hands clean as efforts to supply Sumter sent the Southerners home on April 1, 1861.

183 Any realist could see that the Confederacy's best asset was cotton, a commodity that was needed around the world, that kept the mills going in England and France, and that was expected with certainty to win recognition for the South. "King Cotton Diplomacy," as early Confederate policy was called, had logic, so Davis picked another triumvirate—**184** the Yancey-Rost-Mann Mission—to go abroad and propose cotton for recognition. Davis's men were envoys of odd ineptitude: William L. Yancey's proslavery history limited his usefulness; Pierre Rost spoke French, but his brashness hardly charmed the salon; Dudley Mann's verbose ego sharply restricted his welcome.

185 They arrived in Europe just as Britain and France declared neutrality and granted the Confederacy belligerent rights. Therefore, they claimed success even though they failed to achieve their main commercial objective.

186 Charles Francis Adams, son and grandson of Presidents, the U.S. Ambassador to Britain, and a founder of the Free Soil and Republican Parties, had hailed Lincoln's election as a harbinger of freedom. He represented his country with steadiness, wit, and grace at the Court of St. James's. Fending off Seward's fulminations, upholding Northern interests, fighting against Confederate shipbuilding in England and Europe, Adams did much to prevent Confederate success abroad.

187 José Agustín Quintero, a Cuban whose Southern sympathies and personal connections in northern Mexico made him an important Confederate emissary, was a secret agent sent by Secretary Benjamin from Texas to northern Mexico in 1861. Quintero revived his friendship with Santiago Vidaurri, governor of Nuevo León y Coahuila. A lively cooperation ensued, with Vidaurri offering important supplies to the South and suggesting Confederate annexation of his own state and Tamaulipas.

188 This alliance between Quintero and Vidaurri gave rise to a vital cotton trade between San Antonio and such north Mexican cities as Laredo and Eagle Pass. It lasted throughout the war. Large amounts of military and civilian supplies were traded for thousands of cotton bales hauled hundreds of miles across south Texas.

189 In May 1862, the Rebels did score one notable diplomatic success. That month the Swiss-born Henry Hotze, probably the most effective Confederate agent ever sent abroad, began publishing the London *Index,* a newspaper funded by the Confederacy and dedicated to the truth as seen with Rebel eyes. Ably edited, the *Index* converted many Europeans to Southern sympathies with its good-humored candor.

1862

THE SECOND
YEAR OF
THE WAR

It had been a long winter. Both warring nations nursed wounds, boasted successes, and pondered their next moves.

190 **For the Confederacy, the winter seemed colder than usual, with a north wind blowing across the land and buffeting the coasts.** Defending over 3000 miles of coastline posed large problems.

191 Working without precedent, the Union Navy joined with army units in August 1861 to capture important bases on the Confederate coast. A joint operation took Fort Clark and Fort Hatteras and dominated Pamlico Sound. In November the entrance to Port Royal fell, along with Beaufort, South Carolina, and some signif-icant sea islands; the important Confederate post at Roanoke Island fell in March 1862.

192 Federal bases on the Carolina coast anchored the growing blockade squadrons seeking to choke the rebellion. They were to serve an equally disturbing function as staging areas for river incursions into the Southern heartland, a land cut with rivers often used for commerce.

193 Riverine operations, as they were known at the beginning of the war, had a long military history under less imposing names, but efforts to turn Southern rivers into avenues of invasion turned into a different kind of war. It was fought by boats,

Foundry at Federal naval station, Hilton Head, South Carolina, 1862.

Federal gunboats near Memphis, Tennessee, on June 5, 1862, the day before they defeated the Confederate flotilla and took Memphis.

marines, sailors, cavalrymen, slaves, cotton, all kinds of people in unsung and often bloody forms of combat, from the coast to the Mississippi, the Red, the Ohio, Tennessee, Cumberland, Roanoke, James, Potomac, and Yazoo Rivers.

194 Both navies grew during 1862. Northern blockade squadrons expanded in scope and size. The North Atlantic and the Eastern and Western Gulf Squadrons menaced most of the Confederate sea outlets. Southern efforts centered on building blockade-running vessels and on commissioning privateers as well as cruisers, such as the *Sumter* (q.v.) and the *Alabama* (q.v.).

195 Both sides geared toward war as the governments concentrated on finances, transportation, agricultural production, on all aspects of the new science of logistics, on diplomacy, and on organizing armies larger than any in American history.

196 Lincoln's and Davis's initial calls for volunteers intensified into a constant demand for men. Armies grew beyond the relatively small ones of First Bull Run, and campaigns swirled around Richmond, in the crucial central area along the Mississippi, even in west Texas, and around the old Spanish settlements near Santa Fe.

197 Confederate diplomacy shifted focus to commercial interests, while Northern diplomats continued their attempts to isolate the South. By the end of the year the Confederacy's future seemed cloudy but not hopeless. The North was nursing serious wounds to armies and morale.

EASTERN LAND BATTLES

**198 General Ambrose Burnside and Commodore L. M. Goldsborough worked together in February and March 1862 to capture the important

Confederate position at Roanoke Island, at the entrance to Albemarle Sound, North Carolina. Southern reaction to the loss of Roanoke ran from disbelief to anger to depression. Twenty-five hundred men were gone, along with a vital strategic position. No matter that the new Union amphibious combination put 13,000 troops up against the island; the loss was unacceptable because it exposed main rail lines connecting the Deep South with Virginia. Dereliction, inefficiency, skullduggery, crime, treason—all these misdeeds were attributed to Secretary of War Benjamin, because he apparently had refused to send gunpowder to the island until too late.

199 Twenty-five years after the war, evidence showed that Benjamin had no powder to send, corroborating that woeful lack would have given vital intelligence to the North. "For the want of a nail" pretty clearly described the South's condition early in 1862, as the war settled into dead earnest.

200 **In April a far worse defeat battered the Confederacy.** On April 29, 1862, New Orleans fell to a combined land-water campaign led by General Benjamin F. Butler and Flag Officer David Glasgow Farragut. Farragut's fleet passed the formidable Confederate Mississippi bastions 201 Fort Jackson and Fort St. Philip, and anchored at the panic-stricken city. Defenders under 202 General Mansfield Lovell were far too few to man the massive works around the city.

203 General Lovell had been asking for help for some time; instead, his men were steadily siphoned off to other Confederate armies. With what he had, he did almost more than possible. The loss of one of the Confederacy's world-famous landmarks and control of the Mississippi's mouths staggered the South and thrilled the North. A young New Orleans girl wrote in her diary, on April 25, "We are conquered but not subdued."

204 **Stonewall Jackson's famed Shenandoah Valley campaign began with a defeat, at Kernstown, Virginia, on March 23, 1862.** As he took his small force down the Valley (the Shenandoah River flowed north), he encountered a Union force under Brigadier General James Shields. Inadequate reconnaissance led Jackson, with 3500 men, to attack a force of 9000 men. Jackson, compelled to withdraw, learned a lesson; he never again attacked without proper scouting.

205 Kernstown ranked as a Confederate strategic success, however, since it prompted Washington to send a Federal army under Major General Nathaniel P. Banks (q.v.) to counter Jackson's threat to the Union capital. Even more dangerous was Lincoln's decision to keep General Irwin McDowell's (q.v.) force from joining McClellan's peninsular advance on Richmond. Jackson attracted nearly ten times as many Union soldiers as he had in

his army, thereby keeping them from other service.

206 Jackson schemed in strategic terms and plotted grand tactics. He needed more men to deal with the Federals who were clotting the Valley, but he would use those he had to function as confusers and worriers. Aided by Major General Richard S. Ewell's (q.v.) 7000-man brigade, Jackson, at the end of April 1862, feinted a move southeast toward Richmond, put his men on the Virginia Central Railroad, and moved west through Staunton to join Brigadier General Edward (Allegheny) Johnson's (q.v.) 2000 men.

207 Jackson fought the Battle of McDowell, in Virginia, on May 8, 1862, and defeated a 6000-man force under Brigadier General Robert Milroy. The battle did not run entirely according to plan, since it cost the Rebels more losses than the Yankees. But the results were splendid. Milroy hastily retreated northward in the South Branch Valley and was unable to join Major General Banks in the Shenandoah.

208 Jackson then turned to take on Banks. Joined by Ewell, Jackson surprised a 1000-man Union outpost at Front Royal on May 23, 1862, and captured most of the survivors. Jackson hoped to cut off Banks by getting between him and Winchester, but Banks slipped ahead.

209 Jackson rushed Banks's entrench-

ments at Winchester on May 25, drove the hapless Federals out of the Shenandoah Valley, and marched to threaten Washington at Harpers Ferry.

210 Lincoln personally plotted the bagging of Jackson. He ordered Shields to return from east of the Blue Ridge and told Frémont to join him at Strasburg. That junction, he hoped, would neatly bottle up Jackson's army. The plan failed.

211 Rapid marches by Jackson's "Foot Cavalry" eluded Lincoln's snare.

212 Jackson, in remarkable dual battles, turned victoriously on the united forces of Shields and Frémont at Cross Keys and Port Republic, on June 8 and 9, 1862.

213 In a dazzling campaign that lasted little more than a month, Jackson's 17,000 men had outfought, outmaneuvered, and outmarched more than 70,000 Yankees. His reputation spread around the world.

214 When the campaign ended in the Valley, Jackson's army moved to defend Richmond. McClellan's timorous advance had finally threatened Richmond from the peninsular approach, and Joe Johnston moved the Confederate army from Manassas to oppose Little Mac's force of over 110,000 men, who were moving glacially up between the York and James Rivers from old Revolutionary positions at Yorktown and Williamsburg.

215 At Seven Pines (also called Fair Oaks) in Virginia, Joe Johnston attacked

Federal entrenchments at Seven Pines (also called Fair Oaks), Virginia, June 1, 1862.

McClellan's advancing legions. In a two-day action, from May 31 to June 1, 1862, several confused attacks failed to destroy the exposed Federal positions, and the situation remained essentially unchanged, except that Johnston suffered a debilitating wound.

216 The most important result of the Seven Pines fighting was a change in command of the Confederate army. Robert E. Lee replaced Johnston on June 1, and as he regrouped an army he barely knew, Lee daringly plotted to recoup its fortunes.

217 Lee's reputation was not very high that June. His campaign in western Vir-ginia had fizzled; his engineering operations around Charleston lacked glamor; his important work as a kind of chief of staff to President Davis after Manassas was unknown. Still, many thought him talented, and some relief greeted his promotion.

218 **Large numbers of men clotted around Richmond.** President Davis and the Confederate government brought together 90,000 men around the capital, and General Lee received important information about enemy dispositions from a rising star of the Rebel cavalry, James Ewell Brown (Jeb) Stuart.

Confederate Major General James Ewell Brown (Jeb) Stuart.

219 On a four-day "Ride Around McClellan," Jeb Stuart's 1200 men rode around the enemy's right flank, raided deep behind McClellan's front, then rode on around his left flank into Richmond. Suddenly famous, Stuart brought Lee invaluable information about terrain, enemy strength, and troop dispositions. He may, however, have alerted McClellan to his exposed flanks. Still, the ride was one of the great adventures of the Civil War—and Stuart would do it again in October!

220 Varina Davis received a worried letter from her husband, the President, as the opposing legions grew: "We are preparing and taking position for the struggle which may be near at hand. The

stake is too high to permit the pulse to keep its even beat . . . A total defeat of McClellan will relieve the Confederacy of its embarrassments in the East."

221 Lee tried to keep the odds fairly even. He sent reinforcements to Jackson just before calling him to Richmond. The ruse worked. Lee collected units from Virginia and planned a vast flanking move-

First Lady of the Confederacy Varina Howell Davis, who later wrote a two-volume biography of Jefferson Davis.

The Chickahominy River, June 1862.

ment around McClellan's exposed right, north of the Chickahominy River. Uncharacteristically, Jackson arrived late for the Seven Days' Battles around Richmond. **Since Jackson was missing, 222 Gen-**

General Daniel Harvey Hill, C.S.A.

eral Daniel Harvey Hill began the Seven Days' Battles by attacking Union positions at Mechanicsville, north of Richmond. He ran into strong resistance from 223 General Fitz John Porter's big corps, which repulsed a major Rebel attack late in the day. Costs were high: 1484 Confederate casualties out of some 14,000 men engaged, to 361 for the 15,000 Federals on the field.

224 During the night, Porter withdrew to a strong position near Gaines's Mill, and McClellan, seeing enemies everywhere, began shifting his base from the Pamunkey River to the James.

225 **On Friday, June 27, Jackson's men, though they arrived late, delivered the breaking blow against Porter's positions at Gaines's Mill.** McClellan ordered Porter to hold at any cost to provide cover for the Union change of base, and Porter's men, atop a semicircular ridge, beat off furious Rebel attacks through ravines, across fields, and in swamps.

About dark, 226 General John Bell Hood's (q.v.) Texas Brigade, aided by 227 General George Edward Pickett's (q.v.) men, broke the Union line. Darkness and confusion prevented total disaster for the Union as Federals retreated across the Chickahominy and joined the Union main body. Again, Confederate losses outran those of the Federals: 8750 out of some 57,000 engaged to 6837 casualties for the 36,000 Federals.

Now the Rebels were well on

Ruins of Gaines's Mill, which gave its name to the encounter in the Seven Days' Battles fought on June 27, 1862.

McClellan's right and rear. Had he made a serious effort, he could have rushed into Richmond, but, too concerned for his flank, he botched the opportunity.

228 On June 28, McClellan apparently panicked. Assuming that the battle was lost, he moved the blame from his shoulders to Lincoln's. In a bitter telegram, McClellan complained of too few men and a general failure of support from the government—but while he complained, he continued moving his army toward the James, contracting his exposed right. Some fighting marked the day at Golding's Farm and Dispatch Station.

229 Confusion jumbled Confederate efforts to push on during Sunday, June 29. As Confederate units crossed the Chickahominy in pursuit, some were delayed by mixed orders from army head-

quarters (Jackson had received orders to hold at Grapevine Bridge). Others, plagued by poor maps, struggled to find the enemy and one another. Rebels pressed the Yankee rearguard at Savage's Station, captured 2500 sick and wounded, but failed to achieve a decisive victory.

230 Monday, June 30, saw some of the hardest, most confused action of the Seven Days' campaign. The battle of that day is known by at least eight names: White Oak Swamp, Frayser's Farm, Glendale, Nelson's Crossroads, Charles City Crossroads, New Market Road, Willis's Church, and Turkey Bridge. Lee, his coordination weak, tried to attack McClellan from the north, across the boggy White Oak Swamp, and from the west. Jackson's doings that day have long been a puzzle. He seemed lethargic, nearly asleep, showed none of the drive

White Oak Swamp, which McClellan's men crossed on a single long bridge they then destroyed before the Confederates could use it.

that he had in the Valley, and let a battle go on across the swamp without trying to help.

231 McClellan, at last aware of what was happening, foiled the attacks and withdrew to a strong position on Malvern Hill. On this decisive day Lee missed a chance to cut McClellan's army in two. Richmond, though, had been saved by a major and successful Confederate offensive, although McClellan still outnumbered the triumphant Lee.

232 Determined to wreck McClellan

Below: Brigadier General J. H. Martindale (seated) and the staff of the 5th Corps, whose men bore the brunt of the Confederate attack at Malvern Hill, July 1, 1862.

and hurl him into the James, Lee rashly attacked **233** Malvern Hill on July 1. Confederate drives, disjointed and uncoordinated, were barely supported by artillery that was no match for Union cannon on the hill. All the Southern attacks ended in a welter of blood. Still, McClellan retreated farther, to his new base at Harrison's Landing.

234 The costs of the Seven Days' Battles were staggering. Confederate losses amounted to about 20,000: 3286 killed, 15,909 wounded, 946 missing out of a total of about 88,000. Federal losses came to almost 16,000: 1734 killed, 8062 wounded, and 6503 missing from an army of some 115,000.

235 The Seven Days' Battles created vastly different reputations: Lee was the hero, McClellan the goat, and Jackson the puzzle.

236 With McClellan effectively tethered along the James, quarreling with Lincoln, Lee wasted no time in addressing a new threat.

237 **General John Pope's Army of Virginia moved south of the Potomac to relieve pressure on the Army of the Potomac.** This army, comprising McDowell's, Banks's, and Frémont's commands and such other detachments as could be gathered, swelled to about 75,000 men during July and August 1862. When Pope first invaded Virginia, he issued debasing orders to his men and to the citizens of Virginia that set new standards for military bombast. One of them, headed "Headquarters in the Saddle," sparked a famous quip from Lincoln: "Pope has his headquarters where his hindquarters ought to be."

238 While many wondered about Jackson, Lee gave him nearly half of the remaining army and detached him to deal with Pope. Lee clearly realized that his Presbyterian deacon functioned better in independent command. Jackson marched promptly and was engaged by Pope's advance elements under Banks. Checked at first, Jackson pushed reinforcements to a desperate conflict and finally drove Banks's men from the field in a battle variously named Cedar Mountain, Slaughter Mountain, Cedar Run, Cedar Run Mountain, and Southwest Mountain. Jackson's personal exposure saved a battle ill fought by both sides.

239 Banks took 8000 men into battle and lost 2381; Jackson, who finally deployed 16,800, took 1341 casualties. The battle's main result was to make clear Pope's major effort in central Virginia, and soon McClellan's men along the James were being transported north to help Pope.

240 **On August 13, Lee moved to help Jackson and thus** began the Second Manassas Campaign. Pope slowly drew back to the Rappahannock River toward McClellan's reinforcing troops, skirmished with Rebel cavalry, and tried to determine Lee's intentions.

Federal soldiers repairing damage done by Stuart's cavalry at Catlett's Station, August 22, 1862.

Manassas Junction, August 26, 1862, where Jackson's men looted the Federal dumps and destroyed any supplies they could not carry away.

241 At Catlett's Station, on June 22, General Jeb Stuart (now commanding all cavalry of the new 242 Army of Northern Virginia, soon to be called Lee's Army), captured Pope's baggage train, containing all his papers. On August 26, General Fitzhugh Lee's Gray troopers captured Manassas Junction, a major Union supply point, as Jackson—again detached with a large corps—marched around Pope's right flank. Lee followed, with General James Longstreet's corps.

243 Pope, baffled, rested his army and waited for developments. They came as Jackson's men captured or destroyed the Manassas dumps and then moved to a strong position in a railroad cut near the old Manassas battlefield, between Pope's army and Washington. A sharp, bloody fight at 244 Brawner's Farm on Thursday, August 28, focused Pope's attention on Jackson, and a slow Union concentration began.

245 Elements of Pope's army launched the Battle of Second Manassas (called Second Bull Run by the Union) with a piecemeal attack against Jackson's entrenched line on August 29, 1862. Jackson beat off repeated assaults, even though he was hard-pressed at times. In fact, some his men ran out of ammunition and had to throw rocks at the enemy. By the end of the day Lee and Longstreet were in position to hit the Union left flank in the morning. Pope, having convinced himself that the Rebels would retreat, struck Jackson hard but reeled under

Battlefield of Second Manassas (Second Bull Run), August 29–30, 1862.

Longstreet's flank drive, which threatened to envelop his whole army. Heavy fighting around the Henry House Hill (the scene of bitter struggle during First Manassas) kept open Pope's lines of retreat and prevented total destruction of his army. Defeated, he retreated toward Washington with a fierce rearguard action at **246** Chantilly (or Ox Hill), Virginia, on September 1, 1862.

247 Casualties were enormous on both sides as the war showed the power of modern weaponry. From August 27 to September 2, Confederate losses cannot have been fewer than 1400 killed, 7600 wounded, and nearly a hundred missing, for a total close to 9000 out of a force of nearly 50,000. Federal losses were about 1700 killed, 8300 wounded, nearly 6000 missing, or about 16,000 out of the 75,000 men engaged.

248 As Pope's defeated legions straggled into the Federal capital, Lincoln considered ways to save the city and perhaps the war. With serious misgivings, and against heavy Cabinet opposition, Lincoln put McClellan back in command of Union forces around Washington. Although the President doubted the general's fighting qualities, he admired the man's ability to rebuild morale.

249 President Davis and General Lee pondered how best to capitalize on the expulsion of the enemy from Virginia. Convinced, as Napoleon had been, that the weaker side must be the more aggressive, Lee pressed for the invasion of Maryland.

Carrying war to the enemy would encourage the South, discourage the North, impress foreign powers, and perhaps add another slave state to the Confederacy. At least it might recruit thousands of Marylanders to the ranks.

250 Gray soldiers began crossing the Potomac at fords around Leesburg on Thursday, September 4, as the Maryland campaign began. The crossing took three days, and on September 6, Stonewall Jackson's corps marched into Frederick, which they found closed and empty, like a "churchyard." Few recruits appeared, and Maryland seemed curiously unfriendly.

251 From Frederick, on September 9, Lee issued General Order No. 191, daringly dispersing his army westward. Jackson would take a major force to eliminate the 12,500-man Federal garrison at Harpers Ferry; other units would hold mountain passes in western Maryland and establish a possible reconcentration point for Lee's army. At about three in the morning of September 10, Jackson and his staff rode through Frederick. John Greenleaf Whittier to the contrary, Barbara Frietchie did not show her "old gray head" that morning, but a few curious onlookers heard the general ask directions to so many places that no one could tell where he was going.

252 McClellan suddenly knew where Lee was going—only because of a fluke. During the morning of September 13, two Union soldiers, strolling along Frederick's streets, picked up three cigars wrapped in a copy of Lee's General Order No. 191. When they turned it in, McClellan appraised it with some caution; it seemed too good to be true. But he began a concentration beyond Frederick with uncharacteristic speed. By the time Stuart told Lee of the 253 **Lost Order,** skirmishing had begun along some of the mountain passes east of Hagerstown.

254 Lee faced ruin. With his men dispersed—Longstreet near Hagerstown, Stuart at South Mountain, Jackson at Harpers Ferry, D. H. Hill's rearguard division strung along various passes—Lee considered the idea of retreating piecemeal across the Potomac. But he clung to hope, despite fierce fighting in the passes on the night of September 14–15. General Lafayette McLaws's (q.v.) men, holding the southern end of South Mountain and covering Harpers Ferry escape routes, were attacked, and Lee realized the army would have to concentrate somewhere.

255 **Jackson eased the danger.** Late on September 14, he told Lee that Harpers Ferry would probably fall the next day, and Lee hoped that McLaws could escape to Harpers Ferry and join Jackson. Where should they gather? Lee decided on the small village of Sharpsburg, Maryland.

256 Harpers Ferry fell to Jackson early on September 15, and he began marching toward Sharpsburg, where Lee had collected about 18,000 men along a lazy creek called Antietam, which branched off

from the Potomac. On September 16 and 17, one of the bloodiest battles of the Civil War raged along that creek—Antietam to those of the Blue persuasion, Sharpsburg to wearers of the Gray.

257 McClellan mismanaged his battle from the start. With more than 75,000 men on the field against Lee's—at most—40,000, the Little Napoleon fed in his divisions bit by bit, which permitted Lee's thinner legions to defeat them. But there were terrible moments when Rebel lines seemed to evaporate at the Corn Field near the Dunkard Church on Lee's left, then in the center at the Bloody Lane, and

Burnside's Bridge outside Sharpsburg, where General Burnside's Federals crossed Antietam Creek.

Confederate casualties of Hooker's charge, along the Hagerstown Pike, after one of the bloodiest days of the war, September 17, 1862.

at last on the right, as McClellan shifted his point of attack. At a critical moment in the afternoon of September 17, when General Burnside's men were about to cross a vital bridge (known ever since as Burnside's Bridge) to turn the weak Rebel right, General Ambrose Powell Hill's (q.v.) Light Division arrived from Harpers Ferry and ended the Yankee attack.

258 So fearsome were the sounds along the Antietam that they were remembered. People in Shepherdstown, a few miles away, across the Potomac, heard "the incessant explosions of artillery, the shrieking whistles of the shells, and the sharper, deadlier, more thrilling roll of musketry; while every now and then the echo of

some charging cheer would come, borne by the wind, and as the human voice pierced that demoniacal clangor we would catch our breath and listen."

259 Other voices tolled the wages of the war's worst day. A Pennsylvania soldier said, "No tongue can tell, no mind conceive, no pen portray the horrible sights I witnessed this morning"; a Wisconsin man felt it all as a "great tumbling together of all heaven and earth."

260 Barely staving off disaster, Lee's men held their positions during the night, and on September 18, Lee hoped McClellan would try again. Such a drive would have finished the Army of Northern Virginia, because McClellan had 24,000 unengaged men on the field, in addition to 12,000 who had arrived during the night. Convinced at last that defeat was probable, Lee withdrew to Virginia during the night of September 18–19, 1862.

261 Both sides had botched the battle. Lee should not have fought at Antietam with so few, nor held on against rising odds on September 18. McClellan failed to coordinate his full strength anywhere on the field, wasted his legions one by one, and failed to attack on September 18, when victory was in his hands.

262 Lincoln anguished over McClellan's failure to push Lee. In part, the awful cost of battle explained McClellan's reluctance: out of 75,000 men when the battle began, McClellan lost about 12,400; Lee,

Lincoln's visit to the Antietam camps, October 8, 1862. To his right, Allan Pinkerton who set up the army's secret service. To his left, General John A. McClernand.

out of about 40,000 on the field, lost 14,000.

263 McClellan had missed opportunities, but the Confederates had failed by not sustaining their invasion. On the coattails of that thin success, and despite a concurrent Confederate invasion of Tennessee and Kentucky by Braxton Bragg (q.v.) and General E. Kirby Smith (q.v.), Lincoln issued his Preliminary Emancipation Proclamation. The war, as Lincoln feared, had begun to change the nature of the old Union.

264 McClellan did not change. Despite President Lincoln's distress about his failure to push Lee, McClellan stalled for weeks, complaining always. On October 25, 1862, a complaint about horses sparked one of the President's famous quips: "I have just read your despatch about sore tongued and fatiegued [sic] horses. Will you pardon me for asking what the horses of your army have done since the battle of Antietam that fatigue anything?" The next day, McClellan crossed his men into Virginia—to Lincoln's wry enjoyment. Still, Lee kept his men distributed around northern Virginia and waited for a serious thrust from his hesitant opponent.

265 Lincoln's patience finally snapped on November 5, and he replaced Little Mac with General Ambrose E. Burnside (q.v.), who did not want the job. McClellan's controversial military career was over, but many in his army dreaded his departure. Burnside reorganized the forces and began moving toward Fredericksburg, Virginia, in mid-November. Lee countered by sending Longstreet's corps to hold Marye's Heights, overlooking Fredericksburg. A quick Federal push would have caught Lee's army divided, but Burnside paused to collect more men and supplies while Jackson was joining Lee's lines. Federal troops began crossing the Rappahannock River to Fredericksburg on December 11 and 12, against heavy opposition from sharpshooters.

266 On Saturday, December 13, Burnside launched the Battle of Fredericksburg. Union frontal assaults against impregnable Confederate positions above the town and against Jackson's lines on the

Surgery in the field. Without antiseptic measures, the incidence of infection was high and the loss of limbs frequent.

Confederate right were foolhardy and disastrous. One Yankee soldier said that "it was a great slaughter pen . . . they might as well have tried to take hell." Burnside's losses amounted to 12,653 out of more than 110,000 men. Lee lost 5309 out of nearly 72,000.

267 Lee, from a vantage point above Marye's Heights, made a comment that showed a hidden side of himself: "It is well that war is so terrible—we should grow too fond of it!"

268 Burnside fumed in defeat as Northern morale sagged and winter promised more discomfort to the Army of the Potomac.

WESTERN LAND BATTLES

269 It sometimes seemed as though two wars were raging in 1862. In the eastern theater of war, the Army of Northern Virginia largely held its own and dominated the Army of the Potomac. The point is made in a book published in 1978 **270**: *Our Masters the Rebels: A Speculation on Union Military Failure in the East, 1861–1865,* by Michael C. C. Adams.

271 Affairs in the sprawling West were different. There, after initial successes at Wilson's Creek, Missouri (q.v.), and in Kentucky, Confederate forces either played catch-up or were beaten, which has led many historians to believe that the war was lost in the West. The argument is likely to continue; there are valid points to be made by both sides.

272 An initial Confederate success at Middle Creek, Kentucky, on January 10, 1862—General James A. Garfield (q.v.), the future President, failed to beat the Confederates under General Humphrey Marshall (q.v.)—was followed nine days later by a serious defeat.

273 Confederate strategy called for holding a line from Cumberland Gap to Columbus, Kentucky, on the Mississippi, in order to stabilize the northwestern frontier. Resources were limited, leadership uncertain, the stakes high.

Two major battles raged in Kentucky during the war. 274 The first had a confusion of names to match the action itself: Mill Springs, Fishing Creek, Somerset, Logan's Cross Roads, Beech Grove.

275 On January 19, 1862, Confederate General George B. Crittenden launched a night advance in the rain against a threatening Federal force under General George H. Thomas (q.v.). From a weak position, Crittenden tried to seize success by sending his flamboyant subordinate **276** General Felix K. Zollicoffer to attack. Zollicoffer briefly drove off the enemy, but his white raincoat attracted fatal bullets. Thomas reinforced his confused men, and finally the Rebel line broke and straggled across the river. Zollicoffer was considered

Brigadier General Felix K. Zollicoffer, C.S.A.

a hero for earlier actions and was mourned across the South.

277 Breach of the Kentucky line threatened all the Confederate West, now commanded by President Davis's admired friend General Albert Sidney Johnston (q.v.). Johnston, responsible for a vast area but short of men and arms, called for help from Richmond as he tried a shadow defense by scattering small units at important points.

At Cairo, Illinois, **278** General U. S.

Grant prepared to change the nature of the war. Deciding to shred Johnston's thin defenses, Grant launched a combined land-river operation against Fort Henry on the Tennessee River. Using troop transports and gunboats, he landed north of the fort on February 4, while gunboats reconnoitered the fort, which lay just south of the Kentucky-Tennessee border.

279 **On February 6, 1862, General Lloyd Tilghman sent most of Fort Henry's garrison overland to Fort Donelson on the Cumberland River.** Staying with a few defenders, Tilghman

and his men scored fifty-nine hits on the passing boats, but they surrendered when high water threatened their gunports. Grant's infantry arrived after the fight. He had opened an important river highway into the South, but still had to deal with the far stronger Fort Donelson, which could block interior infiltration.

280 Wasting no time, Grant reconnoitered Fort Donelson on Friday, February 7, while his gunboats churned back down the Tennessee to the Ohio, from which they would approach the fort upriver.

281 Johnston, threatened with the col-

Federal naval station at Mound City, near Cairo, Illinois.

Federal gunboat *Cincinnati,* a flat-bottom ironclad built by Captain Eads and commanded by Flag Officer Foote, began the bombardment of Fort Henry on February 6, 1862.

lapse of his whole line, rushed reinforcements to Fort Donelson and planned ways to stem the Yankee tide. Davis had sent him General P. G. T. Beauregard (q.v.) as a

kind of second in command—in large part because he wanted the argumentative general out of Virginia and out of his hair. Beauregard's strategic sense would indeed be of help to Johnston. He was appalled by the Western situation. With the main line broken, with Grant threatening Fort Donelson from land and water, with Union forces gathering, Beauregard saw concentration as Johnston's only hope. Meanwhile, there was Fort Donelson— and the woeful news of the fall of Roanoke Island, North Carolina.

282 Grant could not get his expedition together as quickly as he had hoped, but some of his men moved overland toward Fort Donelson on February 11, 1862. Confederate reinforcements were

Federal Eads-built ironclad *Pittsburg* first went into action at Fort Donelson, where she was hit forty times. Later took part in the Red River expeditions.

pouring into the fort ahead of enemy gunboats. Fighting began on February 13, but reinforcements arrived for both sides, and the fort had a new commander, **283** General John B. Floyd, former Virginia governor and U.S. Secretary of War.

284 Gunboats bombarded Fort Donelson on February 14, 1862, with poor results. The fort's guns were stronger than Fort Henry's and drove the ships downstream. At night, the Confederate generals, including Gideon J. Pillow (q.v.) and Simon B. Buckner (q.v.), agreed to try a breakout the next day. Pillow's men attacked at 5 A.M., broke the Union right, opened the road to Nashville, and returned to the fort. Disturbed by the near disaster, Grant worked to strengthen his line while the Rebel leaders debated surrender and argued furiously about who would have the dubious honor of offering his sword. Floyd and Pillow decided to escape, and the command fell to Buckner, who knew Grant and hoped for generous terms.

285 During the night of February 15–16, 1862, Nathan Bedford Forrest angrily took his men away from the fort, and early in the morning three hundred hapless reinforcements arrived just in time to surrender.

286 Loss of the river forts cost the Confederacy Kentucky, opened Tennessee to Union operations, proved the value of combined operations, and made a national hero of "Unconditional Surrender" Grant.

287 Lincoln's pleasure at Federal West- ern successes dimmed harshly on the afternoon of Thursday, February 20. William Wallace (Willie) Lincoln, aged twelve, died in the White House.

288 The Federals pushed their Western successes as General Don Carlos Buell's (q.v.) army occupied Nashville on February 25, 1862, and General Henry W. Halleck (q.v.), commanding Northern forces in the West, ordered Grant to advance from his well-won positions toward Mississippi. A falling-out between Halleck and Grant demoted Grant to local command. Halleck, standing well with Lincoln, received enlarged duties: **289** the new Department of the Mississippi, comprising the Department of Missouri, the Department of Kansas, and part of the Department of the Ohio.

290 **"We have suffered great anxiety,"** President Davis wrote to Sidney Johnston on March 12, 1862, "because of recent events in Kentucky and Tennessee." He added, "I suppose the Tenn. or Mississippi River will be the object of the enemy's next campaign, and I trust you will be able to concentrate a force which will defeat either attempt." Goaded by Davis, by widespread grumbling, and by the energetic Beauregard, Johnston began to pull together himself and his command. Beauregard gathered men from Columbus, Kentucky, **291** Island Number 10 on the Mississippi, and Corinth, Mississippi. Davis, through skillful use of roads, railroads, and rivers sent reinforcements. By late March, Johnston concentrated at Corinth, where he could join Beauregard and prepare to attack Grant's exposed ranks near Pittsburg Landing, Tennessee.

292 Johnston issued orders for an advance on April 3, 1862, from Corinth toward Pittsburg Landing, with an attack to take place on April 4. Delays, confusions, and heavy rain forced postponement, and as the army approached Grant's camps on April 5, most hopes for surprise were gone—but Johnston was determined to attack on April 6.

293 Incredibly, surprise did prevail as Rebels came streaming into Yankee camps near Shiloh Church early that Sabbath morning. Rolling through blossoming peach trees, the Rebels drove wildly

During the Battle of Shiloh, in Pittsburg Landing, when the cannonade began on April 6, 1862, Grant moved his headquarters to the *Tigress* (middle vessel) on the Tennessee River.

disorganized units ahead of them, and a roaring victory seemed theirs. Grant, not on the field, rushed to the fighting, and stubborn Union resistance here and there—at Sunken Road, the church itself, Bloody Pond, Peach Orchard, especially at Hornet's Nest—delayed Johnston's evenly distributed lines of attack, mixed the units, and spread confusion. Still, by fierce fighting, the Gray lines nudged the Bluecoats closer to the Tennessee River in a shrinking semicircle.

294 Around two-thirty in the afternoon of April 6, Johnston, wounded in the leg, died from loss of blood that may have been preventable. Command passed to Beauregard, who kept the push going. Grant's whole army faced destruction if one more Rebel attack was launched. Around dusk, Beauregard tried to organize a final rush to the river. Confusion and fading light made it impossible, and during the night heavy reinforcements from Buell's army stabilized Grant's lines.

295 A renewed Yankee attack on the morning of April 7 drove Beauregard's tired men, but they rallied near the Peach Orchard and held on for expected reinforcement by General Earl Van Dorn's (q.v.) troops from across the Mississippi. When word came during the afternoon that Van Dorn was not coming, Beauregard pulled his army back, broke off the battle, and slowly fell back to Corinth.

296 Shiloh, or Pittsburg Landing, ranked as the costliest battle of a still-young war. Grant lost on the field 13,000 out of a total of 60,000. Confederate losses were 10,500 out of an army of about 40,000. Technically, the Federals won Shiloh because the Rebels left the field—but Grant could hardly boast of a victory in the wake of such wasteful surprise, and Beauregard could claim, at least, that he had not been driven away. But so high had been Southern expectations that Shiloh came as a crushing defeat.

297 **On June 27, 1862, General Braxton Bragg officially took command of the Department of the West,** replacing an ill and unfairly criticized Beauregard. Another friend of President Davis, Bragg had been appointed a full general for his service at Shiloh, where he had served in corps command as a kind of chief of staff late in the day.

298 Bragg, aware of President Davis's predicaments, decided that a swift advance into Kentucky would restore the Confederate left flank along the Mississippi.

Federal steamships at Pittsburg Landing a few days after the Battle of Shiloh.

299 **Once he made the decision, Bragg moved his army rapidly from Tupelo, Mississippi, to Chattanooga.** The 776-mile move involved six railroads and detours through Mobile, Montgomery, Atlanta, and everything went smoothly in one of the best uses of railroads during the war. On August 28, Bragg began a major incursion into central Tennessee. He planned to recover the whole state as well as Kentucky by forcing Buell's (q.v.) army northward.

300 Plans called for Bragg's men to join the Army of Kentucky under General E. Kirby Smith. Smith had crossed into the Blue Grass state from Tennessee with about 7000 men in mid-August. On August 30, he fought 301 a battle at Richmond, capturing almost 4000 Bluecoats and nearly annihilating an equal Union force.

302 **Bragg pushed on, as did Smith, while Lee crossed into Maryland,** and Lincoln realized that a two-pronged Rebel offensive threatened the Union. President Davis knew, even better than his generals, the importance of the great Confederate drives, and he sought to gain every advantage from the risks run. Mounting fear in the North could touch off rumors of a 303 "Northwest Conspiracy" and bring other states to the Confederacy—or certainly stir up serious troubles by the Copperheads 304, the name given to several organized groups of Southern sympathizers in the North.

305 Bragg might conceivably invade

Ohio and cut Northern communications between East and West. Whatever the outcome, recruits surely would join by the thousands. So Davis issued careful orders to Lee, Bragg, and Smith: **306** Proclaim peaceful intentions to the invaded areas and remind the people that the Confederacy was fighting only in self-defense and had no conquests in mind. Remind them, too, that free navigation on the Mississippi will not be infringed and that the Confederacy would welcome them in the just cause of independence.

307 Bragg issued a bombastic proclamation on September 5: "Tennesseans! Your capital and State are almost restored without firing a gun. You return conquerors. Kentuckians! the first great blow has been struck for your freedom." There was some truth to this, since Buell had evacuated northern Alabama and moved to Murfreesboro, Tennessee.

When Bragg bypassed Buell's army and moved directly toward Kentucky, Governor Oliver P. Morton (q.v.) of Ohio called for volunteers to repel a possible invasion. By September 12, Smith's army came within fifty miles of Louisville; it reached the Ohio across from Cincinnati on September 15 but then fell back.

308 A dangerous breach widened between Bragg and Smith, since both were army and department commanders. As Bragg triumphantly bagged a Federal garrison of 4000 men at Mun-

fordville, Kentucky, on September 17, Smith worried lest his smaller command would put him under Bragg. Bragg, in turn, assumed that would indeed be so, and President Davis surely hoped jealousies would not ruffle operations. As Bragg moved toward Frankfort, determined to install **309** Richard Hawes as Confederate governor of the state, Kirby Smith kept his distance. Bragg went himself to Frankfort to meet Smith and attend the ceremonies—which were unceremoniously interrupted by Yankee troops. Smith's men and one of Bragg's divisions went south; Bragg rejoined the bulk of his army near Perryville.

310 Bragg fought his main Kentucky battle at Perryville on October 8. It was a weird affair, made more weird by an "acoustic shadow" that left parts of the field unaware of, and uninvolved in, the heavy fighting. (Due to the unusual phenomenon, the sounds of the battle were not heard by others on the field, creating confusion among the troops.) Perryville began with a Confederate attack that pushed Buell's left flank back two miles. **311** Quickly, General Philip Sheridan's division successfully counterattacked and a stalemate developed. **312** Casualties were heavy—about 4200 Federals out of 23,000 engaged, against 3400 Rebels out of 16,000 engaged—and Bragg began retreating southeast.

313 Grant began operations against Vicksburg at the end of October 1862.

Right: Union General John A. McClernand, Commander of the Army of the Mississippi, 1862–1863.

Trouble erupted between Grant, the new commander of the Department of the Tennessee, and 314 General John A. McClernand, an Illinois politician and friend of Lincoln's, whom the President had ordered to recruit men in Indiana, Illinois, and Iowa for the expedition against Vicksburg. Grant pursued his own campaign by capturing the rail hub at Holly Springs, Mississippi, in mid-November, and in mid-December he took command of a reorganized army, with McClernand as one of his corps commanders, and con-

Vicksburg, halfway between Memphis and New Orleans, was the strongest natural defensive position on the Mississippi River.

tinued preparations to take the Confederacy's main bastion on the Mississippi.

315 General Earl Van Dorn's 3500 troopers foiled Grant's plans by capturing Holly Springs on December 20, taking 1500 prisoners and some $1.5 million worth of supplies. Grant found himself forced back to La Grange, Tennessee, unable to cooperate with 316 General William Tecumseh Sherman's movement toward Chickasaw Bluffs, north of Vicksburg. Unaware at first of Grant's problems—because 317 Forrest's 2100 raiders attacked Grant's supply lines in mid-December and cut Union telegraph lines in all directions—Sherman continued his advance and attacked the formidable Confederate works on December 29. He met a brutal repulse and lost almost 1800 men out of his 31,000, while Rebel losses were 207 of 14,000 engaged. Grant's first try for Vicksburg failed, but he knew, somehow, that he would get it.

318 **On October 30, General William Starke (Old Rosy) Rosecrans assumed command of the Army and Department of the Cumberland, replacing Buell.** This was the result of Washington's discontent with action in the West. Rosecrans felt pressure to push the Rebels out of middle Tennessee.

On November 20, Braxton Bragg assumed command of the officially constituted 319 Confederate Army of Tennessee, comprising three corps under Generals Kirby Smith (q.v.), Leonidas Polk (q.v.),

Federal soldiers outside quarters in Memphis, soon after Grant's failed attempt, on December 29, 1862, to take Vicksburg by way of Chickasaw Bluffs.

and the quiet, steady 320 General William Joseph Hardee (q.v.), author of a widely used book on tactics. Bragg felt pressed to consolidate the Confederate western flank with a major victory.

Rosecrans, after frustrating delays caused by daring Rebel cavalry raids on his communications, advanced from Nashville with 42,000 men on December 26, 1862. Bragg, his 36,000 men deployed astride 321 Stone's River, about a mile north of Murfreesboro, Tennessee, plotted attack. The armies bivouacked a few hundred yards apart on the night of December 30, and a duel of bands filled the air with strains of "Dixie," "Yankee Doodle," and, finally, with the nostalgia of "Home Sweet Home."

Bragg planned to attack the Union flank at dawn on December 31, roll it up against the river, and cut off the Yankee line of retreat. The eerie Rebel yell woke the surprised Yankees, as it had done at Shiloh, and suddenly two Union divisions broke and fled. Bragg's cavalry raided Rosecrans's ammunition and supply stores while disaster threatened the Army of the Cumberland. Rosecrans resolutely rallied his men as he rode his lines; Sheridan's division, in the right center, held its front long enough for a new line to form by the Nashville Pike—a line that stopped the Rebel drive by noon. A patch of woods called the Round Forest became the linchpin of the entire Union position as 322 General George H. Thomas's (q.v.) corps held it firmly through the long afternoon.

Memories of that day were filled with the loudest sounds of battle—so loud that men picked cotton to stuff in their ears—with flashes of anguish, heroism, desperation, excitement, horror. Bragg claimed a great victory in a telegram to Richmond and stated that "the enemy is falling back." They were not.

Against advice, Rosecrans stayed on the field, and the two armies faced each other on the first day of 1863. On January 2, Bragg launched a fierce attack on the Union left, east of the river; it first succeeded and then wilted under artillery fire.

Rosecrans received supplies; Bragg did not. Bragg's generals grumbled against him, and, in one of his strange despondencies, he retreated behind Duck River on the night of January 3–4.

323 **Stone's River (also called Murfreesboro) ranked among the costliest of battles.** The Federals lost 31 percent of their men, and the Confederates suffered 33 percent killed, wounded, or missing. One Southern survivor of that fiery cauldron wrote, "I am sick and tired of this war, and . . . I don't think it ever will be stopped by fighting, the Yankees cant whip us and we can never whip them, and I see no prospect of peace unless the Yankees themselves rebell and . . . refuse to fight any longer."

Rosecrans snatched success from disaster; Bragg threw away a victory. The North exulted at a success in the West after so many failures, and the South pondered a year of waste and danger.

FAR WESTERN OPERATIONS

In May 1861, 324 **Henry Hopkins Sibley, born in Louisiana and famous for designing a military tent and stove, resigned from the U.S. Army, went to Richmond, and talked to President Davis. Sibley sold Davis on the idea of seizing New Mexico Territory as a prelude to conquering Colorado and perhaps California.** With the rank of brigadier general, Sibley went to Texas, recruited an expedition in San Antonio, and marched toward New Mexico in early 1862 with about 2600 men. After a difficult march across the alkali flats north of El Paso, properly called the Jornada del Muerto, Sibley's men attacked a Union force under Colonel E. R. S. Canby (q.v.) at 325 Valverde, on the Rio Grande. The small, hard fight on February 21, 1862, opened the way for the Texans to bypass Fort Craig on their way to Santa Fe.

Sibley, notoriously fond of strong drink, apparently visited friends or relatives in Santa Fe after sending a scouting column eastward. That column ran into Federals at 326 Glorieta Pass (Pigeon's Ranch), fought a pitched battle on March 28–29, and after early success had to retreat when its wagon trains were burned. Defeat at Glorieta ended Sibley's expedition, and he began a bitter winter retreat to Texas as Confederate dreams of a Western empire faded.

In early March a big force under 327 General Samuel Curtis (q.v.) pushed General Sterling Price (q.v.) out of Missouri. General Earl Van Dorn (q.v.), commanding the Confederate Arkansas troops, joined Price and decided to attack Curtis as soon as possible. The Federals were entrenched north of Fayetteville, so Van Dorn wisely did not choose a frontal assault but sought to flank Curtis and hit him from the north at Pea Ridge, or Elkhorn Tavern, Arkansas. Confident—he boasted, "I must have St. Louis and then

Huza!"—Van Dorn led a composite force of some 14,000 Missouri militia, Arkansas, Texas, and Cherokee Indian troops.

On a cold, clear Friday, March 7, 1862, the Rebels got behind Curtis and attacked from 328 Elkhorn Tavern. The Yankees changed front, attacked, but by afternoon were on the defensive. They stubbornly fell back, then advanced, and the swaying action went on for most of the day. Two Confederate generals fell almost simultaneously—329 Ben McCulloch and 330 James McIntosh—which confused the Rebel ranks. Nightfall found Curtis reorganized, waiting for attack, and Van Dorn

Brigadier General Benjamin McCulloch, C.S.A.

Brigadier General James McIntosh, C.S.A.

taking a defensive position around the tavern.

On March 8 Van Dorn's men, subject to heavy artillery fire and low on ammunition, retreated and soon abandoned the field. Curtis won a battle he should have lost; Van Dorn fought a tactically flawed battle, squandered his superior numbers, and lost the decisive battle for Missouri. 331 Casualties: Union, about 1400 killed, wounded, and missing out of about 11,000 engaged; Confederacy, about 800.

332 **The results of Elkhorn Tavern, or Pea Ridge, were significant.** Confederate hopes for Missouri dwindled; Van Dorn's men would not relieve pressure on Sidney

Johnston nor join him for Shiloh, and Van Dorn's men were finally shifted east of the river, an indication that Richmond had written off the Trans-Mississippi, since no more men came that year, nor generals, nor major fighting.

333 **In August 1862, a massacre on the Nueces River in Texas showed the depth of the divisions in parts of the South.** Sixty-one pro-Union Germans from the Fredericksburg area organized into a company and marched toward Mexico in order to avoid Confederate conscription and oppression. Betrayed, they were surprised on the morning of August 10 by ninety-four Texas partisan rangers, near Fort Clark. Incited by the bloodthirsty Captain James Duff, the rangers annihilated the Germans; thirty-two were killed and wounded in the fight, seven more were killed trying to cross the Rio Grande, and nine survivors were later executed. Only two attackers were killed and eighteen wounded. This massacre inflamed the already strong anti-Confederate feeling in many Texas German settlements.

334 **Rebel General Earl Van Dorn wrecked General Grant's first attempt to take Vicksburg by raiding the huge Yankee supply base at Holly Springs, Mississippi, on December 20, 1862.** Van Dorn's cavalry roared into the town, captured about 1500 Federals, and destroyed supplies valued at more than $1.5 million. This unexpected loss foiled Grant's plan to

SEA BATTLES

Chickasaw Bluffs, where Sherman was unable to take Walnut Hill, a natural fortress two hundred feet high.

join General Sherman's expedition down the Mississippi to Chickasaw Bluffs.

335 **After Grant's first attack on Vicksburg failed,** a second, under General William T. Sherman (q.v.), foundered at the Battle of Chickasaw Bluffs on December 29, 1862. General Sherman's expedition from Memphis reached the bluffs on December 28, and the next day he attacked the nearly impregnable position. General John C. Pemberton's defenders, outnumbered by more than two to one, easily held their ground, and Sherman took a costly beating: 1776 casualties out of 31,000. Rebel losses were 207 out of 14,000.

Southern hopes rose briefly at the exploits of a new and powerful warship, the 336 C.S.S. *Virginia.* Secretary Mallory (q.v.) authorized construction of an armored vessel in June 1861, but engines and boilers could not be found or constructed in time to float an ironclad before the Union finished one. Mallory accepted the suggestion of the ordnance expert 337 Lieutenant John M. Brooke and the naval constructor John L. Porter to raise the

John M. Brooke, C.S.N., inventor of the Brooke rifled gun, which was part of the *Virginia*'s armament.

Norfolk Navy Yard, where the *Merrimack* was refitted as the South's first ironclad, the *Virginia*.

sunken *Merrimack* at the Norfolk yard for conversion into the South's first ironclad. Commissioned on February 17, 1862, as the C.S.S. *Virginia,* with Commodore Franklin Buchanan (q.v.) commanding, this formidable warship attacked the Union fleet at Hampton Roads on March 8, rammed and sank the big U.S.S. *Cumberland,* turned on the U.S.S. *Congress,* and set it afire with hot shot.

By dark, the Union fleet was in trouble; two ships had been destroyed and three run aground, likely to be finished off the next day. Buchanan had been wounded, and Lieutenant Catesby Jones was now in command of the *Virginia.*

Sallying out Sunday morning, March 9, to finish the Union armada, the *Virginia*

met the 338 U.S.S. *Monitor,* which had arrived hastily in the glow of the fire from the *Congress.* Four hours of fierce bombardment produced no victor. But then a shot into the pilot house temporarily blinded the *Monitor's* captain, and the ship veered out of action. The *Virginia,* short of ammunition and vulnerable to a falling tide, returned to Norfolk.

Under Captain Josiah Tattnall (q.v.), the *Virginia* continued to threaten the Union fleet. After the evacuation of Norfolk, the *Virginia* had to be burned, on May 11, 1862, because its deep draft prevented its being withdrawn up the James River.

339 **The battle between the** *Virginia*

Gunports of the Federal ironclad *Monitor*'s revolving turret.

340 The U.S.S. *Monitor,* the "cheese-box on a raft" or "tin can on a shingle," changed the basic design of ironclad ships. Built in response to the C.S.S. *Virginia,* the *Monitor,* designed by the Swedish-born engineer John Ericsson, was constructed in three months. Powered by steam, displacing 1200 tons with deck awash, the *Monitor* made a difficult target; only its 140-ton rotating turret, covered with eight layers of one-inch iron plates, rose above deck. The turret enabled gunners to fire from any direction, thus eliminating the need to maneuver the ship into firing position.

During the battle with the *Virginia,* the *Monitor*'s captain, Lieutenant (later Admiral) J. L. Worden, took the brunt of a shot to the pilot house; blinded by smoke

and the *Monitor* changed the nature of naval warfare; the age of sail faded in the wash of a great technological revolution.

Union naval officers on deck of the *Monitor.*

and powder, his face lacerated, he gave the order to "sheet off" and assess damages. Command was passed to Chief Engineer A. C. Stimers.

Owing to the flush deck (which prohibited internal ventilation), iron construction, and steam power, temperatures inside the hull were often searing, but the fact that the *Monitor* seemed invulnerable to any ship on the ocean prompted the Union to construct dozens of copies, all of them classed as monitors. None of them was especially seaworthy, however, as demonstrated by the prototype itself, which sank, in December 1862, during a gale off Cape Hatteras, North Carolina.

John Ericsson, designer of the *Monitor*.

341 On July 15, 1862, the C.S.S. *Arkansas* descended the Yazoo River, engaged three Union vessels, disabled one, and pursued the other two into the Mississippi. Work on this unusual vessel had begun in October 1861 at Memphis. The *Arkansas* had a straight-sided casemate covered with T-rails; it was 165 feet long, thirty-five feet wide, carried ten guns, drew eleven to twelve feet, and had a crew of two hundred. In the Mississippi, the *Arkansas* steamed slowly through the combined fleets of Flag Officers Charles Davis and David Farragut. Although it was hit several times, the *Arkansas* reached Vicksburg and, after repairs, sailed on August 3 to cooperate in an attack on Baton Rouge. There, engine failure forced the crew to

set her on fire. The *Arkansas*'s daring exploit humiliated Farragut and his river flotilla.

Admiral J. L. Worden, U.S.N.

SPECIAL UNITS

Marines were used by both sides. 342
U.S. Marines served as naval police forces
and as infantry for amphibious landings.
Under a colonel commandant, the corps
reported to the Secretary of the Navy; it
boasted 1892 officers and men as the war
began. Half the captains and many of the
lieutenants went South with secession; even
so, the corps grew and did important service. One battalion served at First Bull Run
(First Manassas), and Marines were in every
riverine action. They served, too, as auxiliary
police during the New York draft riots
(q.v.) in 1863. By the end of the war, the
U.S. Marine Corps numbered over 4000.

Members of the United States Marine
Corps, 1865.

343 **The Confederate Marine Corps
was created by the Confederate Congress in March 1861.** Under Colonel
Commandant Lloyd J. Beall, the corps
served in small units aboard ships, in river
operations, at naval installations, and in
some coastal defenses. One Marine battalion marched with Lee's army in the Appomattox campaign. Numbering only 350
officers and men in 1861, the corps
expanded to over 500 by 1864. Estimates
put the total enrollment through the war at
over 1200.

344 **Necessity forced the weaker side
to be daring, and the Confederacy
tried to use technology to offset the
odds.** The Confederate Navy, under the
skilled scientific eye of the world famous
oceanographer Matthew Fontaine Maury,
created in June 1861, a torpedo bureau,
officially called the Naval Submarine
Battery Service, under the Bureau of
Ordnance and Hydrography. This service
perfected various kinds of marine torpedoes, which were credited with destroying more Union ships than any other
weapon.

345 **Antipersonnel mines (land mines
or "subterra shells") were used against
McClellan's men** on the Peninsula of
Virginia in 1862, to the horror of many
on both sides. McClellan threatened to
march Confederate prisoners ahead of his
men unless the mines were removed.

These weapons, invented by General Gabriel Rains, were later widely used.

346 Balloons were used by both sides, more extensively by the Union. Most famous were those made by Professor Thaddeus S.C. Lowe, which were called on during early campaigns in Virginia and in the Peninsular campaign. He organized the army's Balloon Corps and is credited with designing the first "aircraft carrier," the coal barge U.S.S. *George Washington Parke Custis,* which he used for several ascensions. Aerial observation expanded the Federals' knowledge of the battlefields, and on at least one occasion provided artillery fire control. Confederate efforts to shoot down Union balloons were the first instances of antiaircraft fire.

Professor Thaddeus S.C. Lowe ascending in an observation balloon, May 1862.

Only one documented instance of Confederate ballooning is recorded. 347 Langdon Cheves and Charles Cevor of Savannah used silk, made gas proof with naphtha-treated gutta percha, and floated their craft over the James River in 1862. Rumors of other Rebel balloons are unconfirmed though romantic.

348 During one of the early air operations near Richmond in 1862, Count Ferdinand von Zeppelin watched closely. An aeronaut himself, he later invented the dirigible, known as the Zeppelin, that was used in World War I.

349 Zouaves were relied on by both sides throughout the war, especially in the early campaigns. Taking their name

Thaddeus S.C. Lowe using engineering maps to explain the military applications of aerial observation to his father before the Battle of Seven Pines (Fair Oaks).

Members of the 4th Michigan Infantry in Zouave uniform.

from a Berber tribe, and originating in Algeria in the 1830s, the Zouaves dressed in colorful pantaloons, short open jackets with complicated stitches, white gaiters, and a turban, fez, or tasseled cap. Zouave units were often listed under individual names: Louisiana Zouaves (Tigers), Corcoran's Zouaves (164th New York), Fire Zouaves. Hard fighting became their hallmark. The Louisiana Tigers began with a tough reputation; they were recruited mainly from the rowdiest elements of the French, Italians, and Creoles in New Orleans. The 11th New York Fire Zouaves, comprising members of New York City's fire brigades, did yeoman service.

350 **Proud names for proud units were bestowed by both sides.** Examples include the Davis Guards, the Richmond Grays, the Wisconsin Iron Brigade, the Stonewall Brigade, and the fashionable Washington Artillery of New Orleans. Among the most interesting of these units was the Mozart Regiment, a group of New York musicians talented in strings and chords and soon proficient in the tunes of glory.

351 **Several groups of free blacks mustered to serve the Confederacy** but were used mainly as home guards. Why did they serve the slave cause? Because, in the beginning, Lincoln and the North had vowed to save the Union and not disturb slavery, and many of the free blacks shared the Southern abhorrence of Northern materialism.

352 On August 25, 1862, Union Secretary of War Stanton (q.v.), gave permission to the Southern Department commander to "receive into the service of the United States" 5000 black soldiers for training as guards. Made part of Union doctrine by the Emancipation Proclamation, in January 1863, black recruiting continued through the rest of the war. Black units fought well, were usually led by white officers, and struggled against several forms of discrimination. By the war's end some 180,000 African Americans were in Union ranks. Close to 37,000 black troops were casualties, a casualty ratio 40 percent higher than for white troops.

353 The three and a half million Southern blacks were vital to the Rebel war effort. Working as military laborers, they allowed white men to be soldiers, and tending home front matters—usually loyally—they helped to sustain Confederate supplies and support morale. The Confederate Congress sought to codify the use of slave labor by prescribing rules for recruitment in the Act to Regulate Impressments, passed on March 26, 1863.

354 A few Rebels thought from the beginning of the war that slaves as well as free blacks should serve in Confederate ranks. This opinion gained strength as the forces ran short of whites. Toward the end of 1863, General Patrick Cleburne raised the question among Joe Johnston's generals in the Army of Tennessee. Although President Davis squelched the idea, he left the door open for discussion, and in November 1864 he told a reluctant Congress that "a broad moral distinction exists between the use of slaves as soldiers in defense of their homes and the incitement of the same persons to insurrection against their masters," and announced that he supported drafting of the slaves. When General Lee wrote in January 1865 that he thought "we should employ them without delay," congressional opinion shifted. Still, not until March 1865 did a draft bill pass; freedom was not promised but assumed. Only a few black infantry companies wore the Gray as soldiers.

355 Both sides found ways to use wounded men. The U.S. Veteran Reserve Corps, well organized, helped to staff non-

combat areas. The Confederate Invalid Corps was not as well organized or equipped, but its members did service in hospitals, prisons, and depots.

ARMY LEADERS, 1862

356 Nathaniel Prentiss Banks (U.S.), born in Waltham, Massachusetts, on January 10, 1816, was a lawyer, politician, the speaker of the U.S. House of Representatives, and governor of Massachusetts. In January 1861, Lincoln appointed him major general of volunteers. Although he

Union Major General Nathaniel Prentiss Banks.

was ridiculed by West Point graduates for his lack of ability, Banks used his vast political influence to help the Union cause. After being defeated by Stonewall Jackson in the Shenandoah Valley campaign of 1862, defeated once again by Jackson at Cedar Mountain in August, Banks moved west. At Port Hudson, in 1863, he ordered futile attacks, but the post had to surrender in the wake of Vicksburg's fall. In 1864, Banks initiated the ill-fated Red River campaign. These losses incurred Grant's wrath, and he replaced Banks with General E.R.S. Canby. Banks was given the thanks of Congress for the part he had in gaining Port Hudson, and he left the army in August 1865. He died in Waltham on September 1, 1894.

357 **Braxton Bragg (C.S.), born in War-renton, North Carolina, on March 22, 1817,** graduated from West Point in 1837, served against the Seminoles, and earned commendations for his actions in the Mexican War. On March 7, 1861, he became a brigadier general in the Provisional Army of the Confederate States, with command of the coast from Mobile to Pensacola. He commanded A. S. Johnston's 2nd Corps at Shiloh and was appointed a full general in the Confederate Regular Army as of April 6, 1862. In June of that year he replaced Beauregard as army commander and led the ill-fated Kentucky expedition from August to October. Bragg defeated Rosecrans at Murfreesboro, Tennessee, at the beginning

General Braxton Bragg, C.S.A.

of 1863, but abandoned his victory in a strange wave of lassitude. In September 1863 he scored another major victory against Rosecrans, this time at Chickamauga, and laid siege to Chattanooga. Grant defeated Bragg at Lookout Mountain and Missionary Ridge and forced him into north Georgia. His subordinates lost confidence in him, and he gave up command of the Army of Tennessee. President Davis, ever his friend, called Bragg to Richmond to take charge "of the military operations in the armies of the Confederacy." Although the appointment was unpopular, it had a sound basis. Bragg was not a good battle commander, but he was a fine organizer and a master of logistics. After Lee became general-in-chief, he sent Bragg to join J. E. Johnston in North Carolina, where he bungled the defense of

Fort Fisher. He died in Galveston in September 1876. Bragg ranks among the most controversial of Confederate generals, in part because his abilities were undermined by his thorny personality and odd moments of dereliction.

358 Simon Bolivar Buckner (C.S.), born on April 1, 1823, in Kentucky, graduated from West Point in 1844. After winning two brevets in the Mexican War, he resigned and became a businessman in Chicago. As adjutant general of Kentucky when the war started, he struggled to maintain the state's neutrality. Both North and South offered him rank as brigadier general, and in September 1861 he

Lieutenant General Simon Bolivar Buckner, C.S.A.

accepted the South's offer. Left to surrender Fort Donelson, he became a prisoner of war but was exchanged and took command of a division in Bragg's Kentucky expedition. When he was shifted south, he strengthened Mobile's defenses between December 1862 and April 1863. From May to August he commanded the Department of East Tennessee and then led a corps at Chickamauga. He was transferred to the Trans-Mississippi Department as lieutenant general and chief of staff to Kirby Smith, from September 1864 to the war's end. He died on his estate near Munfordville on January 8, 1914.

359 Don Carlos Buell (U.S.), born in present-day Lowell, Ohio, on March 23, 1818, graduated from West Point with the class of 1841, which contributed twenty generals to the Civil War. Distinguished service in the Mexican War earned him two brevets, and for thirteen years he served in the Ohio adjutant general's department. Commissioned brigadier general on May 17, 1861, he helped to train McDowell's army. McClellan sent him to lead a force into east Tennessee from Kentucky, and his plans were of help in Grant's campaign against Forts Henry and Donelson. His arrival, though late, stemmed the Rebel tide at Shiloh. Some historians regard him as an advocate of "soft war," along with McClellan, but his operations against Bragg in Kentucky were sound and important. Buell's failure to pursue Bragg swiftly, however, cost him his command,

Union Major General Don Carlos Buell.

and a military commission investigated his conduct without recommendations. Mustered out of volunteer service in May 1864, he resigned his regular commission on June 1. Grant later unsuccessfully recommended his recall, and Buell turned to civilian work in the coal and iron business and had some success as an inventor. He died near Paradise, Kentucky, in November 1898.

360 Ambrose Everett Burnside (U.S.) was born at Liberty, Union County, Indiana, on May 23, 1824, the son of a former South Carolina slave owner who had freed his slaves when he moved to Indiana. A West Point graduate, class of 1847, Burnside had an uneventful career and resigned from the army in 1853 in order to manufacture a breech-loading rifle of his own invention. He organized the 1st Rhode Island Infantry Regiment at the outbreak of war, commanded a brigade at First Bull Run (First Manassas), and was commissioned brigadier general of volunteers in August 1861. Lincoln, who liked him, sent him on an expedition against the North Carolina coast, which proved a great success and won him promotion to major general in March 1862. His punctilious interpretation of orders may have cost him the chance to smash the weak Confederate right opposite what was called Burnside's Bridge at Antietam. On November 10, 1862, he replaced McClellan as commander of the Army of the Potomac, a task he had not sought. Aware of the need for success, Burnside moved toward Richmond via Fredericksburg and, on December 13, 1862, threw his whole army against the virtually impregnable Rebel works. He took nearly 13,000 casualties. Almost maddened by failure, Burnside tried an abortive winter campaign against Lee, which won a descriptive name: the Mud March. Lincoln relieved Burnside but gave him command of the Department of the Ohio, where he overreacted to loyalty problems by ordering the death penalty for anyone aiding the Confederacy. However, Burnside redeemed himself by a fine defense of Knoxville against Longstreet in the autumn of 1863. Restored to command of his old 9th Corps, Burnside failed to support the

Commander of the Army of the Potomac Burnside (standing center) and staff at Warrenton, Virginia, November 14, 1862.

Crater attack at Petersburg in July 1864, and that error clouded his career. He resigned in April 1865, enjoyed a successful business career, and was elected to the U.S. Senate from Rhode Island. He died at Bristol, Rhode Island, in September 1881.

361 Benjamin Franklin Butler (U.S.), born in Deerfield, New Hampshire, on November 5, 1818, was short, had a cast in one eye, but was gifted with dynamism and resourcefulness. After graduating from Colby College, in Maine, in 1838, Butler taught school in Lowell, Massachusetts, was admitted to the bar in 1840, and developed a lucrative criminal practice. Politics lured him; he attended the Charleston Democratic Convention in 1860 and voted fifty-seven times to nominate Jefferson Davis as President of the United States. He later backed the John Breckinridge branch of the split Democratic ticket. A militia general, Butler received a brigadier general's commission from Lincoln in May 1861, but his military career was badly damaged by a serious defeat at Big Bethel and never revived. He coined the term "contraband-of-war" for slaves who fled to Union lines. When he occupied New Orleans and began a long, some say infamous, stay as military governor, he also issued the Woman Order. That order labeled any female who insulted a Union

Union Major General Benjamin Franklin Butler.

soldier as a "woman of the town," and it created a furor—especially among the city's prostitutes—and won him the sobriquet "Beast." Jefferson Davis declared him an outlaw. Accused of profiteering—a reasonable charge—Butler nonetheless kept New Orleans orderly. In 1863, having been given command of the Army of the James, Butler managed to get himself bottled up at Bermuda Hundred Neck by a much smaller force under Beauregard. He was sent home in January 1865 to "await orders" and resigned on November 30. He became a Radical Republican and, until 1875,

served in Congress, where he managed to win the enmity of both parties. Back in Congress in 1878 as a Greenbacker, he carried that banner into the presidential election of 1884. He died in Washington, D.C., on January 11, 1893.

362 Edward Richard Sprigg Canby (U.S.) was born in Boone County, Kentucky, on November 9, 1817, and graduated next to last in the West Point class of 1839. He fought the Seminoles and assisted in Indian removals and won two brevets in the Mexican War. On frontier duty when the Civil War began, he became a colonel of the 19th Infantry Regiment and took command of the

Union General Edward Richard Sprigg Canby.

Department of New Mexico. He opposed H. H. Sibley's invasion in February 1862. His cautious tactics irritated many, but he did send Sibley's demoralized Texans scattering. In May, he was appointed brigadier general, the rank he held when he commanded New York City during the draft riots in 1863. Promoted to major general in May 1864, he was put in charge of the vast Military Division of West Mississippi. He planned the capture of Mobile, which surrendered on April 12, 1865, earning him the thanks of President Lincoln. Canby accepted the surrender of Richard Taylor's and Kirby Smith's commands. After the war, during which he was promoted to brigadier general in the regular U.S. Army, he served in department commands and was put in charge of the Division of the Pacific in 1873. While negotiating peace with the Modoc Indians on April 11, 1873, Canby was wounded by the Modoc Captain Jack and killed by another warrior.

363 **Samuel Ryan Curtis (U.S.) was born in Clinton County, New York, on February 3, 1805,** and was appointed to West Point from Ohio. He graduated with the class of 1831 but resigned on June 30, 1832, after doing brief service in Indian Territory. For several years he worked in Ohio and then fought in the Mexican War under Zachary Taylor. He moved to Iowa, became a lawyer, and was elected to Congress in 1856. As a colonel of the 2nd Iowa

Union Major General Samuel Ryan Curtis.

Regiment, Curtis entered Federal service and was appointed a brigadier general on May 17, 1861. Victory at Pea Ridge in April 1862 brought him the rank of major general and command of the Department of the Missouri. Curtis's political troubles with the governor of Missouri prompted his assignment to the Department of Kansas and from there to the Department of the Northwest. He worked at making peace with the Indians after the war and helped to construct the Union Pacific Railroad. He died in Council Bluffs on December 26, 1866.

364 **Richard Stoddert Ewell (C.S.) was born in the Georgetown section of Washington, D.C., on February 8, 1817.** He graduated from West Point in 1840, served in the Southwest, and was brevetted

Lieutenant General Richard Stoddert Ewell, C.S.A.

for gallantry in the Mexican War. After being commissioned a brigadier general in the Confederate Provisional Army, on June 17, 1861, he rose rapidly: major general, January 24, 1862; lieutenant general to succeed Stonewall Jackson, May 23, 1863. An aggressive, careful commandeer, Old Bald Head won renown at First Manassas (First Bull Run), and as a brigade and division leader under Jackson in the Shenandoah Valley campaign, the Seven Days' Battles, and Second Manassas, where he lost a leg at Groveton. Equipped with a wooden leg, he commanded the 2nd Corps from Gettysburg (where he did not shine) to Spotsylvania. Illness compelled a short leave, and he returned in charge of Richmond's

defenses. On being captured at Sayler's Creek, Ewell was imprisoned at Fort Warren. After his release, he spent his last years farming near Spring Hill, Tennessee, where he died, on January 25, 1872.

365 Nathan Bedford Forrest (C.S.) was born in Bedford County, Tennessee, on July 13, 1821. At the time of the war's outbreak, he was a wealthy planter and slave trader. Still, he enlisted as a private in the 7th Tennessee Cavalry and used his own money to raise and equip a mounted battalion. He extracted his men from Fort Donelson before its surrender and commanded a cavalry brigade in the Army of Tennessee in June 1862. He saw to the

Lieutenant General Nathan Bedford Forrest, C.S.A.

capture of a Union garrison, with its supplies, at Murfreesboro, which helped his promotion to brigadier general on July 21, 1862. His derring-do in December wrecked Grant's West Tennessee supply lines. Bold fighting by his men—often dismounted—saved the Confederate rail line between Chattanooga and Atlanta in May 1863. A fight with Bragg won Forrest an independent command, and he became a major general in December 1863. Famous, his reputation occasionally won battles for him. That fame was tarnished by the ruthless killing of Northern blacks and prisoners at what became known as the Fort Pillow Massacre on April 12, 1864.

At Brice's Cross Roads, Mississippi, June 10, 1864, Forrest showed the highest tactical brilliance. He commanded all of Hood's cavalry during his Tennessee operations in November and December 1864 and was promoted to lieutenant general on February 28, 1865—just in time to lose his last major fight, at Selma, Alabama, in April. After the war he was a railroad executive, a planter, and first grand wizard of the early Ku Klux Klan. He died in Memphis on October 29, 1877.

366 Famed for his pithy recipe for military success—get there first with the most—Forrest probably ranks as the best natural American soldier of the nineteenth century, certainly as America's most able cavalry leader.

367 James Abram Garfield (U.S.) was born in Cuyahoga County, Ohio, on November 19, 1831. He lost his father early, but was determined to get an education and worked his way into Williams College. He graduated in 1856 and became a schoolmaster. Then he entered the Ohio senate as an ardent free-soil Republican. When the war started, he helped recruit the 42nd Ohio and served as its lieutenant colonel and colonel by December 1861. A devoted student of military manuals, he became a fine organizer. While serving in Kentucky under Buell, Garfield did reasonably well and was promoted to brigadier general in January 1862. He fought at Shiloh and Corinth, and in the spring of 1863 became chief of staff to Rosecrans. After Chickamauga, Garfield reached the rank of major general, apparently in tandem with his election

Major General James A. Garfield, later twentieth President of the United States.

to the U.S. House of Representatives, where he served nine terms before his election as twentieth President of the United States, in 1881. On July 2, 1881, he was shot by a deranged office-seeker and died at Elberon, New Jersey, on September 6, 1881.

368 Ulysses Simpson Grant (U.S.), eighteenth President of the United States, was born Hiram Ulysses, at Point Pleasant, Ohio, on April 27, 1822. The congressman who nominated Grant to West Point reported him as Ulysses Simpson, and it was under that name that he graduated in 1843, twenty-first in the thirty-nine-man class. Twice brevetted in the Mexican War, Grant settled unhappily into humdrum army life in the Northwest, drank too much, and resigned on July 31, 1854. Various jobs occupied him for several years, and his fortunes faded. Not until June 17, 1861, did he get a commission as colonel in the 21st Illinois. Through his friendship with Congressman Elihu Washburne, he became a brigadier general in August 1861. His ill-starred effort at Belmont, Missouri, faded from memory as he hammered at the center of the Rebel line above Nashville. His campaign against Forts Henry and Donelson made him famous, and his dogged determination brought him the lasting admiration of President Lincoln. Grant made several abortive attempts to take Vicksburg; after each failure, he simply started again. When he did take the bastion in 1863 and routed

General-in-Chief Ulysses S. Grant during the Wilderness Campaign of 1864, later eighteenth President of the United States.

Bragg's army at Chattanooga in November of that year, Lincoln tapped him for higher things. In March 1864 he became General-in-Chief of the Armies of the United States. In that role he devised the double offensive that pinned down both main Confederate armies in 1864 and brought about their surrender in April 1865. While Sherman pinned down Johnston's Army of Tennessee in Georgia, Grant located the headquarters of the Armies of the United States, near Meade's army headquarters, and directed the heavy Wilderness fighting in May and June 1864. That serious action brought an outcry against "Butcher Grant." The Army of the Potomac suffered several setbacks in that campaign, but Grant refused to retreat and kept turning Lee's right closer to Richmond. He said that he intended to fight it out on that line "if it . . . [took] all summer." After accepting Lee's surrender at Appomattox Court House, in April 1865, Grant remained in the army and in 1866 became a full general. When he was elected President of the United States in 1868, he found the job extremely difficult, and scandals rocked his administration. After his presidency Grant's fortunes declined, and his last years were plagued by penury and illness. His last months were marked by a heroic fight against throat cancer while he worked to finish his splendid *Personal Memoirs,* a legacy for his family. The volumes were published by Mark Twain and earned more than $400,000. He died in Mount McGregor, New Jersey, on July 23, 1885.

Was Grant a great general? Absolutely. Some critics attack his brutal style ("My terms are unconditional surrender . . ."), his costly frontal-assault tactics (Vicksburg, Missionary Ridge, the Wilderness, Cold Harbor), and argue that shrewder strategy would have saved lives. Some admirers argue that Grant was the first of the "modern" generals who understood mass, force, and firepower. Grant's greatness lay in that rare human quality: a firm grasp of the obvious. He knew the Union had more of everything than the Confederacy and that

victory would come when the North mustered its strength and hurled it simultaneously at the Confederate armies. Tactically, he agreed with Bedford Forrest—get there first with the most. Strategically, he agreed with Lincoln, who understood that the Union had "the *greater* numbers, and the enemy has the *greater* facility of concentrating forces," and that the Union had to find "some way of making *our* advantage an overmatch for *his.*"

369 Henry Wager Halleck (U.S.), born in Westernville, New York, on January 16, 1815, ran away from home, was adopted by a grandfather, and attended

Union Major General Henry Wager Halleck, General-in-Chief, July 1862 to February 1864.

Union College, where he was awarded Phi Beta Kappa, and West Point. He was third in the class of 1839 and had distinguished himself by being appointed an assistant professor while he was still a student. Engineering interested him, and he studied New York Harbor works and many in France. His *Report on the Means of National Defense* took him to the Lowell Institute in Boston, where he delivered lectures later published as *Elements of Military Art and Science.* His studies led him into military history, and he translated Jomini's life of Napoleon, *Vie Politique et Militaire de Napoléon Recontre par Lui Meme* (1827). Mexican War service—largely political administration in lower California—earned him rank as a brevet captain in the engineers. He resigned from the army in 1854 to enter the law, but he returned as a major general on August 19, 1861. "Old Brains," as he was known, did not do well and earned the derision of Welles, McClellan, even of Lincoln, who finally tabbed him as "little more than a first-rate clerk." The successes of his subordinates in the West made Halleck look good, but when he took command in person, his deficiencies were painfully apparent. Sloth and fussiness were his hallmarks, and Lincoln finally brought him to Washington as general-in-chief, which caused a change in his nickname to "Old Wooden Head." He came to function as a kind of interpreter of military matters to Lincoln and of Lincoln's pithy orders to denser generals. After the war he held routine department commands and died in Louisville, Kentucky, on January 9, 1872.

370 **William Joseph Hardee (C.S.), born in Camden County, Georgia, on October 12, 1815, graduated from West Point in 1838.** Twice brevetted for gallantry in Mexico, Hardee served a commandant of cadets at the military academy and wrote a standard military textbook, *Rifle and Light Infantry Tactics,* which was read widely by

Lieutenant General William Joseph Hardee, C.S.A.

both Union and Confederate armies. He resigned from the U.S. Army in January 1861, became a Confederate brigadier in June, and rose to major general in October 1861. He raised an Arkansas regiment, which he took to A. S. Johnston's assistance just before Shiloh. Bragg put him in command of one of his army wings for the Kentucky campaign and Murfreesboro. In October 1862, when he was a lieutenant general, he led a corps at Chattanooga and did so again in the Atlanta campaign of 1864. Toward the end of the war he tried to scratch together a force to halt Sherman in Georgia and South Carolina but failed. Forced to surrender Savannah and Charleston to Sherman, Hardee went with the remnants of the Army of Tennessee and surrendered in April 1865. Widely acknowledged as one of the best Confederate corps commanders, Hardee did fear responsibility, which led him to decline command of the Army of Tennessee after the fall of Chattanooga. He might have done well; certainly better than Bragg. After the war he ran a plantation in Selma, Alabama, and died at Wytheville, Virginia, on November 6, 1873.

371 Ambrose Powell Hill (C.S.), born in Culpeper, Virginia, on November 8, 1825, graduated from West Point in 1847, fought in the Mexican War and against the Seminoles, and resigned to join the Confederacy, in March 1861, as colonel of the 13th Virginia. His talents in organization and discipline won him a

brigadier's commission in February 1862, and his fine performance at Williamsburg brought him praise. On May 26, he became a major general, with command of the largest division in the Confederacy. "Little Powell"—five feet nine and 145 pounds—gained fame in the Seven Days' Battles. Tired of waiting for Stonewall Jackson, Hill launched a costly attack on his own at Mechanicsville, suffered severe losses at Gaines's Mill, and, together with Longstreet, at Frayser's Farm. Hill's troubles with superiors began with a skirmish with Longstreet, who put him under arrest. Lee transferred him to Jackson, but

Lieutenant General Ambrose Powell Hill, C.S.A.

they proved nearly as incompatible. Jackson badgered Hill continuously about poor marching discipline in the advance against John Pope, though it was Hill's arrival at a critical moment that probably saved the Battle of Cedar Mountain. His staunch defense of the railroad cut at Second Manassas brought Stonewall's personal praise. During the Maryland campaign Jackson fumed again about Hill's slow marching and arrested him for insubordination. Released temporarily, Hill did well at Harpers Ferry; it was his forced march to Sharpsburg that prevented the destruction of Lee's army. Relations between Jackson, the corps commander, and Hill, a division commander, deteriorated into undignified charges and countercharges—both were practiced at feuding—to Lee's despair. Hill failed to close an important gap in his line at Fredericksburg, a spot that Jackson had noted would probably attract attack, and the feud intensified. It ended with Jackson's death. Hill, after the army reorganization following Chancellorsville, took command of the new Third Corps as a lieutenant general. Some of his men began the Battle of Gettysburg, though Hill himself rested in an ambulance some distance away. He did well on the retreat to Virginia, but in October 1863 he launched a hopeless attack against heavy Union entrenchments at Bristoe Station and suffered his worst and bloodiest defeat. Again, he seemed staunch at the Wilderness fighting the following May, although a strangely recurring illness removed him briefly from the field. Uneven performances in May and June were balanced by his courageous fighting in the Siege of Petersburg, where he turned back every Union attack with style and economy. When Lee's line finally broke, on April 2, 1865, Hill was killed while trying to hold his position.

Recent scholarship shows that Hill suffered the deteriorating effects of gonorrhea, contracted in 1844, and that kidney failure induced uremia, with worsening effects as the war persisted. Nonetheless, sick, irritable, prickly though he was, Little Powell was one of the finest Confederate battle commanders, a fact acknowledged by both Jackson's and Lee's calling for him on their deathbeds.

372 Daniel Harvey Hill (C.S.), born in York District, South Carolina, on July 12, 1821, graduated from West Point in 1842 and won two brevets and a regular promotion in the Mexican War. On resigning from the army in 1849, Hill taught mathematics at Washington College and at Davidson. He was head of the North Carolina Military Institute when war erupted and became colonel of the 1st North Carolina Infantry; he fought successfully enough at Big Bethel to win a brigadier's promotion. He also fought well on the Peninsula under J. E. Johnston and in the Seven Days' Battles under Lee. After a brief try at department command in North Carolina, which he did not enjoy, he rejoined Lee's army.

A carper who looked the part, Hill

tangled with most of his superiors and openly criticized Lee for mismanaging battles. His thorny personality negated such good qualities as personal courage and strong battle leadership and incurred resentment and distrust. Unfairly accused of losing Lee's Lost Order, he felt his important stand at South Mountain was underappreciated, but he nonetheless led a marvelous stand at Sharpsburg's Bloody Lane. Lee did not, however, recommend him for corps command after Maryland, and a resentful Hill threatened to resign in January 1863. Stonewall Jackson, his brother-in-law, urged him to stay in the service. He was transferred to the West, led a corps at Chickamauga, and quarreled furiously with Bragg. That persuaded President Davis to withhold Hill's promotion to lieutenant general. He spent the rest of the war seeking vindication and holding small assignments. He surrendered with J. E. Johnston in April. Back in North Carolina after the war, Hill published a monthly magazine, *The Land We Love,* and a weekly newspaper, *The Southern Home.* He continued feuding with Lee. In the 1870s and early 1880s he was president of two universities; he died in Charlotte on September 24, 1889.

373 John Bell Hood (C.S.), born in Owingsville, Kentucky, on June 1, 1831, graduated from West Point in 1853, and served in California and Texas before resigning, on April 17, 1861. Then began a meteoric rise, as Hood moved quickly

General John Bell Hood, C.S.A.

through Confederate regimental, brigade, and division commands. A brigadier in March 1862, he fought on the Peninsula, with distinction in the Seven Days' Battles, when his Texas Brigade stormed the heights at Gaines's Mill (and won a special place in Lee's heart). On October 10, 1862, he became a major general and proved to be a superb brigade commander who rose to the challenge of division command. He missed Chancellorsville, but he led a division at Gettysburg and took a bad wound in the left arm. When he was transferred to Tennessee with Longstreet's corps, Hood fought at Chickamauga, where he lost his right leg, a wound that damaged him physically and mentally. As a lieutenant general, after February 1, 1864,

Hood commanded a corps under Bragg—whom he disliked and distrusted—and soon became involved in the army's intrigues against superiors. When J. E. Johnston replaced Bragg, Hood continued his personal sniping, and during the Atlanta campaign of 1864 he sank to the worst insubordination by going around Johnston with complaints to President Davis. His conniving brought him an army command—despite Lee's doubts—when Davis relieved Johnston on July 17, 1864. With his army entrenched around Atlanta, Hood, a newly promoted temporary full general, determined to give Davis the battle he wanted to save the Deep South's major city. Costly attacks at Peachtree Creek, Ezra Church, Atlanta, and Jonesboro crippled the army and lost Atlanta on September 1, 1864. In a bold move, Hood turned north to cut Sherman's communications and entice him out of Georgia. Sherman left him to Union forces near Nashville. Poorly planned and brutally costly battles at Franklin and Nashville in November and December wrecked and routed Hood's army. He asked to be relieved and never returned to the field. Sad-eyed, long-faced, Hood gazes yearningly from history. Bold, brave, and gallant, he lacked those things he bartered for ambition: moral courage, honesty, character, the stuff of great commanders. In New Orleans, after the war, he married Anna Marie Hennen, did well in the cotton business, but spent bitter years writing an apologia for his war, *Advance and Retreat*.

Before it was published, yellow fever had closed the cotton exchange, ruined Hood, killed his wife and daughter in August 1879, and killed him a few days later, on August 30.

374 **Edward Johnson (C.S.), born in Salisbury, Virginia, on April 16, 1816, graduated from West Point in 1838,** fought gallantly in the Seminole and Mexican Wars, and resigned to enter Confederate service in June 1861. He was promoted to brigadier in December 1863 and served in the Allegheny Mountains, west of Staunton, Virginia, soon becoming known as "Allegheny" Johnson. His distinguished service at Greenbrier River, Allegheny Mountain, and McDowell confirmed his sound reputation; Stonewall Jackson greatly admired Johnson. He was wounded at

Major General Edward Johnson, C.S.A.

McDowell and became a major general in February 1863, after which he command-ed Stonewall Jackson's old division in Lee's army at Gettysburg, through the Mine Run Valley, the Wilderness, and Spotsylvania. There, in the desperate May 1864 fighting at the Bloody Angle, Johnson and 2500 of his men were cap-tured. After he was exchanged in August, he commanded an Army of Tennessee division, but was captured at Nashville in December. He was released in July 1865, took up farming in Virginia, and enjoyed various civic organizations. Still a bache-lor, he died in Richmond on March 2, 1873.

375 Fitzhugh Lee (C.S.), born in Fairfax County, Virginia, on November 19, 1835, graduated in 1856 from West Point, where his uncle Robert E. Lee was serving as superintendent. He had earned honors at the academy in horsemanship. He was wounded on the Indian frontier and joined the West Point faculty in 1860. After resigning from the U.S. Army in May 1861 he served as adjutant to General R. S. Ewell at First Manassas (First Bull Run) and was commissioned lieutenant colonel of the 1st Virginia Cavalry in August. A merry man, like his commander, Jeb Stuart, Lee enjoyed taunting old U.S. Army friends when he raided their camps. In the action known as Stuart's Ride Around McClellan, he won high com-mendation. In July 1862, he was promoted to brigadier and served with Lee's army

Major General Fitzhugh Lee, C.S.A.

during the Second Manassas and Sharps-burg campaigns. His scouting activities at Chancellorsville helped show the way for Jackson's march around Hooker's right flank. In September 1863, Fitz Lee became a major general and was put in command of the 2nd Division of the Cavalry Corps. He did distinguished service in 1864 at Yellow Tavern (he took command after Stuart's mortal wound), at Spotsylvania, and at Trevilian Station, and was given command of the Cavalry Corps after Wade Hampton went to North Carolina in Jan-uary 1865. Attendance at an infamous shad bake just before the Battle of Five Forks on April 1 clouded his reputation, but he regained esteem by delaying Sheridan's pursuit of Lee's army toward Appomattox.

He farmed in Virginia after the war, was elected governor in 1885, and served as U.S. consul general in Havana from 1896 to 1898. He wore U.S. Blues again during the Spanish-American War as a major general, and died in Washington, D.C., on April 29, 1905.

376 Robert Edward Lee (C.S.) was born at Stratford, Westmoreland County, Virginia, on January 19, 1807, the third son of Ann Hill Carter Lee and the Revolutionary War hero Henry (Light Horse Harry) Lee. First schooled in Alexandria, Robert graduated from West Point, second in the class of 1829, and joined the Engineer Corps. He married Mary Ann Randolph Custis, the only child of George Washington Parke Custis, General Washington's adopted son; the Lees had seven children. Routine engineering assignments won Lee renown in the corps, and outstanding service in the Mexican War brought him three brevets and Winfield Scott's regard. After serving as superintendent of the U.S. Military Academy (1852–1855), he became lieutenant colonel of the 2nd Cavalry in Texas, but family problems kept him in Virginia through the late 1850s. In October 1859, Lee led a force that crushed John Brown's insurrection at Harpers Ferry. As secession loomed, Scott offered Lee command of an army to halt the rebellion. Lee declined and entered Virginia's service, which became Confederate. Davis, despite Lee's poor showing in an abortive western

Robert E. Lee, wearing a sword and sash given him by ladies of Baltimore and a shirt made by the ladies of Richmond, in 1863.

Virginia campaign, made him a full general in August 1861 and sent him to strengthen South Atlantic seaboard defenses. After J. E. Johnston was wounded at Seven Pines, Davis made Lee commander of what would be the Army of Northern Virginia. Lee's daring Seven Days' Battles, in June and July 1862, saved Richmond. He then planned and executed a campaign that nearly annihilated General John Pope's

Army of Virginia at Second Manassas on August 29–30, and pushed the Federals out of Virginia. His invasion of Maryland ended after a desperate battle at Sharpsburg on September 16–17, 1862. Sound defensive tactics defeated General Ambrose Burnside at Fredericksburg in December 1862. Lee's most complete success came against General Joseph Hooker at Chancellorsville, on May 2–4, 1863. In that battle Lee divided his force in the Virginia Wilderness and sent Stonewall Jackson on a march that smashed Hooker's right flank and nearly enveloped the Army of the Potomac. Victory came at the incalculable cost of Stonewall Jackson's life. Strategic considerations (relief of Vicksburg and possible capture of Washington or another major Northern city) and logistics (Virginia was bare of foodstuffs) led Lee to invade Pennsylvania in June 1863. Ill and fatigued, he fought and lost the nearly decisive Battle of Gettysburg, July 1–3, 1863. Davis refused Lee's subsequent offer to resign, and the general again showed his audacity in the fierce 1864 Wilderness campaigns against Grant and George Meade. At Cold Harbor, on June 3, 1864, Lee's heavily entrenched army mowed down 7000 Yankees in about thirty minutes. The summer campaign cost roughly three Yankees to each Rebel, a ratio too high for the South—since reinforcements were so few. Finally on the defensive, besieged at Petersburg, Lee extended his lines to sustain the siege from July 1864 until April 1865. Attrition thinned Rebel

lines too far, and on April 2 a Yankee breakthrough forced Lee out of Richmond. Although he hoped to reach Joe Johnston's army in the Carolinas, Lee was intercepted, and he surrendered to Grant at Appomattox Court House on April 9, 1865. After the war he served as president of Washington College in Lexington, Virginia, and became a living legend: the embodiment of the good of the Lost Cause. He died on October 13, 1870.

Lee ranks among the greatest of American generals, certainly as a tactical genius. He is sometimes criticized for wasteful attacks, for deviating from President Davis's apparent strategy of the offensive-defensive, and for concentrating too much on Virginia. Lee was guilty of these things, not from recklessness but from a certainty—shared by the President—that the South would have to win on the battlefield, that the inferior side must strike fast and keep the initiative and that daring often humbles strength.

377 **James Longstreet (C.S.), born in Edgefield District, South Carolina, on January 2, 1821, graduated from West Point in 1842,** won brevets for gallantry in Mexico, and resigned from the U.S. Army on June 1, 1861, to become a Confederate brigadier. Attached to J. E. Johnston's army, Longstreet fought at Blackburn's Ford, missed First Manassas, and became a major general on October 7, 1861. He supported Johnston's strategic arguments

Lee's "old war horse," Lieutenant General James Longstreet.

with President Davis, and when Johnston moved the army to the Peninsula in 1862, Longstreet demonstrated his mastery of logistical details. He held stubbornly at Williamsburg in May 1862, did not do well at Seven Pines, but won Lee's admiration for his aggressiveness in the Seven Days' Battles. Lee put Longstreet in command of one wing of the reorganized Army of Northern Virginia. At Sharpsburg, Longstreet solidified his reputation for tenacity by roaming the whole of the exposed Confederate right, encouraging, exhorting, "like a rock in steadiness," an observer noted, "when sometimes in battle the world seemed flying to pieces." At the end of September 17, Lee embraced him with the greeting: "Ah! here is Longstreet; here is my old war horse." Promoted to

lieutenant general, with command of Lee's First Corps in October 1862, Longstreet starred at Fredericksburg, where he improved his formidable positions along Marye's Heights with entrenchments and repulsed some 25,000 Yankee attackers. Detached by Lee early in 1863 to forage south of the James River, Longstreet fed his divisions but showed unexpected caution in engaging Federals in Southern Virginia. He missed Chancellorsville but went with Lee into Pennsylvania. He had advocated concentration in the West to save Vicksburg, but he accepted Lee's decision in the belief that the Rebels would take strong ground, beat off the enemy, and threaten Washington. Lee's decisions to attack on the several days at Gettysburg depressed Longstreet, who had expected Pickett's Charge to fail, and he obeyed orders apathetically. Detached to aid Bragg's army after Gettysburg, Longstreet exploited a gap in W. S. Rosecrans's lines at Chickamauga and nearly wrecked the Union army. Exacerbating his errors at Lookout Mountain by joining the chorus of complaints against Bragg, Longstreet was given an independent assignment to capture Knoxville. He failed, and he tried to blame subordinates for his troubles. Back with Lee's army in the Wilderness campaigns, Longstreet was accidentally wounded by his own men and was kept out of action until October 1864. He commanded the left of Lee's besieged lines at Petersburg and marched with the army to Appomattox.

Always best on defense and counter-attack—he was an early expert at field entrenchments—Longstreet usually proved a superior battle commander. A master of concentration, he rarely delivered a piece-meal counterstroke. Lee trusted him almost as much as he trusted Jackson and relied on him for advice and comfort. Longstreet engaged in some unwise criticism of Lee after the war and suffered the enmity of Jubal Early, who nearly ruined Longstreet's reputation in the pages of the *Southern Historical Society Papers.* Close Republican affiliation further lowered the "war horse" in Confederate veterans' eyes. He was pardoned in 1867 and received several Federal appointments. In 1896 he published *From Manassas to Appomattox,* and on January 2, 1904, he died in Gainesville, Georgia.

378 **Mansfield Lovell (C.S.), born in Washington, D.C., on October 20, 1822, graduated from West Point in 1842 and served with distinction in the Mexican War.** He resigned from the U.S. Army in 1854, became a businessman, and later was deputy street commissioner of New York City. On being appointed a Confederate major general in October 1861, he commanded the defense of New Orleans. His small army, weakened by the detachment of units to other theaters, could not withstand a combined land and sea attack, and Lovell abandoned New Orleans in April 1862. Unjustly blamed for a weak defense (Robert E. Lee praised his

Confederate Major General Mansfield Lovell.

efforts), Lovell finally won exoneration from a court of inquiry. He did commendable duty in a skillful retreat from Corinth, but, the victim of New Orleans rumors and marred by a drunkard's red nose, he was relieved. J. E. Johnston and J. B. Hood vainly sought to get him a corps command in the summer of 1864. Johnston won him an assignment in March 1865, but Lovell did not arrive until after Johnston had surrendered. Skilled, brave, relentlessly luckless, Lovell never had a chance to show his mettle in the Civil War. He returned to engineering duties in New York City after the war and died there on June 1, 1884.

379 **Lafayette McLaws (C.S.), born in Augusta, Georgia, on January 15, 1821,**

Confederate Major General Lafayette McLaws.

graduated from West Point in 1842. Service in the Mexican War yielded to routine assignments and slow promotion. When he resigned from the U.S. Army to join the Confederacy, McLaws had been a captain for almost a decade. After brief quartermaster service in Georgia, he became colonel of the 10th Georgia Infantry on June 17, 1861, and joined the army around Richmond. His sound service there and early in the Peninsular campaign won him a brigadier's appointment in September 1862. The major general's commission he earned dated from May 23, 1862, and made him one of the seniors at that rank. In Longstreet's corps, McLaws won admiration for his defensive dispositions and for maintaining the condition of his men. He was highly regarded as a division leader and he performed brilliantly at Maryland Heights. His was a vital victory in the West Woods at Sharpsburg, and he also tenaciously held the riverfront at Fredericksburg. "He was," noted an observer, "about the best general in the army for that sort of thing." Lee, probably unjustly, lost some confidence in McLaws because of the confused fighting at Salem Church. At Gettysburg, McLaws, in turn, lost confidence in Longstreet and spoke against him. During the Tennessee operations of "Old Pete's" corps, McLaws became the brunt of the failure at Knoxville, and Longstreet brought six charges against him. President Davis exonerated McLaws of the charges and censured Longstreet, but, realizing their relations were impossible, transferred McLaws to Georgia. He surrendered with J. E. Johnston in April 1865. After the war McLaws tried the insurance business, held some appointed positions, but lived poorly, and in 1896 said, "I am without means, having lost all." He died in Savannah on July 22, 1897.

380 **Humphrey Marshall (C.S.), born in Frankfort, Kentucky, on January 13, 1812, was the nephew of the antislavery leader James G. Birney and a relative of U.S. Chief Justice John Marshall.** He graduated from West Point in 1832 and resigned from the Army to become a lawyer. Service in the Black Hawk and Mexican Wars was interspersed

Confederate Brigadier General Humphrey Marshall.

Davis—Marshall won minor actions in the border mountains between western Virginia and Kentucky in 1862. But he was irked at his isolation, so he resigned in mid-June 1862. He was, however, persuaded to keep his commission and to aid in the Confederate Kentucky invasion in September. Marshall joined Kirby Smith's politicking against Bragg and moved his brigade lethargically to the aid of the main Confederate Army. After his insubordinate actions, Marshall took his men back to western Virginia. No one opposed Marshall's second resignation in May 1863, and he moved to Richmond, where he opened a law practice and served as a member of the Kentucky delegation to the Second Confederate Congress, where he generally opposed the Davis administration. Marshall fled to Texas at the end of the war but returned to practice law in Louisville in 1866 and died there on March 28, 1872.

with local political activities and then with membership in the U.S. Congress. A secessionist who hoped to preserve Kentucky's neutrality, Marshall supported Breckinridge in the 1860 election. When Lincoln countered a small Confederate incursion into Kentucky with massive force, Marshall accepted a Rebel brigadier's commission in October 1861. In a perpetual sulk, largely incompetent, devoted to indiscipline, so large (300 pounds) as to strain any mount, critical of superiors—especially Bragg and President

381 Robert Huston Milroy (U.S.), born near Salem, Indiana, on June 11, 1816, graduated in 1843 from Captain Partridge's Academy in Norwich, Vermont, and served as captain of the 1st Indiana Volunteers from 1846 to 1847. He left a law practice in Rensselaer, Indiana, for Union service in 1861, and fought with McClellan in western Virginia. He served as a brigadier of volunteers in September 1862 and became a major general in March 1863. He fought Stonewall Jackson in the Shenandoah Valley, a campaign that made him famous as the butt of a comment by Confederate General R. S. Ewell. Receiving a confusing communication from his new commander, Jackson, which said that through the aid of Providence Milroy's wagon train had been captured, Ewell exploded, "What has Providence to do with Milroy's wagon train?" During the Gettysburg campaign, Milroy, with 6000 to 8000 men, was outsmarted by Ewell's corps and lost many killed, 3400 prisoners, and twenty-three guns. He was investigated but exonerated of dereliction, and he served later in the war with George Thomas at Nashville. After Appomattox, Milroy served as a trustee of the Wabash and Erie Canal Company and became an Indian agent in Olympia, Washington, where he died, on March 29, 1890.

382 George Edward Pickett (C.S.), born in Richmond, Virginia, on January 28, 1825, graduated last in the West Point class of 1846 and served gallantly in Mexico and in the West. He returned to Virginia at the outbreak of war and first served as an infantry captain. Pickett received quick promotion to colonel, and, because of his West Point background, became a brigadier on January 14, 1862. He led a brigade commendably in Longstreet's division at the Battle of Seven Pines and in the Seven Days' Battles but was wounded at Gaines's Mill and was out of action until October 1862. Promoted to major general that month, Pickett was at Fredericksburg and went on the Suffolk

campaign with Longstreet—and spent much time courting LaSalle Corbell, whom he later married. When he arrived at Gettysburg late on July 3, 1863, the second day, Pickett led the charge that forever bears his name. At about 3:00 P.M., after a two-hour cannonade, Pickett's division as well as units from the Third Corps (between 12,000 to 15,000 men) advanced across a mile of open ground against the entrenched Yankees. Artillery, chopping away at the attackers, was augmented by rifle fire as the range closed, and only a small group broke through the Union lines. They were wiped out. Pickett lost at least half of his force within an hour. He never forgave Lee for ruining his division. Pickett earned some criticism for brutality

Major General George Edward Pickett, C.S.A.

against Unionists in North Carolina, but in May 1864 he distinguished himself by helping bottle up General Benjamin Butler (q.v.) at Bermuda Hundred. An emotional breakdown took him out of action for a time, but he returned to the defense of Petersburg. Charged with defending the vital junction at Five Forks on Lee's extreme right, Pickett attended the same ill-timed shad bake on April 1, 1865, that had hampered the career of Fitzhugh Lee. His division was destroyed while he was away. During the retreat to Appomattox on April 8, Lee dismissed him from command, but he surrendered with the army at Appomattox. He fled to Canada after the war to escape possible war crimes charges, but returned to Virginia by 1866. He worked as a life insurance salesman in Norfolk, became increasingly embittered, and died there on July 30, 1875.

Pickett, whose fame rests on a gallant futility, is hardly a shining hero. He was, though, unusually popular among his enemies. At Cold Harbor, Grant had campfires lighted in honor of Pickett's newborn son, and when Lincoln visited Richmond in early April 1865, he called at Pickett's house.

383 **Gideon Johnson Pillow (C.S.), born in Williamson County, Tennessee, on June 8, 1806, graduated from the University of Nashville in 1827** and entered law practice with James K. Polk, later President, who pronounced him "the shrewdest man I ever knew." Appointed a

Confederate Brigadier General Gideon Johnson Pillow.

brigadier general by Polk in 1846, Pillow made a dismal showing in the Mexican War, though Polk sustained him against General Winfield Scott's complaints. He was a senior major general of Tennessee's army during secession and became a Confederate brigadier on July 9, 1861. In November, he was a division commander at Belmont, Missouri. At Fort Donelson, he was second in command to General John B. Floyd and led a successful breakout attempt through the Union lines, but he and Floyd and Buckner withdrew to the fort, thereby sealing its fate. He and Floyd escaped after command passed to Buckner. His reputation ruined, Pillow spent months trying to vindicate his ineptitude; even brigade command at Murfreesboro in 1863 did not resurrect him. He served with the Confederate conscript service and, finally, as the last commissary general of prisoners. Bankrupt after the war, he practiced law with former Tennessee governor Isham G. Harris. William T. Sherman assessed him brutally as "a mass of vanity, conceit, ignorance, ambition, and want of truth."

384 Leonidas Polk (C.S.) was born in Raleigh, North Carolina, on April 10, 1806. After being educated by private tutors, he entered the University of North Carolina but, because he wanted to be a soldier, switched to West Point, from which he graduated in 1827. Among the friends he made there were Albert Sidney Johnston (q.v.) and Jefferson Davis. Religious enthusiasm took him from the army into the Episcopal ministry in December 1827. By 1830, he was a deacon and became missionary bishop of the Southwest (Alabama, Arkansas, Louisiana, Mississippi, Texas) and, in 1831, bishop of Louisiana. In June 1861, Davis appointed the almost mystically handsome minister a major general, and Polk became the "Bishop-Militant," commanding west Tennessee and eastern Arkansas. In his defense of the Mississippi, Polk made a colossal blunder: he invaded Kentucky but occupied only Columbus, leaving strategic

Episcopal bishop and Confederate Lieutenant General Leonidas Polk.

Paducah to swift Yankee control. Polk's ineffective invasion lost Kentucky to the North. He then commanded Sidney Johnston's First Corps at Shiloh. A presidential favorite, Polk became a lieutenant general in October 1862 and involved himself in insubordinate efforts to unseat Braxton Bragg. Bragg tried to replace him, despite Davis's resistance and Polk's irritating ability to slough off guilt onto subordinates. After Chickamauga, where Polk was slow, Bragg, himself sloughing responsibilities, sacked Polk, and Davis shifted him to a department command. With J. E. Johnston's army, Polk was killed by an artillery shell at Pine Mountain, Georgia, on June 14, 1864.

385 John Pope (U.S.), a collateral

Union Major General John Pope.

descendant of George Washington and related by marriage to Mary Todd Lincoln, was born in Louisville, Kentucky, on March 16, 1822. He graduated from West Point in the star-studded class of 1842, earned two brevets in the Mexican War, and was appointed brigadier general of volunteers, as of June 14, 1861. He captured New Madrid and Island No. 10 in March and April 1862. A major general in March, he commanded the left wing of the Union advance on Corinth after Shiloh. In June 1862 he received command of all U.S. forces in the East, other than McClellan's neutralized forces near Richmond. As commander of the Army of Virginia, Pope moved to relieve

McClellan. Flushed with importance, Pope issued a series of bombastic orders that embarrassed the government and infuriated the enemy. He was so confused and outmaneuvered by Jackson and Lee that he lost the Second Bull Run (Second Manassas) campaign and blamed others for his errors; he ruined the career of General Fitz John Porter (q.v.) by charging him with disobedience of impossible orders. When he was sent to command the Department of the Northwest, Pope did well against the Sioux in Minnesota. As a career officer, he served in various commands and became a major general in October 1882. In 1886 he retired; he died in Sandusky, Ohio, on September 23, 1892.

386 Fitz John Porter (U.S.), born in Portsmouth, New Hampshire, on August 31, 1822, graduated from West Point in 1845, won two brevets for gallantry in the Mexican War, taught artillery at West Point from 1849 to 1855, and served in Utah from 1857 to 1860. He was commissioned a brigadier of volunteers as of May 1861 and served in the Shenandoah until McClellan brought him to Washington to help train his army. That was the start of Porter's lasting bond with McClellan. Porter led the 5th Corps brilliantly during the Seven Days' Battles, withdrew his corps across the Chickahominy, and held firmly at Malvern Hill. As a major general, Porter led his corps in the Second Bull Run (Second Manassas) campaign. He despised Pope and fulmi-nated against him. In the complicated operations around Manassas, Pope, un-aware of the situation, gave Porter orders that were impossible to implement. In the bitter aftermath of that failed campaign, Pope court-martialed Porter for disobedi-ence, disloyalty, and misconduct. Porter, relieved of command in November, arrested, tried, and found guilty by a com-mission determined to discredit McClel-lan, was cashiered in January 1863 and devoted his life to vindication. He was at last exonerated by a special board in 1879 and was then praised for saving the army at Second Manassas. His case, however, became snarled in postwar politics, and Porter waited until 1886 for a special act restoring him to the army and making par-tial amends for perhaps the greatest injus-tice done to a Federal commander in the Civil War. Porter died in Morristown, New Jersey, on May 21, 1901.

387 **Sterling Price (C.S.), born in Prince Edward County, Virginia, on September 20, 1809, was educated at Hampden-Sydney College, studied law, and moved with his parents to Missouri in 1830.** There, he was elected to the legislature, then to Congress. Price led a Missouri reg-iment in the Mexican War, was promoted to brigadier general, and became military governor of Chihuahua. In 1853 he was elected governor of Missouri. A moderate Unionist, Price became president of the state convention that voted against seces-

Major General Sterling Price, C.S.A.

sion in 1861, but he was disenchanted by the extreme Unionists. Price—affection-ately known as Old Pap—took charge of the state militia in May 1861 and tried to maintain neutrality. As Union forces gath-ered, Price took the militia to southwest-ern Missouri, where, aided by Confederate troops under General Ben McCulloch, he defeated General Nathaniel Lyon (q.v.) at Wilson's Creek (q.v.) and moved on to capture 3000 Federals at Lexington, Mis-souri, after which he retreated to Arkansas. After the battle of Elkhorn Tavern (q.v.), Price opposed transferring his men to Mississippi, but he accepted rank as a Con-federate major general. The campaign he led at Iuka and Corinth was fruitless; back in Arkansas, he botched an attack on Helena in 1863. He was, however, successful in aiding General E. K. Smith (q.v.) to repulse a Federal expedition against Camden in 1864. He invaded Missouri in the fall with about 12,000 men but was pushed out at Westport in October and retreated to Texas. He fled to Mexico after the war and founded the Confederate Carlota Colony. In 1866, he returned to Missouri and died in St. Louis on September 29, 1867.

388 William Starke Rosecrans (U.S.), born in Delaware County, Ohio, on September 6, 1819, had little formal

Union Major General William Starke Rosecrans.

education but graduated from West Point in 1842 and did routine engineering duties until he resigned in 1854. A volunteer on McClellan's staff in April 1861, Rosecrans became a regular brigadier general on May 16, commanded a brigade at Rich Mountain, and helped to push Robert E. Lee's troops from western Virginia. He participated in the Corinth operations after Shiloh and took command of the Army of Mississippi under Grant's overall direction. When he was promoted to major general in October 1862 (after some complaints over relative date of rank), Rosecrans relieved Don Carlos Buell (q.v.) in Kentucky and soon commanded the new Army of the Cumberland. "Old Rosy" repulsed Bragg's (q.v.) army at Murfreesboro. Late in June 1863, Rosecrans, as one historian put it, "inaugurated a campaign of maneuver—as brilliant as any in American military annals—which forced the Confederates . . . into the fortified railroad center of Chattanooga and then by a skillful feint up the Tennessee, out of the town." (Ezra J. Warner, *Generals in Blue: Lives of the Union Commanders* [Baton Rouge: Louisiana State University Press, 1964], p. 411.) Severely defeated by a heavily reinforced Bragg at Chickamauga, September 19–20, 1863, Rosecrans was relieved by Grant and put in command of the Department of Missouri in 1864. He resigned from the army on March 28, 1867. President Johnson appointed him minister to Mexico in 1868, but President Grant removed him in

1869. He lived in California and in 1880 was elected to Congress, where he served as chairman of the Military Affairs Committee. He left in 1885 and was register of the Treasury until 1893. He died in California on March 11, 1898.

389 **Philip Henry Sheridan (U.S.) was born (according to his memoirs) in Albany, New York, on March 6, 1831, and graduated from West Point in 1853.** The war's outbreak found him a second lieutenant, 4th Infantry, but he became General H. W. Halleck's (q.v.) quartermaster after Shiloh. Appointed colonel of cavalry—he hated riding—in May 1862, he began a spectacular career. He was made a brigadier as of July 1, 1862, fought hard during Bragg's Kentucky ventures, and became a major general after Murfreesboro. His command suffered heavily at Chickamauga, but two months later he stormed the apparently impregnable Missionary Ridge—to Grant's delight. Grant put Sheridan in command of the cavalry of the Army of the Potomac in May 1864. In the campaign against Richmond, Sheridan's troops killed Jeb Stuart at Yellow Tavern, were defeated at Trevilian Station, but became the darlings of reporters in need of victories in the midst of that summer's carnage. Sheridan took charge of a mixed field force (about 45,000) in August 1864 and scourged the Shenandoah Valley— and, incidentally, Jubal Early's small army. In mid-October, with Sheridan absent in Washington, Early surprised and nearly

Major General Philip Henry Sheridan, 1864, in the hat he wore on the famous ride when he rallied Union troops with the words "We're all right . . . we'll whip them yet!"

wrecked the Union force at Cedar Creek. Early did not, however, push his success, which permitted "Sheridan's Ride" to rally his men, save the battle, and push to waste the Valley. Promoted to a regular major general, lauded by Congress, Sheridan joined Grant, smashed Lee's right at Five Forks, captured a large part of Lee's men at Sayler's Creek, and cut off Lee's retreat at Appomattox. He was put in charge of the Fifth Military District (Louisiana and Texas), but his harsh Reconstruction policies forced President Johnson to remove him six months later. During Grant's presidency, Sheridan became a lieutenant general and held several posts, often against hostile Indians. He observed the Franco-Prussian War in 1870–1871, became commanding general of the U.S. Army in 1884, and was appointed a full general in June 1888. He died in Nonquitt, Massachusetts, on August 5, 1888.

390 William Tecumseh Sherman, next to Grant the most famous Union general, was born in Lancaster, Ohio, on February 8, 1820, and enjoyed an unusual upbringing by friends. His brother John was a long-sitting U.S. representative, senator, and Cabinet member. Sherman graduated from West Point in 1840 and was brevetted for service in the Mexican War. After resigning from the army in 1853, he went into banking in San Francisco; when the bank failed, he failed again in law practice in Leavenworth, Kansas. In 1859 he accepted the superintendency of the Louisiana State Seminary of Learning and Military Academy (later Louisiana State University). Secession caused him to resign in January 1861, and Sherman worked briefly in St. Louis, but in May rejoined the U.S. Army as a colonel in the 13th Infantry. He commanded a brigade at First Bull Run (First Manassas), and on August 7, 1861, became a brigadier general—ranking seventh in the service and seven ahead of U. S. Grant (q.v.). After being sent to Kentucky, he allowed his short temper to earn him the reputation of an eccentric, even a madman. His division was surprised at Shiloh, but he fought well and won promotion to major general in

Union General William Tecumseh Sherman in 1864, before his march through Georgia to the sea.

May 1862. His command participated in several attempts to take Vicksburg, suffered a defeat at Chickasaw Bluffs, but helped take Arkansas Post. He also commanded a corps under Grant during the main drive at the South's Mississippi bastion. He fought at Chattanooga, and after Grant took command of the U.S. Army in 1864, "Cump" Sherman commanded all U.S. forces in the central area. Sherman's campaign against J. E. Johnston at Atlanta and his subsequent "March through Georgia" set new standards of hard war. His "bummers" burned Confederate facilities, ruined Rebel railroads with "Sherman's neckties" (rails softened over fires and twisted around trees), captured Savannah, and moved on to Charleston against the remnants of Rebel forces collected in the wake of Hood's disastrous Tennessee venture. After a minor check at Bentonville, North Carolina, Sherman accepted Johnston's surrender at Durham Station on April 26, 1865. He ended the war as a major general in the regular army, was twice thanked by Congress, and became a lieutenant general in 1866. When Grant was elected President, Sherman was named a full general and commander of the army. He helped to establish the Command School at Fort Leavenworth, one of the important acts of his career. He requested retirement in February 1884 and became a popular speaker. Sherman died in New York City on February 14, 1891, and in his funeral procession, his arch opponent, General Joseph E. Johnston (q.v.), marched bareheaded, and, as a result, died of pneumonia.

391 Henry Hopkins Sibley (C.S.), born in Natchitoches, Louisiana, on May 28, 1816, graduated from West Point in 1838. Service in the Seminole War, in the Utah Expedition against the Mormons, and brevets in the Mexican War made him a highly experienced officer. He resigned from the U.S. Army on May 13, 1861, and became a Confederate colonel on May 16 and a brigadier on June 17. He persuaded Jefferson Davis to support a campaign to New Mexico, but Sibley turned it into a

Brigadier General Henry Hopkins Sibley, C.S.A.

disaster. A victory at Valverde and a defeat at Glorieta Pass in February and March 1862 forced him to a terrible winter retreat through mountainous country, and few of his men survived. Thereafter he had no major commands. Charges were twice filed against him, and his reputation for drinking mounted. Sibley, famous for designing a tent used by both armies early in the war, served in Egypt from 1869 to 1873. He died in Fredericksburg, Virginia, on August 23, 1886.

392 Edmund Kirby Smith (C.S.), born in St. Augustine, Florida, on May 16,

General Edmund Kirby Smith, C.S.A.

1824, graduated from West Point in 1845 and won two brevets for gallantry in the Mexican War. He served on the West Point mathematics faculty from 1849 to 1852 and then transferred to frontier action with the 2nd U.S. Cavalry. He held a Texas post against secessionists, but resigned when Florida seceded. There he served under J. E. Johnston in the Shenandoah Valley, became a brigadier on June 17, 1861, and was badly wounded at First Manassas (First Bull Run). As a major general he commanded the District of East Tennessee, won a major victory at **393** Richmond, Kentucky, on August 30, 1862, during Bragg's western invasion, which he failed to support enthusiastically. On being promoted to lieutenant general in October 1862, Smith commanded the Trans-Mississippi Department. A full general in the

Provisional Army in February 1864, Kirby Smith (as he was known) won the Battle of Mansfield, Louisiana, in April 1864 and repulsed General N. P. Banks's (q.v.) Red River expedition. He maintained a defensive posture in his department and made few efforts to aid the main theater of war. After surrendering on May 26, 1865, Smith went into business, then into education, and was a professor of mathematics at the University of the South, Sewanee, Tennessee, from 1875 until his death, on March 28, 1893—the last of the Confederacy's full generals.

394 James Ewell Brown (Jeb) Stuart, born in Patrick County, Virginia, on

Major General Jeb Stuart, leader of Lee's Cavalry.

February 6, 1833, graduated in 1854 from West Point, where his fellow cadets contrarily nicknamed him "Beauty." Serving largely on the frontier, Stuart was an aide to Robert E. Lee in the Harpers Ferry raid that captured John Brown in 1859. With Virginia's secession, Stuart became a colonel of the 1st Virginia Cavalry and did well under J. E. Johnston in the Shenandoah. Fine service at First Manassas was rewarded with a brigadier's promotion in September 1861, and Stuart's initial claim to fame came with his "Ride Around McClellan," the carefully planned three-day triumph in mid-June 1862. A major general in charge of Lee's cavalry by July 1862, Stuart grew more famous with each exploit. He was a superb scout, a fine intelligence officer, and a close friend of Stonewall Jackson's—and he knew how to advance his image. He raided Pope's (q.v.) communications during the Second Manassas campaign, seized massive stores, captured important Union documents, and supported Jackson's front. His men screened Lee's army during the Maryland campaign, and his horse artillery ably sustained Lee's right at Fredericksburg. During the Chancellorsville campaign, he helped direct Jackson around Hooker's flank and took command of Jackson's corps when both Jackson and A. P. Hill (q.v.) were wounded. While Lee was moving toward Pennsylvania, Stuart's command was surprised by Yankees at Brandy Station, on June 9, 1863, and

nearly bested. He failed Lee during the Gettysburg campaign by going on a raid to revive his dampened spirits after Brandy Station. And he also failed to beat Union cavalry behind Gettysburg when Pickett was attacking the Union front on July 3, 1863. The supposition is that, had Stuart been present during the Pennsylvania invasion, Lee would have fought elsewhere. Mortally wounded after intercepting Sheridan's cavalry at Yellow Tavern on May 11, 1864, Stuart, surrounded by admirers, died in Richmond the next day.

His death came at the beginning of Rebel decline in cavalry and fortunes. At Yellow Tavern he had about a third as many men as Sheridan, yet his men outfought the enemy. Men and horses, however, were growing scarce. His legend remains. A grand and daring "bold dragoon," Stuart ranks among America's greatest horse soldiers.

395 **George Henry Thomas (U.S.), born in Southampton County, Virginia, on July 31, 1816, was nearly killed in Nat Turner's slave insurrection of 1831.** After graduating from West Point in 1840, Thomas served in the artillery, fought against the Seminoles, was brevetted twice in the Mexican War, and served on the Texas frontier under Robert E. Lee, A. S. Johnston, and William J. Hardee until the outbreak of war. Although he had sought an appointment to the Virginia Military Institute in January 1861, he stuck with the

Union. He commanded a brigade in the Shenandoah during First Bull Run (First Manassas) and became a brigadier on August 17, 1861. On being transferred to the West, he defeated Felix Zollicoffer (q.v.) in January 1862, fought at Shiloh, was promoted to major general as of April 25, then served with Halleck (q.v.), Buell (q.v.), and Rosecrans (q.v.) at Corinth, Perryville, Murfreesboro, and Chickamauga. There, during the rout of Rosecrans's army, he held a vital hill on the Union left long enough to cover that retreat, and was known afterward as the "Rock of Chickamauga." His men participated in the storming of Missionary Ridge in November 1863. During Sherman's Atlanta campaign, Thomas commanded the Army of the Cumberland, which made up more than half of Sherman's force. Detached to fight Hood in Tennessee, Thomas won an action at Franklin on November 20, 1864, and virtually destroyed Hood's army at Nashville in December 1864. He was promoted to major general in the regular army and thanked by Congress; then he commanded the Department of Tennessee until 1867 and, in 1869, the Division of the Pacific. On March 28, 1870, he died in San Francisco.

George Thomas was one of the most important Union commanders; he never failed at a crucial moment.

396 **Earl Van Dorn (C.S.) was born near Port Gibson, Mississippi, on September 27, 1820, and graduated from West Point in 1842.** He earned two brevets in the Mexican War and by 1861 was a major in the 2nd U.S.

Union Major General George Henry Thomas.

Major General Earl Van Dorn, C.S.A.

Cavalry, under A. S. Johnston and R. E. Lee. Joining the South, he was appointed colonel, then brigadier general in June 1861, when he served in Texas. As a major general, he was sent to Virginia and became commander of the Army of the West in the Trans-Mississippi area in January 1862. Although he was daring and aggressive, he lost the battle of Elkhorn Tavern in April 1862 and hence was unable to aid A. S. Johnston at Shiloh. He was defeated at Corinth after Shiloh but was given charge of General John C. Pemberton's (q.v.) cavalry. His dashing raid on U. S. Grant's (q.v.) supply base at Holly Springs, Mississippi, in December 1862, stalled a major Union thrust at Vicksburg and stands as Van Dorn's best achievement. He was murdered by a Dr. Peters (possibly a jealous husband), at Spring Hill, Tennessee, on May 7, 1863.

397 **Stand Watie, who was born in Georgia on December 12, 1806, was a three-quarter-blood Cherokee Indian.** After being educated at a mission school, he led the faction of the Cherokee Nation that supported the Confederacy. A colonel of the 1st Cherokee Mounted Rifles, he fought at Wilson's Creek and Elkhorn Tavern, then in several skirmishes in the West. He was commissioned a brigadier in May 1864 and remained loyal to the South. In fact, he was one of the last to surrender—on June 23, 1865. A planter and businessman after the war, Watie died in

Brigadier General Stand Watie, Cherokee leader who commanded Indian troops for the Confederacy.

present-day Delaware County, Oklahoma, on September 9, 1871.

398 **Watie was helped in organizing a regiment by his nephew Elias C. Boudinot, son of Cherokee Chief Killa-kee-nah.** Boudinot changed his name while he was studying in Connecticut and Vermont. He became editor of the Fayetteville *Arkansan* and the *True Democrat*. A secessionist, he fought as a lieutenant colonel at Elkhorn Tavern, and from 1863 to the end of the war was an Indian Territory delegate to the Confederate Congress.

NAVAL LEADERS, 1862

399 Franklin Buchanan (C.S.) was born in Baltimore, Maryland, on September 17, 1800. He received a naval commission in January 1815, became a lieutenant in 1825 and a commander in 1841. He was the first superintendent of the U.S. Naval Academy at Annapolis and he served in the Mexican War and also commanded Matthew C. Perry's flagship during the Japan expedition in 1852. After joining the Confederacy, in August 1861, Captain Buchanan made all personnel assignments and aided Secretary Mallory (q.v.) in formulating naval policy. As a flag officer, he took charge of the James River defenses in February 1862. With the new ironclad C.S.S. *Virginia,* Buchanan attacked the Union fleet at Hampton Roads on March 8, 1862. After ramming the U.S.S. *Cumberland,* Buchanan attacked and burned the *Congress.* A leg wound forced him to yield command to Lieutenant Catesby apR. Jones, who maneuvered the *Virginia* against the U.S.S. *Monitor* the next day. Buchanan, confirmed as admiral on August 21, 1862, took command at Mobile Bay, where he worked amicably with army and navy people to build a small fleet of gunboats and ironclads to defend the harbor. In command of the ironclad *Tennessee,* Buchanan fought valiantly against Admiral David G. Farragut's (q.v.) attack on August 5, sustained frequent ramming, but when the *Tennessee*'s rudder chains were cut and the smokestack shot away, Buchanan—whose

Confederate Navy Admiral Franklin Buchanan (left), the *Virginia*'s first commander, and his successor, Captain Josiah Tattnall.

leg had been broken during the fighting— gave permission to strike colors. He was imprisoned at Fort Lafayette, New York, until an exchange was arranged in February 1865. Buchanan was on his way to Mobile when the war ended. After the war he served as president of Maryland Agricultural College (now the University of Maryland), then retired to Easton, where he died on May 11, 1874.

400 David Glasgow Farragut (U.S.) was born in Knoxville, Tennessee, on July 5, 1801. When, in 1810, he was adopted by Captain David Porter, he took the name David and entered the navy as a boy. Service taught him the

Admiral David Glasgow Farragut, U.S.N.

essence of life at sea and the intricacies of command; under a tutor, Farragut became a skilled linguist. He served against Caribbean pirates, and in 1825, as a lieutenant, he was assigned to the Norfolk navy yard. He was a commander by 1841 and captain by 1855, and he served at Mare Island and in command of the *Brooklyn.* He stuck by the Union and, as a flag officer, commanded the Western Gulf Blockading Squadron. He cooperated effectively with army forces, took his fleet past Confederate forts covering the mouth of the Mississippi on April 24, 1862, and participated—with his adoptive brother David Dixon Porter (q.v.)—in the capture of New Orleans on April 26. Popular with his men and his army colleagues, Farragut won acclaim as the "Old

Salamander" for his work on both land and sea. After going upriver to bombard Vicksburg, Farragut withdrew before that bastion's heavy guns and turned his attention to Mobile, which was of special importance, now that New Orleans had been captured. Farragut launched an attack on August 5, 1864, against Admiral Franklin Buchanan's (q.v.) small ironclad and wooden fleet. When his leading ship, the *Tecumseh,* was sunk by a "torpedo" (a mine), Farragut ordered, "Damn the torpedoes! Full speed ahead!" He carried the outer harbor and supporting forts. But Farragut's health soon weakened and he took no further command. A grateful country created the rank of vice admiral for him and, in July 1866, he became the first full admiral. He died at Portsmouth, New Hampshire, on August 14, 1870.

401 David Dixon Porter (U.S.) was born in Chester, Pennsylvania, on June 8, 1813. The son of a naval officer, he became a midshipman in 1829, served as lieutenant in the Mexican War, and even brought camels from the Mediterranean for army use in the desert. In 1861, as a commander, he joined the blockaders at the Southwest Pass of the Mississippi. He proposed sending a flotilla of mortar-bearing flatboats up the Mississippi to shell New Orleans into submission and urged that this expedition be commanded by his adoptive brother, David G. Farragut (q.v.). After the New Orleans success, Porter operated against Vicksburg, then supported

Admiral David Dixon Porter, U.S.N.

McClellan's (q.v.) campaign on the Virginia Peninsula. Once he was switched west again, he took a prominent part in capturing Arkansas Post in January 1863. As commander of the Mississippi squadron, he ran his fleet past Vicksburg's guns in May 1863 and transported Grant's army across the river for the campaign that took Vicksburg. He was promoted to rear admiral and thanked by Congress for "opening the Mississippi River." Porter then cooperated with General N. P. Banks in the luckless Red River campaign, from March to May 1864. In command of the North Atlantic Blockading Squadron, Porter assembled the largest fleet ever

assembled during the Civil War and captured Fort Fisher on January 15, 1865, effectively closing the Confederacy's last port. He served as superintendent of the U.S. Naval Academy from 1865 to 1869, succeeded Farragut as admiral in 1870, and died in Washington, D.C., on February 13, 1901.

402 Josiah Tattnall (C.S.), born near Savannah, Georgia, in 1795, was a midshipman in the U.S. Navy in 1812, had a successful career, and served as a flag officer commanding the East India Squadron in 1857. In 1859 he became famous for stating that the reason he had helped British and French ships against Chinese forts was that "blood is thicker than water." He resigned during secession and became a captain in the Confederate Navy in March 1861. For some time, he commanded a fleet of four small vessels in defense of Georgia and South Carolina waters and then replaced Frank Buchanan (q.v.) in command of the C.S.S. *Virginia* in March 1862. He tried to bring the *Monitor* to battle, but when the entire Union blockading force moved against him, Tattnall refused combat. After the *Virginia* was blown up to prevent its capture following the loss of Norfolk, in May, Tattnall was court-martialed but exonerated. He commanded Savannah Naval Station and attached vessels from July 1862. Relieved of squadron command in March 1863, Tattnall continued to head the naval station. After the war he went to Nova Scotia but returned to

Savannah in 1868 as port inspector and died there on June 14, 1871.

SOME NORTHERN WAGES OF WAR

403 Lincoln did not want the war to become a great, sweeping change agent—but it did. And as it did, it swept many things into the ash heaps of history and sent new things into a future that changed the world. It seemed as though the war had released some American furies that broke beyond the past into an age of force. The change wafted from the battlefields to the walks of commerce, the halls of law, and the changing manners of men.

404 A "second American System" developed in the North, a system much like the one Henry Clay had advocated in the 1820s. Absence of laissez-fairest Southerners in Congress cleared the way for much nationalistic legislation—railroad expansion, banking changes, different land laws—that opened a different future for America.

405 A main feature of the system was the necessity to pay for beating the Rebels. Old-line financial conservatives dreaded anything approaching easy money; according to them, the war was to be paid for by taxes and excises, but the costs rose higher than anyone had guessed, so fast payments had to be made. An empty Treasury loomed as a stark possibility. The Union

devised innovations; as one historian put it, "Republican economics thus became part of wartime patriotism" (Phillip S. Paludan, *A People's Contest: The Union and Civil War, 1861–1865* [New York: Harper & Row, 1988], p. 127).

New sales techniques were devised to sell bonds. **406** Jay Cooke, a wealthy citizen of Philadelphia who had sold that city's entire early 1861 $2 million bond issue, became a kind of bondseller's bondseller. He volunteered to help the Union and launched a nearly superhuman effort. By putting together a massive campaign—advertisements, editorials, cultivation of editors, public announcement of the names of "patriots" who contributed, night sales offices for workers, suggested sermons for clergymen—Cooke created an image of the nation rising to meet a great cause. In the wake of Bull Run, Cooke raised another $2 million in Philadelphia, and by August 1861 New York financial circles subscribed $35 million and Boston financiers another $10 million. Cooke's national sales campaign made buying bonds a public enterprise.

407 Although Treasury Secretary Salmon Chase (q.v.), a believer in hard money, only reluctantly supported paper money, on February 25, 1862, Congress passed the Legal Tender Bill, authorizing $150 million in noninterest-bearing notes that were to be legal tender for everything except import duties, which still had to be paid in specie. The bill broke an old government policy of dealing only in gold or silver. Greenbacks joined the mass of paper issued by the government and by state and local banks. Feared though they were, greenbacks did not ruin the Union's economy—only $450 million worth were issued during the war—though they contributed to doubling the cost of living by January 1865. And they represented a pronounced shift in philosophy: the government became "activist" in creating a national currency.

408 Taxes paid for most of the Union war. In the August 1861 tax bill, Congress levied the country's first federal income tax; every annual income over $800 was taxed at 3 percent.

409 An excise tax, levied in July 1862, raised most of the money for the war—ten times more than the income tax—and hit the small consumers hardest, because they could not pass the cost on to consumers, as did businesses.

410 A national banking system took its place despite much laissez-faire opposition. Linked to a national currency, backed by bonds, and of limited issue, it appealed to those Democrats and Republicans who feared greenbacks. Lincoln lobbied personally for the bill; Jay Cooke persuaded Senator John Sherman to support it as a unifying measure in national defense; and it squeaked by. State bank notes were still issued, but by 1865 were squeezed out.

411 War changed the attitude toward many things, not least toward tariffs. Ever since the so-called Tariff of Abominations in 1833, U.S. tariff policies had trended downward. War, though, brought loud cries for more money. Late in 1861 the Republican congressional majority passed the Morrill Tariff Act and reversed the downward trend. By 1864, tariff levels were double those of 1857. Some manufacturers wanted higher tariffs to offset higher taxes; even labor leaders became supporters.

412 Western lands were opened up. Republican election promises included small farms that all people could afford, and Lincoln signed the Homestead Act in May 1862, to go into effect on January 1, 1863. It stated that any twenty-one-year-old loyal citizen or head of a family could claim up to 160 acres of land for a small fee. After five years that the settler spent in improving the land, it passed to him. Veterans got title after one year.

413 Railroad land grants blazed the trail for homesteaders. War proved the necessity of railroads, and Congress encouraged their construction through generous land grants. Precedent helped; in 1850 the Illinois Central had benefited from the first land-grant law, which gave big tracts to be sold to finance more miles of track. And in June 1862 Lincoln signed the Union Pacific Railroad Bill. Vast tracts of land (15.5 million acres given as 400 feet of right-of-way, buffered by ten alternating sections of land per mile) were given to two rail construction companies to build a line from Omaha, Nebraska, to Sacramento, California, and tie the Union together with a belt of iron.

414 Most of the future rested on education. Lincoln knew it, as did most members of Congress. For some time Justin H. Morrill of Vermont harangued the House of Representatives on the obligation of government to help education. The Northwest Ordinance stood as a firm precedent, but since that effort in the 1780s, there had been only tinkering. Growth and experience showed the need for agricultural instruction and a more highly skilled work force. Efforts to pass a federal land-grant act in the 1850s had failed, but in June 1862 Congress passed Morrill's land-grant college act, which gave thirty thousand acres of public land to every state for every senator and representative in Congress. Proceeds from the sale of these lands would support colleges "to teach such branches of learning as are related to agriculture and the mechanical arts," as well as military tactics. The act covered future states as well as those temporarily in rebellion. A national educational system was on the horizon.

SOME SOUTHERN WAGES OF WAR

415 Jefferson Davis never doubted that war would change many aspects of life. He feared that it would banish much virtue from the Southern way of things, that it would erode morals, economies, graces, maybe even slavery itself. He guessed, too, that the changes were likely to run squarely against such sacred beliefs as states' rights and cause complications for the Confederate government. He was right. As his war effort expanded, he pushed a "Confederate system."

416 Mary Chesnut, the witty and wise wife of a former U.S. senator from South Carolina, told her daily diary that "this Southern Confederacy must be supported now by calm determination and cool brains. We have risked all and we must play our best, for the stake is life or death." Davis agreed wholeheartedly.

417 Southern changes came in support of a new national life. The "permanent" constitution of the Confederacy resembled the U.S. Constitution but offered some differences and improvements. The African slave trade was prohibited, but the slave system already established in the country was protected. The President of the Confederacy, elected to a six-year term, could not succeed himself. He could exercise the item veto in appropriation bills and had, in effect, more power than the President of the United States. The Southern Congress had its wings clipped by a provision prohibiting the appropriation of money without a specific request from the Executive branch, and some hints

of the parliamentary system appeared in the document. Significantly, the Constitution stood as the supreme law of the land, a fact that former states-righter Jefferson Davis used to sustain the Confederacy.

418 On April 16, 1862, the Confederate Congress passed the first general draft law in American history. By then the government knew that unless it could exercise some form of force, the Southern armies might melt away. The first of the twelve-month volunteers were nearing the end of their time and were talking loudly of going home. Recruiting had slackened. New regiments had to be mobilized and trained by veterans—hence "An Act to Further Provide for the Public Defence," which made all white men between eighteen and thirty-five draftable unless they were exempted. And exemptions were steadily curtailed as the war progressed. Substitutes could be hired in the first years, and later **419** "the twenty-slave law" exempted one white male for every twenty blacks. "Details" from conscripted ranks were made at the War Secretary's discretion and were an attempt to manage the South's manpower problem. Modern estimates indicate that approximately 82,000 conscripts were enrolled east of the Mississippi. The twenty-slave law, enacted on October 11, 1862, combined with paid exemptions, led to a rising complaint of "a rich man's war and a poor man's fight."

420 Paying for the war posed several problems for the South. Secretary of the Treasury Memminger, a hard-money man, like his Northern counterpart, believed that taxation was the soundest way to raise funds. However, the Confederate Congress failed to follow his lead and instead levied light burdens while turning to bonds and paper money. The first bond issue, of $15 million, was quickly sold out, but it exhausted most of the $27 million worth of specie in the country. A Rebel experiment—**421** the ingenious Produce Loan, which allowed farmers to pledge proceeds from their crops in return for bonds—raised only some $34 million.

422 Congress authorized $100 million in treasury notes the first year and $400 million more in 1862, so the debasement of the currency assumed an alarming rate. Counterfeiting further debased money, and gradually the South slipped toward a barter economy.

423 One in eight blockade runners was caught in 1862.

ODDITIES

424 Ivan Vasilovitch Turchinoff (John Basil Turchin), commanding one of Don Carlos Buell's (q.v.) brigades, captured Athens, Alabama, in April 1862. Apparently in reprisal for the townspeople shooting at his lead regiment, Turchin allegedly told his men, "Now, boys, you stops in this Rebel town this night and I shut mine eyes for von

Union Brigadier General John B. Turchin (Ivan Vasilovitch Turchinoff).

Woman Order, which declared that any New Orleans woman who was insulting or contemptuous toward Union soldiers would "be regarded . . . as a woman of the town," was what earned Butler the nickname "Beast." Many Northerners, too, were shocked by the financial scandals in his management of the city. A Rebel acrostic caught the feeling:

> *Brutal and vulgar, a coward and knave;*
> *Famed for no action, noble or brave;*
> *Beastly by instinct, a drunkard and sot;*
> *Ugly and venomous, on mankind a blot;*
> *Thief, liar, and scoundrel in highest*
> *degree;*
> *Let Yankeedom boast of such hero[e]s as*
> *thee;*
> *Every woman and child shall for ages to*
> *come,*
> *Remember thee, monster, thou vilest of*
> *scum.*

hours." When nothing happened and the town remained unburned, he sent out another message: "I shut mine eyes for von hours and a half." Mayhem resulted—fires, looting, even reported rapes—and Turchin's reputation plummeted. Court-martialed and about to be cashiered, he was saved by his wife, who persuaded Lincoln to forgive the charges and make him a brigadier. In that higher role he did distinguished service at Chickamauga and Missionary Ridge.

425 General B. F. Butler's notorious

426 Another infamous order, with some of the lasting repercussions of Butler's, was General Grant's Jew Order. General Order Number 11, 1862, branded Jews "as a class violating every regulation of trade" and expelled them from Grant's department within twenty-four hours. Intended to attack spiraling speculation along the Mississippi, this ill-considered order damaged Grant's reputation for years. Lincoln revoked the order in January. He said that although he did not oppose expelling "traitors and Jew peddlers" who trafficked

St. Charles Hotel, New Orleans, headquarters of Major General Benjamin F. Butler, Commander of the Federal Military Department of the Gulf.

with the enemy, he could not approve it, since the order "proscribed an entire religious class, some of whom are fighting in our ranks."

427 The Great Locomotive Chase, one of the famous Civil War adventures, began early on the morning of April 12, 1862, at Big Shanty, Georgia. James A. Andrews, with one other civilian and twenty-two Union volunteers, cut out the engine *General* from a northbound train on the Western and Atlantic Railroad. Intending to burn the bridges south of Chattanooga, Andrews pushed hard.

Three Rebel trainmen pursued Andrews and his men, first by foot, then in borrowed engines, and then in the southbound engine **428** *Texas* near Adairsville, Georgia. In full reverse—sometimes at sixty miles an hour, *Texas* chased the raiders so closely that no real damage was done to bridges or tracks, and the *General* ran out of steam near Ringgold. Andrews and seven men were tried and hanged; eight others escaped from jail in Atlanta. The last six, exchanged as prisoners of war,

Locomotive *General* commandeered by James Andrews and others, who were captured by the Confederates and tried as spies for their efforts to cut telegraph wires and burn bridges.

were the first recipients of the U.S. Medal of Honor.

429 **Rebel efforts to find nitre supplies inspired one of the war's most** popular pieces of doggerel. One method of making nitre was to leach dirt from smokehouses, barns, caves, and even outhouses. A zealous agent of the Nitre and Mining Bureau is said to have run the following notice in a Selma, Alabama, newspaper:

The ladies of Selma are respectfully requested to preserve all Chamber lye collected about their premises, for the purpose of making Nitre. A barrell will be sent around daily to collect.

> John Harralson, Agent
> Nitre and Mining Bureau
> C.S.A.

Confederate Army poets were inspired to respond:

John Harralson, John Harralson,
You are a wretched creature;
You've added to this cruel war
A new and curious feature.
You'd have us think, while every man
Is bound to be a fighter;
The ladies—bless the pretty dears—
Should save their pee for Nitre.
John Harralson, John Harralson,
Where did you get the notion,
To send your barrel 'round the town
To gather up this lotion?
We thought the girls had work enough
In making shirts and kissing;
But you would put the pretty dears,
To patriotic pissing!!
John Harralson, John Harralson,
Pray do invent a neater
And somewhat less immodest mode
Of making your Saltpetre.
For 'tis an awful thought, John,
Gunpowdery and cranky;
That when a lady lifts her skirts,
She shoots a bloody Yankee!

A Union version then appeared:

John Harralson, John Harralson,
We've read in song and story;
How women's tears, through all the years,
Have moistened fields of glory.

But never was it told before,
Amid such scenes of slaughter,
Your Southern beauties dried their tears,
And went to making water.
No wonder, John, your boys are brave.
Who would not be a fighter,
If every time he lifts his gun
He shoots his sweetheart's nitre.

And what on earth could ever make
A Yankee soldier sadder,
Than dodging bullets fired from
A pretty woman's bladder?

They say there was a subtle smell,
That lingered in the powder;
And as the smoke grew thicker and
The din of battle louder,
That there was found in this compound,
One serious objection:
A soldier could not sniff it
Without getting an erection!

430 At the war's beginning, various inventions were presented to both sides. President Lincoln, who had an interest in unusual inventions, is rumored to have received a proposition to build a huge ship with giant clawlike arms on each side. The idea was to have it run up behind a Rebel ship, scoop up the ship in the claws, and deposit it, intact, into a cavernous hold.

Another involved a large, revolving wheel of mallets that would strike cannonballs set on a tee-like base. Ranges were unpredictable, but the economy in powder was a benefit.

431 In 1862, Dr. Richard J. Gatling tried to interest Lincoln in his idea for a six-barrel machine gun. Lincoln's interests were elsewhere, but General Ben Butler ordered a dozen of the guns. Gatling's reputation as something of a Copperhead, however, worked against his gun's acceptance.

432 One inventor proposed a balloon, with an iron plate on the basket bottom, that would allow a Union soldier to fly over Rebel positions and drop grenades and bombs. No one took him up on it.

A Union telegraph office in the field.

433 U.S. ordnance officers were slow to accept change and scoffed at a rocket-driven torpedo, which, in fact, showed some similarities to modern guided missiles.

434 Skepticism also greeted an idea to obviate the need for military bridges. Someone suggested that each soldier be equipped with a paddle and small canoes for his feet. He could then glide over the water.

435 **Telegraph communications changed the tempo of war.** Both sides used telegraphs for some battlefield communication and for remote management of the war when tactical use became possible in 1862. The North had most of America's fifty thousand miles of telegraph line before the war. During the war, the South suffered severe shortages of battery acid, which hampered military and civilian communication, especially that of the Confederate States Press Association, which linked correspondents from the armies and the capital to the country.

436 On October 24, 1861, the transcontinental telegraph was finished by Western Union. The last segment, hastened because of the war, ran from Denver across the mountains to Sacramento.

437 **A private calling himself Henry M. Stanley, 6th Arkansas Volunteer Infantry, was captured at Shiloh.** John Rowlands—his real name—quickly joined the Union Army. On being discharged for illness, he joined the Union Navy and deserted in 1866. Later he led a famous expedition into Africa that ended in the deathless greeting "Dr. Livingstone, I presume?"

438 **During the Battle of Cedar Mountain, in August 1862,** the Rebel artillerist Major Snowden Andrews received what everyone believed was a fatal wound. Disemboweled, his viscera rolling in the dust, Andrews was examined by Stonewall Jackson's personal physician, Dr. Hunter McGuire, who lamented that he could not help. "Yes, that's what you fellows all say," Andrews snapped. Stung, McGuire, who knew him well, stopped, cleaned the man's intestines, reinserted them in the abdomen, stitched up the patient, and hospitalized him. One of Jackson's aides asked whether Andrews would live. "Well," said McGuire, "if the good Lord will let the rest of the world take care of itself for a time and devote his attention exclusively to Andrews, he may be able to pull him through, but no one else can!" Andrews lived into the twentieth century.

1863

❦

THE THIRD
YEAR OF
THE WAR

EMANCIPATION

439 Many crises and decisions crowded the war's third year. Lincoln, in what may have been the most important political act of his career, changed the nature and purpose of the war just as the year began. He had tested several emancipation ideas on his Cabinet in the time since Antietam, had issued his **440** Preliminary Emancipation Proclamation on September 22, 1862, which freed slaves in areas not under Federal control and gave rebellious areas until January 1, 1863, to stop rebelling. **441** On New Year's Day 1863, Lincoln gave the North a new war aim when he issued the final Emancipation Proclamation as a necessary war measure. It reiterated freedom for slaves in areas outside Union control, but urged them "to abstain from all violence, unless in necessary self-defense."

Reaction varied. Many Northerners rejoiced in freedom's march, but some balked. A good many Union soldiers, including General McClellan, regarded the proclamation as a breach of faith with the Union cause.

442 Democrats in most Northern states fumed, and some legislatures condemned the action. On January 7, 1863, the Illinois legislature resolved to brand Lincoln's action "as unwarrantable in military as in civil law; a gigantic usurpation, at once converting the war, professedly commenced by the administration for the vindication of the authority of the constitution, into a crusade for the sudden, unconditional and violent liberation of 3,000,000 negro slaves . . . the present and far-reaching consequences of which to both races cannot be contemplated without the most dismal foreboding of horror and dismay. The proclamation invites servile insurrection . . . a means of warfare, the inhumanity and diabolism of which are without example in civilized warfare."

443 The predictable Southern reaction appeared in a Message from President Davis to the Confederate Congress: the proclamation meant the extermination of the black race, encouraged the extermination of slave owners, and proved the "true nature and designs" of the Republicans.

444 Foreign reaction split almost along class lines. Many affluent people in Britain and Europe supported the South; liberals and the less affluent, especially laborers, supported the Union and emancipation.

445 Lincoln prized greatly the Address of the British Workingmen in Manchester, who, at a meeting on December 31, 1862, asked him to "accept our high admiration of your firmness in upholding the proclamation of freedom." In a masterly response, "To the Working-men of Manchester," he wrote that governments cannot always prescribe "the scope of moral results which follow . . . policies. I have understood well that the duty of self-preservation rests solely with the American people," but he knew that "favor or disfavor of foreign nations might have a material influence in enlarging or prolonging the struggle . . . I know and deeply deplore the sufferings which the working-men at Manchester, and in all Europe, are called on to endure in this crisis. It has been often . . . represented that the attempt to overthrow this government, which was built upon the foundation of human rights, and to substitute for it one which should rest exclusively on the basis of human slavery, was likely to obtain the favor of Europe . . . Under the circumstances, I cannot but regard your decisive utterances upon the question as an instance of sublime Christian heroism."

MORE DRASTIC CHANGES IN THE CONFEDERACY

War continued its fine grinding, and President Davis increased the span of his Confederate system. Paying for the war remained the toughest problem. Weak tax laws had clearly failed; new measures produced little.

446 One Rebel innovation appeared as a "tax in kind" on agricultural products; it was really a tithe for the war. Under the provision of a general tax bill, in April 1863, farmers would reserve specific amounts of food for their families and pay a tenth of the remaining yield to the government.

447 Inflation forced the Rebels to invasions of privacy far beyond the draft. Since the Confederate Congress failed to pass a legal tender law and the value of the cash declined, commissaries and other supply agents with the armies resorted to impressing (commandeering) private property. Legalized by An Act to Regulate Impressments in March 1863, which decreed appraised prices for impressed items, the practice alienated growing numbers of Rebels—though without that practice, the war effort would have collapsed quickly.

448 Even the laissez-fairest Rebels came to an income tax. A graduated income levy, included in the general tax bill of April 1863, assessed 1 percent on incomes of $1000 to $1500 and ran to 15 percent on incomes above $10,000.

449 The Rebels, once they were convinced, resorted to such outrages as sales taxes, profits taxes, excise taxes, license taxes on businesses and professions, and a tax on the two most profitable holdings in the South (which should have been taxed at the start of the war): land and slaves.

War costs led to a bold Confederate diplomatic move in March 1863. Since tax bills were generally failures, Congress reluctantly agreed to arrange for a loan from **450** Emile Erlanger & Co. of Paris, which offered to lend the South much money (possibly to corner the postwar Southern credit market, possibly because young Frederick Erlanger was enamored of Confederate Commissioner John Slidell's daughter). Congress, concerned about passing on a heavy debt to the future, borrowed only $15 million. Nonetheless, the Erlanger loan funded important Rebel war purchases in Europe.

451 To make good use of the Erlanger loan, Colin J. McRae, an Alabama businessman and congressman, went to London in May 1863 and centralized foreign purchasing. Stubborn, officious, sometimes irksome to such as Major Huse and the Bermuda contingent, he nonetheless brought system to the disjointed efforts of Confederate and state supply efforts and made the most of the loan. He also helped to coordinate all blockade-running efforts. This was not an easy task, because many private contractors and commission houses, such as Fraser, Trenholm & Co., Saul Isaac, Campbell & Co., and Collie, Crenshaw & Co. of England, vied for the staggering profits.

452 Blockade running made St. George's in Bermuda, Nassau in the Bahamas, and Havana in Cuba important Confederate ports. St. George's probably handled the most Rebel business, since it was a vital transfer point for supplies coming in large ships from England. At St. George's, sleek and swift blockade runners were loaded from Rebel warehouses and scudded toward such ports as Wilmington, North Carolina, sometimes Charleston, South Carolina, or Fernandina, Florida. An eager Bermudian named John Tory Bourne began serving as a Southern commission agent early in 1862 and soon ran a thriving warehousing and trans-shipping business. A Confederate ordnance office was established in Bermuda under Major Smith Stansbury, who, along with Major Norman Walker, a disbursing agent, sent enormous quantities of supplies to the South.

Rebel activities in Bermuda were watched and often countered by the wily U.S. consul, Charles Maxwell Allen.

453 War necessitated other intrusions into old areas of sanctity. Railroads became the essential arteries of war, and even though they were private property, the Confederate government gradually took them over. Repair parts, rails, man-power, money—all were Rebel rail problems.

454 A railroad bureau in the Quartermaster Department tried to work out cooperative arrangements with private lines for government needs, but high profits eroded even high patriotism.

455 In May 1863 Congress passed a secret act (it should have been public) "to facilitate transportation for the Government." It authorized government seizure of the rails. But devotion to laissez-faire was deep in the Southern psyche. Not until late February 1865 did the rails fall under direct control of the Secretary of War.

MILITARY OPERATIONS

456 The Eastern Theater of War remained the focus of most attention during the first half of 1863.

457 On January 26, 1863, Joseph Hooker became commander of the Army of the Potomac. Armed with self-confidence, a good plan, and a fine army, he launched a campaign at the end of April to flank Lee at Fredericksburg and fight him on Union terms.

458 Lee guessed Hooker's intent and sent Stonewall Jackson to meet the Yankees near Chancellorsville. Hooker might have defeated Lee's separated forces, but he lost his nerve and entrenched his men. Lee and Jackson, seeking ways to make

Union Major General Joseph (Fighting Joe) Hooker.

Hooker's entrenchments useless, found an obscure road that led all the way around the Union army. Lee told Jackson to take 28,000 men and turn Hooker's right while Lee held the front with 16,000 men.

459 Jackson's fifteen-mile march across and around the Union front began at 8 A.M. on May 2, 1863. He attacked the Yankees from their right rear at 5:15 P.M. and smashed their line. Hooker, dazed from a blow to the head, lost control of his battle as darkness fell, and the Union lines collapsed in confusion.

460 Jackson scouted beyond his own lines after dark; as he returned, some nervous Rebel fire wounded him severely, and the corps command passed to Jeb Stuart. Hearing that Jackson's left arm had been amputated, Lee said, "He has lost his left arm; but I have lost my right arm."

461 Lee attacked on May 3, but news of the Federals breaking through Jubal Early's defenders at Fredericksburg forced him to send a detachment to protect the army's rear. General John Sedgwick's Union corps was nearly surrounded at Salem Church but managed to escape on May 4. On May 5, Hooker recrossed the Rappahannock. His failure cost 17,000 casualties against Lee's 13,000.

462 Chancellorsville, Lee's greatest victory, came at the inestimable cost of Jackson, who died on May 10. Lincoln's reaction to Hooker's defeat was "My God! My God! What will the country say?"

463 Davis and Lee discussed strategy after Chancellorsville. How best could they relieve Western pressures—especially against Vicksburg—and finish Hooker? Lee, deciding that an invasion of the North would accomplish both purposes, began to move down (north) the Shenandoah Valley on June 9. Jeb Stuart's cavalry—9500 troopers and gunners—were to screen Lee's move.

464 At 5 A.M. on June 9, General Alfred Pleasonton's 11,000 Union men surprised Stuart's men near Brandy Station, northeast of Culpeper, Virginia, and started the greatest cavalry battle in American history. A wild mêlée of shooting, saber-thrusting troops roiled until mid-afternoon, when the Federals retired. Lee's movements were not detected, and Stuart

had a narrow tactical victory (433 casualties to Pleasonton's 1651) but his reputation was dimmed by the surprise pulled off by the Union cavalry, which gained confidence.

465 Lee crossed into Pennsylvania on June 15, 1863, and threatened Harrisburg and Baltimore. Two events affected Lee's plans. The Union army, under a new commander, General George G. Meade, moved swiftly to find Lee, while Stuart went on a glory-seeking raid into Maryland, which left Lee without eyes at a critical time. Early in July, Lee concentrated his army near Gettysburg.

466 Neither commander wanted to fight yet, but a meeting engagement on July 1 started the Battle of Gettysburg. It

Gettysburg, Pennsylvania, with Round Top at the extreme right, Cemetery Ridge running along the center, and Culp's Hill, left foreground.

Dead Confederate sharpshooter in the Devil's Den, Gettysburg. A picture posed by the photographer.

raged for three days, fortunes shifting from day to day, but the odds were with Meade, who had about 85,000 men against Lee's estimated 65,000. The first day ran for the Rebels. Fearsome fighting marked the second day as Rebel attacks tested both ends of Meade's "fishhook" lines.

467 The attacks Lee planned for July 3 were frustrated by enemy action and by poor communication, so, unwisely, he ordered an assault against Meade's center. After a massive artillery duel, the Rebels under General George Edward Pickett (q.v.) began one of gallantry's last great gestures about 3 P.M. Across a mile of open ground, nearly 13,000 men charged into a hail of shells and bullets. By 4 P.M. a small band had breached the Union line, only to fall as **468** Pickett's Charge failed—at a cost of nearly 6000 wounded and perhaps 1000 killed.

469 Lee expected to be attacked on July 4. When he wasn't, he retreated to Virginia. Meade let him go. Both armies were battered: more than 23,000 Bluecoats fell, along with 20,400 Rebels.

470 Lincoln's generalship ran ahead of his generals'. Enemy armies were the objectives, not cities or territory. And he knew that the first week of July 1863 could have ended the war. "We had them within our grasp," he lamented. "We had only to stretch forth our hands and they were ours . . . And that, my God, is the last of this Army of the Potomac! There is bad faith somewhere . . . What does it mean . . . ? Great God! What does it mean?" Had Lee been smashed when Vicksburg fell on July 4, the stuffing would have gone out of the Confederacy. "As it is, the war will be prolonged indefinitely."

471 In the Eastern Theater, fighting languished for a time after Gettysburg. Union and Confederate forces were detached westward as action shifted to the Mississippi Basin.

472 And when a restive General Lee heard that Meade had detached two corps to Tennessee, he marched to attack on October 1863.

Fort Sumter's eastern barracks during bombardment by the Federal blockading fleet, Siege of Charleston, September 8, 1863. Two Confederate soldiers shown on the chimney of the bake oven.

473 At Bristoe Station, Virginia, on October 14, General A. P. Hill, new to corps command, attacked what he thought was a single Union corps, only to run into a second on the field—and into one of the worst traps of the war. In forty minutes, two North Carolina brigades lost 1400 killed and wounded. Lee chastened Hill because of the dead and soon ended the campaign. He noted the command slippage in his army since Jackson's death.

474 **In an action dubbed the Buckland Races, Jeb Stuart and his troopers routed Union cavalry under General Judson Kilpatrick** on October 19, 1863, at Buckland Mills, Virginia.

475 In operations near the Mine Run Valley during the last week of November 1863, Meade, with 85,000 men, tried to turn Lee's 48,500-man right flank, but the Rebels—moving speedily again—greeted him with impregnable trench lines. The

Union Major General Quincy Gillmore studying the map of Charleston in 1863 before beginning his siege.

Federal winter offensive stalled before it started.

476 On August 21, 1863, the Siege of Charleston, South Carolina, began— and lasted 587 days. At the confluence of the Ashley and Cooper Rivers, this famous city, known to Yankees as the **477** Cradle of Rebellion, protected by Fort Sumter in the harbor and by a fortified outlying island, housed important ordnance works and often harbored blockade runners. Several attempts to pierce Charleston's island defenses had already failed.

Left: The "Swamp Angel," used in bombardment of Charleston.

478 Confederate General Beauregard conducted a skillful defense, although the heavy bombardment—heightened by the Swamp Angel, a huge gun that exploded with its thirty-sixth shot—caused civilian flight and wrecked much of the downtown area. Charleston held out until General William J. Hardee evacuated it in mid-February 1865, when Sherman was marching on Columbia.

479 Northerners thought the war was costing too much, killing too many men, and seemed endless. Despite Lee's defeat, the capture of Vicksburg on July 4, and Confederate troubles at Chattanooga, names were drawn on July 11, 1863, for a new Union draft.

480 Draft riots broke out in New York City on Monday, July 13, 1863. Foreign laborers—mainly Irish, the underpaid underclass who could not afford to buy substitutes—roamed in mobs at draft headquarters and businesses. Houses were looted; fires scorched parts of the city, including a black church and orphanage. Racism raged as blacks caught the worst of it. Troops were rushed from Gettysburg, and rioting ended by July 15. At least a thousand people had been killed or wounded and more than $1.5 million worth of property had been destroyed, including the house of James Sloan Gibbons, blamed for writing the recruiting song "We Are Coming, Father Abraham." Riots took place also in Boston, in Portsmouth, New Hampshire, in Rutland, Vermont, in Wooster, Ohio, and in Troy, New York.

481 Men missing their four front teeth were disqualified for service. They wouldn't have been able to bite bullets!

482 Mrs. Mary Jackson, a Richmonder with "strong features, and a vixenish eye," stood up in church on April 2, 1863, brandished a bowie knife and a six-shooter, and demanded food. Calling on other women to join her, she led a mob toward Capitol Square. As it grew, the mob screamed "Bread!" Food stores were sacked, along with clothing, jewelry, and shoe shops. The city hospital lost 310 pounds of beef. Vengeance teetered on revolution.

483 At the height of the food riot, the Richmond City Battalion arrived, and the governor threatened to have the men open fire. Fear momentarily congealed action. President Davis arrived, mounted a dray, and held up his hands for silence. Hisses and catcalls greeted him; he called for order, emptied his pockets of money, then took out his watch and announced a five-minute dispersal ultimatum. The government was staked on stopping the riot. The sullen crowd ebbed at the last moment.

484 The incident led to one of the Confederacy's rare attempts at censorship. An adjutant wrote to the city's editors: "The unfortunate disturbance which occurred to-day is so liable to misconstruction and misrepresentation abroad that I am desired by the Secretary of War to make a special appeal to the . . . press . . . and earnestly request [no] reference directly or indirectly to the affair." Local citizens attributed the trouble to "aliens" and strangers.

485 **President Davis knew there had been other food riots.** In Mobile, for instance, signs with the ominous threat BREAD OR PEACE had mysteriously appeared on street corners. Food shortages troubled other Confederate cities. Why? In a vast agricultural land, what had gone wrong?

486 Logistics had gone wrong. With only 9000 miles of railroad track in use in 1861 (much of it individual coast-to-plantation lines), and with severely limited train and track repair facilities, the South's distribution system broke down. By late 1863, Confederate quartermasters, commissaries, engineers, medical, and ordnance officers found it extremely difficult to move supplies from factories, depots, and farms to army depots and railheads.

487 **Inflation complicated the Rebel supply situation.** Prices rose inconsistently, and the inflation rates had no pattern. Richmond's prices always outran those of the rest of the Confederacy; by 1864 prices in Columbia, South Carolina, were about a fifth of the prices in Richmond. City prices were always higher than those in the country. In 1864, a bushel of corn in rural South Carolina sold for $2.00; in Charleston, $20.00. Cane syrup in Georgia could be

had for $1.00 a gallon; Richmonders paid $50.00. A ham sold in the capital for $350. Speculators took high profits on most foods and dry goods, thereby earning wide hatred. Attempts to control inflation by fixing prices for impressed goods often curtailed production.

488 The most successful Rebel supply agency was the Ordnance Department, under Brigadier General Josiah Gorgas (q.v.). This department provided all ordnance supplies (plus some quartermaster items) to army units in the field. Its functions were complicated by the problems just mentioned, but Gorgas's genius lay in finding resourceful subordinates to work around deficiencies.

Gorgas appointed **489** Colonel John William Mallet, a fellow of Britain's Royal Society and a chemist with Alabama's Geological Survey, to head the Confederate Ordnance Laboratories, with headquarters in Macon, Georgia. James H. Burton, as Superintendent of Armories, brought arms' manufacturing experience from England (along with a set of plans for making Enfield rifles), organized efficient small-arms production units across the South, and stimulated artillery manufacturing. **490** George W. Rains, an able scientist, built and headed the large Augusta Powder Works, which produced enough in quality and quantity to supply most Confederate needs after the war's start, in April 1862. Able officers were assigned as chiefs of ordnance for field armies. Although enemy incursions in late 1864 began to disrupt Gorgas's bureau, it supplied arms and ammunition to the end.

491 Confederate optimism declined in almost direct ratio to inflation, shortages, casualties, and defeat. In sum, the war was costing too much.

492 The churches were bulwarks of the war. Some Northern churches showed only slight patriotic feeling; some hewed to the Union steadily, in the belief that rebellion against God's country was rebellion against God. The Catholic Archbishop John Hughes helped to recruit the Irish 69th New York Regiment, and the fervent minister Henry Ward Beecher (Harriet Beecher Stowe's brother) contributed personally to equipping the Brooklyn Phalanx regiment in his congregation's area.

493 Slavery tortured many Christian souls. They were involved in arguments about whether it was sinful and, if it was, could there be redemption? Several Protestant denominations were divided over the slavery issue before the war. Such notably pacifist congregations as the Quakers and Mennonites resisted war in both the North and the South. Southern churches were generally militant and acted as centers of voluntary efforts in support of troops—and even became sources of brass bells for cannon. Pulpits propped the cause as many ministers became chaplains. Leonidas Polk, the

Episcopal Bishop of Louisiana, even took the field as a general.

494 Since the war ran on transportation, and foreign imports became essential to sustaining the South's battle, blockade runners—initially private enterprises, in addition to a few bought by the Ordnance and Medical Departments—finally came under government control. In March 1864 space was commandeered for government cotton on outgoing ships and for government freight on incoming vessels.

495 Logistics often muddled Federal operations, but abundant resources softened effects. The superb efforts of the U.S. Military Railroads, under temporary Brigadier General Herman Haupt (a railroad engineering genius), in building and repairing lines accounted for much of the Union armies' logistical success. Speedy repairs often countered the daring damage done by Rebel cavalry raids on key rail connections trestles, bridges, and tunnels.

496 The Western Theater of War became the anvil of conflict in 1863. There, Confederate efforts to hold the central front crumbled as U. S. Grant took Vicksburg on July 4 and Bragg was maneuvered out of Chattanooga in early September. Bragg threw away the fruits of his victory at Chickamauga later that month, and his beaten legions streamed

Union Brigadier General Herman Haupt (standing far right), Chief of the Military Bureau of Railways, inspecting the locomotive bearing his name, 1863.

back from disaster at Lookout Mountain and Missionary Ridge in November. By year's end the initiative rested with Grant.

497 After Sherman's failed efforts to reach Vicksburg at Chickasaw Bluffs, General J. A. McClernand (q.v.) and Admiral David Dixon Porter (q.v.) attacked Fort Hindman at Arkansas Post on January 11, 1863. Heavily outnumbered, Brigadier General T. J. Churchill surrendered the fort after a four-hour fight. Union casualties were about 1000 out of

29,000 men; the Confederates lost some 4700 out of 5000 men, most of them taken prisoner. The success thrilled McClernand, galled Grant (who had not authorized the expedition), and did nothing to threaten Vicksburg.

498 Having campaigned for Vicksburg several times, including a long and unsuccessful attempt to dig a channel (Grant's Canal) across an oxbow in the Mississippi, Grant marched along the west side of the river and pressed a Federal fleet to run the formidable Rebel batteries. Tar barrels and flares illuminated the river on the night of April 16, 1863, as Admiral David Porter's twelve ships approached. Eleven ships made it safely through a fearsome bombardment and prepared to bring Grant's men across the river.

499 Grant crossed back to the east bank, starting on April 29 and completing it the next day. His summation was: "All the campaigns, labors, hardships, and exposures, from the month of December . . . were for the accomplishment of this one object." He prepared to move inland from bases at Bruinsburg and Port Gibson, Mississippi, and to live off the country.

500 President Davis, anxious about Vicksburg, explained its importance to Governor Harris Flanagin of Arkansas on April 3, 1863. If the Confederacy lost control of the Mississippi's east bank, "the Western part of the country must inevitably fall into the power of the enemy. The defense of the fortified places on the Eastern bank is therefore regarded as the defense of Arkansas quite as much as that of Tennessee, Mississippi, and Louisiana."

501 To confuse Vicksburg's defenders, Grant sent Colonel Benjamin Henry Grierson on a diversionary cavalry raid through the heart of Mississippi and Louisiana. Staring on April 17, 1863, from La Grange, Tennessee, Grierson led 1700 troopers (the 6th and 7th Illinois and the 2nd Iowa) on an 800-mile trek that took seventeen days. Frequently

Brigadier General Benjamin F. Grierson, chin in hand, with his staff, after his cavalry raid into the heart of the Confederacy.

engaged, he eluded most major resistance, wrecked two railroads, destroyed much property, and reached Baton Rouge on May 2. He was rewarded with a brigadier's commission.

502 Confederate General Joseph E. Johnston, trying to stop Grant, collected troops near Jackson, Mississippi, but could muster only 12,000 men by May 13. As department commander, he ordered General Pemberton to join him. Pemberton, confused about Grant's intentions, delayed, and Johnston had to seek other reinforcements.

503 One of J. E. Johnston's brigades, under Brigadier General John Gregg, fought Major General John A. Logan's division of James McPherson's corps at the Battle of Raymond, Mississippi, on May 12, 1863. After several desperate hours, Gregg retired toward Jackson. Each side lost about 500 men.

504 Grant inserted John A. McClernand's corps between Jackson and Vicksburg, then sent McPherson's and William T. Sherman's corps toward Jackson. On May 14, 1863, General J. E. Johnston evacuated the Mississippi capital. Johnston again ordered General J. C. Pemberton to join him in an attack on Grant, and Pemberton finally moved, on May 16. About midday, he met McPherson's troops at the 505 Battle of Champion's Hill (Baker's Creek). In this important and close engagement, Pemberton's Confederates finally retreated toward Vicksburg. Grant had 2441 casualties out of 29,000; Pemberton, 3851 out of nearly 20,000.

506 Pemberton fought one more battle at Big Black River, on May 18, 1863. Deployed on the east side, he waited for a missing division, only to be attacked and driven in disorder across the river, leaving 1700 men stranded.

507 **Grant began the Siege of Vicksburg on May 18, 1863, as his troops crossed the Big Black River and took positions in front of heavy Confederate entrenchments.** On that day, President Davis asked the Mississippi militia and civilians to join General J. E. Johnston, whom he urged to join Pemberton and attack Grant. John-

Vicksburg. Fort Castle, in the background, overlooked the Mississippi River and was defended by "Whistling Dick," one of the Confederacy's most powerful guns.

ston tried to find more men to harass Grant's besiegers but failed.

508 Overconfident after his brilliant overland campaign, and eager to avoid a prolonged siege, Grant attacked Pemberton's well-defended lines. The Federals were repulsed and lost about a thousand men. Grant tried a heavier attack against a three-mile stretch of Rebel works on May 22. Deep ravines, felled trees, and cleared Confederate fields of fire held up the advance, but General Sherman's men briefly reached the top of some log breastworks, and General John McClernand's troops took short hold of a few positions. Still, the assault failed, at a cost of 3199 casualties out of 45,000 engaged. Pemberton counted fewer than 500 lost. Instead of attacking again, Grant began a formal siege. Citizens and Confederate troops endured constant bombardment from gunboats and artillery; many civilians took refuge in caves along the river bank.

509 By the end of June, with food scarce and munitions dwindling, morale sagged in Pemberton's army. Many soldiers petitioned him on June 28: "If you can't feed us, you had better surrender." Thinking he might be able to get favorable terms on Independence Day, Pemberton sought out Grant. Unconditional surrender was Grant's demand, but the garrison would be paroled. On July 4, 1863, Pemberton yielded some 29,000 men—and Vicksburg.

Grant's brilliant campaign (generally considered the best of the war) captured Vicksburg at a cost of not quite 10,000 Union men. It inflicted 10,000 casualties on the enemy, and the Federals captured 37,000 men (fifteen generals among them), 172 cannon, and 60,000 good rifles.

510 **Heavily fortified Port Hudson, Mississippi, was the other anchor of the Confederate link to the Trans-Mississippi.** General N. P. Banks (q.v.) began a campaign on May 14 to capture it, and thereby give the Union full control of the Mississippi River. His army marched in two columns against Port Hudson, one from west of the Mississippi, and began siege operations by May 21. About 4500 Confederates, under Major General Franklin Gardner, repulsed an attack by 13,000 Federals on May 27. On June 14 Banks called for a surrender. When he was refused, he attacked again—this time with about 6000 men against 3700 effective Confederates. In the failed assault Banks lost 1792 and Gardner 47. Gardner surrendered his enfeebled garrison to Banks's 33,000 on July 8, after learning of Vicksburg's fall.

511 **With Vicksburg and Port Hudson safely in Union hands, Lincoln announced that "the Father of Waters again goes unvexed to the sea."** **512** On July 16, 1863, the steamer *Imperial* arrived

Confederate fortifications on the eighty-foot bluff overlooking the Mississippi at Port Hudson, Louisiana.

in New Orleans from St. Louis, the first boat to make the trip in over two years. Cut in twain, the Confederacy now began a precarious dual existence.

Confederate officials pondered the fullness of fate 513 in the first week of 1863. Lee's and Pemberton's failures had cost the South some 50,000 men and 70,000 stands of arms, many of them the prized British Enfield rifles. More woeful news came from the Confederate Army of Tennessee.

514 On the third major war front, General William Starke Rosecrans (q.v.) had lurked with his army facing Bragg

near Murfreesboro, Tennessee. In the months after the battle there, Rosecrans had countered several of Bragg's cavalry raids with equally fruitless raids of his own. Relentlessly goaded from Washington, he finally advanced his 63,000-man Army of the Cumberland on June 23, 1863. Moving swiftly, manuevering instead of fighting, he ran Bragg's Kentucky campaign in reverse, and by June 30 he flanked the Rebels to Tullahoma. By July 4, Bragg's 45,000 men fell back on Chattanooga. Rosecrans's brilliant strategic success was outshone by Gettysburg and Vicksburg.

515 Chattanooga was the most strategic site in the war in early July 1863. In Union hands, it opened inner-line avenues into Georgia and other parts of the Deep South and dangled the prospect of cutting the Confederacy into three parts.

Three Confederate cavalry leaders—Forrest, Morgan, and Wheeler—claimed much Federal attention during 1863. Their operations disrupted several Union campaigns and frightened a good many civilians.

516 General Nathan Bedford Forrest, the most formidable and notorious of the trio, plagued Union operations in several parts of Tennessee, capturing infantry near Spring Hill in March, defeating Colonel Abel Streight's command in May, threatening Triune in June, raiding different places, and earning Lincoln's concern. He seemed larger than life to both friends and ene-

mies, and his 1864 ventures would confirm the image.

517 Surrounded by romantic legend, General John Hunt Morgan achieved fame as one of the most dashing Rebel cavalry raiders, though his deeds did not achieve the important results that Forrest's did. A series of raids in Tennessee and Kentucky in 1862 brought early recognition, and his raid north of the Ohio in 1863 caused fear among many Northern citizens. A verse celebrated his impact:

Morgan, Morgan, Morgan!
And Morgan's terrible men,
With Bowie knives and pistols,
Are galloping up the glen!

Many a Northern mother threatened her balky children with seizure by Morgan.

He was captured during his famed Ohio raid (he forced the declaration of martial law in Cincinnati), but he and some of his officers escaped from the Ohio State Penitentiary in November 1863.

518 General Joseph Wheeler won fewer laurels but did more fighting than Morgan and nearly more than Forrest. Commander of the Army of Tennessee's cavalry when he was only twenty-six, Wheeler fought in 127 battles, including all of the Army of Tennessee's big ones, was wounded three times, and had thirty-six staff officers fall by his side and sixteen horses shot from under him.

Lieutenant General Joseph Wheeler, C.S.A.

He captured the U.S. gunboat *Slidell* on the Cumberland River on January 13, 1863, hit the Louisville and Nashville and the Nashville and Chattanooga Railroads in Tennessee in April, and from September 30 to October 17 broke Rosecrans's communications in Tennessee by raiding McMinnville, threatening Wartrace, Shelbyville, Nashville, and wrecking railroads and bridges.

519 **On July 14, 1863, while draft riots raged in New York and elsewhere,** an anguished President Davis assessed recent defeats in a letter to a friend: "In proportion as our difficulties increase, so must we all cling together, judge charitably of each other, and strive to bear and forbear, however great may be the sacrifice and bitter trial." On July 15 he wrote that "the clouds

are truly dark over us." To Lee, he wrote on July 28, "If a victim would secure the success of our cause I would freely offer myself." And in a gesture occasioned by worry, he announced on August 1 that all soldiers absent without leave, together with those who had not reported for duty, would be granted pardon and amnesty if they joined up within twenty days. On August 2 he told Lee that "it is painful to contemplate our weakness when you ask for reinforcements."

520 **On August 8, 1863, General Robert E. Lee offered to resign.** He recognized the discontent stemming from Gettysburg, he told President Davis, and said "I, therefore, in all sincerity, request your excellency to take measures to supply my place." Davis refused the resignation: "Our country could not bear to lose you."

Davis showed considerable forbearance toward Lee. The President's plan had called for a strategic defensive, but Lee had pursued an aggressive offensive in Pennsylvania. In 1877 Davis would remember that Lee "knew that I did not see why that battle [Gettysburg] must have been fought then and there, but did not explain the necessity."

521 **President Lincoln, happy about Vicksburg ("Grant is my man and I am his the rest of the war"),** Port Hudson, and Gettysburg, nonetheless had worries of his own. Victory seemed to bring about lethargy. Lincoln knew that after their two disasters, the Rebels were weak enough for knock-out punches. While Meade hesitated, Grant, who lacked scope for more at the moment, reorganized, and Rosecrans sat before Chattanooga, asking for men. Nonetheless, President Lincoln proclaimed August 6, 1863, a day of thanksgiving for victories.

Once the Union draft got under way, in March 1863, the riots began in New York and other cities. 522 Governor Horatio Seymour of New York asked Lincoln, on August 3, 1863, to suspend the draft in his state. Acutely aware of the crisis caused by conscription, Lincoln nevertheless stuck to his guns and refused.

523 **General W. S. Rosecrans's Army of the Cumberland finally began moving toward Chattanooga from Tullahoma on August 16, 1863,** while General Ambrose E. Burnside marched from Lexington, Kentucky, toward east Tennessee. Rosecrans planned to trap General Braxton Bragg's Army of Tennessee between the two Union forces, so Confederate authorities hurriedly sought reinforcements for Bragg from the Deep South.

Confused by Rosecrans's quick feints and his crossing of the Tennessee River, and "the popping out of the rats from so many holes," 524 Bragg evacuated Chattanooga on September 9, 1863, but, no mean strategist himself, he planned his own ruses. "Deserters" told of Rebel disorganization and retreat. Rosecrans took

the bait and divided his three corps to catch Bragg's army at different mountain passes. Bragg schemed to hit each corps separately.

525 Confederate railroads rallied and took a dramatic part in Bragg's operations. Davis and Lee, in early September 1863, decided to send General James Longstreet's two divisions from Lee's army to Bragg: 12,000 men. Because Union General Ambrose E. Burnside took Knoxville on September 2, 1863, Rebel reinforcements had to swing 965 miles south through Atlanta. The move, which began on September 9, took almost ten days.

526 Rosecrans's army, outflanking Bragg's, entered Chattanooga on September 9, 1863; some of the troops pursued retreating Rebels.

527 Bragg intended to cut off parts of Rosecrans's army as it tried to cut through the mountain passes behind the Confederates. Widely separated, Rosecrans's corps were vulnerable, and Bragg planned well. His corps and division commanders were slow to carry out his orders, however (some of them disliked him), and several opportunities to trap the Federals were missed between September 10 and September 17.

528 On September 19, Bragg attacked Rosecrans along Chickamauga Creek. Some of Longstreet's men had already arrived, and fighting raged heavily on the Confederate right against troops under 529 General George H. Thomas (ever after known as "the Rock of Chickamauga")

General Braxton Bragg, C.S.A.

Union Major General George H. (Pap) Thomas, the "Rock of Chickamauga."

while Bragg tried to get between the Federal troops and Chattanooga. Nightfall found Rosecrans entrenching and Bragg reorganizing as more of Longstreet's men arrived.

Confederate General Leonidas Polk, leading the Confederate right wing, attacked about 9 A.M. on September 20 and pushed Thomas back to a fortified line, where the fighting raged until noon. Longstreet drove into the Union center, found a gap in the line (Rosecrans had mistakenly sent a division to reinforce Thomas), and caused a panic that swept most of Rosecrans's army, and the general himself, in a rout toward Chattanooga.

Bragg had won Chickamauga at high cost. Each side lost almost 28 percent of its

strength: Federal casualties, 16,170 out of 58,000; Confederates casualties, 18,454 out of 66,000.

530 Rosecrans retreated into Chattanooga while Bragg occupied high ground around the city. Instead of trying to crush Rosecrans's army—and in spite of news that reinforcements were being rushed to Rosecrans (in another great rail transfer of the war)—Bragg began a siege.

531 Insubordination flickered in the Army of Tennessee. Bragg and Polk argued about Chickamauga, and other generals joined against Bragg. Controversy flared in the press, and on October 3, 1863, President Davis wrote to Bragg, "The opposition to you both in the army and out of it has been a public calamity in so far that it impairs your capacity for usefulness."

532 An alarmed Jefferson Davis made a swing from Richmond through South Carolina and Georgia to visit Bragg's army. He hoped "to be serviceable in harmonizing some of the difficulties." In Atlanta and Marietta, Georgia, on October 8 and 9, the President praised Georgia's troops and earned cheers. But with the Army of Tennessee, on October 10, he botched his pacifying mission. Discovering that Bragg had sacked two corps commanders, Davis brought the top generals to an interview in Bragg's presence. Did they think the army needed another commander? In response to a unanimous yes, Davis, without explanation, kept Bragg in command.

533 President Lincoln's worries about Rosecrans (since Chickamauga, Lincoln thought he had acted "stunned like a duck hit on the head") led him to put U. S. Grant in command of the Military Division of the Mississippi. Grant replaced Rosecrans with General George H. Thomas and proceeded to lighten Bragg's siege.

534 President Davis had suggested to Bragg that Longstreet's corps be detached and sent to recapture Knoxville. Longstreet had too few men and knew it—15,000 were not enough. And the detachment would reduce Bragg's army to 45,000 against a rising Union tide of 60,000 men. But off went Longstreet, on November 4, 1863. Bragg waited, and Lincoln and Grant worried.

535 Longstreet fought near Knoxville on November 16, and General Ambrose E. Burnside withdrew into the city to stand siege. On November 22, Bragg weakened his army further by sending General Simon B. Buckner's corps to Longstreet. Meanwhile, General William T. Sherman's four U.S. divisions approached Chattanooga.

536 Grant attacked Bragg at Chattanooga on November 23, 1863, sending General George H. Thomas's Army of the Cumberland to take Orchard Knob. On November 24, General Joseph Hooker's three U.S. divisions climbed Lookout Mountain and drove away the Rebels in what became known, erroneously, as **537** the "Battle Above the Clouds." Grant's main assault, on November 25, started badly. Sherman's men struck General Patrick Cleburne's division (one of the best in Bragg's army), on the Union left, while Hooker's men drove on the right to cut off a Rebel retreat, and Thomas's command supported the attack. Cleburne stalled Sherman while Hooker's attack stumbled at a burned bridge over Chattanooga Creek. In midafternoon Grant ordered Thomas to hit the Rebel center and relieve Sherman's drive. Thomas's men reached the lower rifle pits on Missionary Ridge against heavy fire and then, inexplicably, screaming, "Chickamauga!" as they went, swarmed to the top of the hill.

Site of the "Battle Above the Clouds," entrenchments on Lookout Mountain, Tennessee.

Rebel artillery was badly located, and the gunners were afraid to hit their own men coming up the hill.

The Rebels broke and fled across Chickamauga Creek at night. **538** Bragg was appalled. "No satisfactory excuse can possibly be given for the shameful conduct of our troops," he wrote to President Davis. Someone told Grant later that the Confederate leaders had thought the Missionary Ridge position impregnable. After a moment's thought, Grant said, "Well, it was impregnable."

This major strategic victory cost 5824 Union casualties out of 56,000 engaged.

Confederate losses were 6667 out of 46,000 (4146 were taken prisoner). The road to the Deep South sagged open as the Federals topped the year's Western campaigning.

539 Time brought perspective to Bragg. In a rare confession, he wrote to President Davis, on December 1, "The disaster . . . is justly disparaging to me as a commander . . . I fear we both erred in the conclusion for me to retain command here after the clamor raised against me." He yielded command to **540** Lieutenant General William J. Hardee, on December 1, 1863. **541** With Union reinforcements speeding to Burnside, Longstreet, after several abortive attacks, abandoned the siege of Knoxville and moved eastward to Greeneville, Tennessee, on December 6, 1863. It was a sad end of the year for Confederate central operations. Alarmed at the military prospects, President Davis considered sending General Lee to reorganize the Army of Tennessee.

542 Instead, Joseph E. Johnston took command of the Army of Tennessee, on December 16, 1863. It was his proudest moment, and his arrival encouraged the veterans of that often mishandled force.

FAR WESTERN OPERATIONS

543 Using improvised gunboats and artillery, Confederate General (Prince John) Magruder, on January 1, 1863,

retook Galveston, Texas. (It had been captured on October 2, 1862.) The U.S.S. *Harriet Lane* was captured, the U.S.S. *Westfield* destroyed by its crew, and the blockade temporarily lifted. Magruder's victory greatly boosted Confederate morale in the West.

544 **An Englishman traveling through Texas in May 1863** left intriguing pictures of people, places, and war effects on Galveston, where he saw much damage, on Houston, and on other sites in the Trans-Mississippi. His book is *The Fremantle Diary: Being the Journal of Lieutenant Colonel Arthur James Lyon Fremantle, Coldstream Guards, on His Three Months in the Southern States* (reprint ed. by Walter Lord, Boston: Little Brown, 1954).

545 **Lieutenant General E. Kirby Smith, hero of the Battle of Richmond, Kentucky (q.v.),** took command of all Confederate forces west of the Mississippi on March 7, 1863, and would soon command the Trans-Mississippi Department.

546 **On September 4, 1863, Federal General N. P. Banks (q.v.) started an expedition from Louisiana toward the Texas-Louisiana coast** in order to press the Rebels and impress Napoleon III of France, who had imperialistic designs on Mexico.

547 On September 8, 1863, part of Banks's force, under General William B. Franklin, approached the partly finished Fort Griffin at Sabine Pass, Texas. Lieutenant Dick Dowling's 43-man Davis Guards and a few cannon smashed the lead gunboats, took 400 prisoners, and repulsed a force that grew in memory from 1500 to 15,000! The Confederate Congress passed resolutions of thanks to Dowling and his men and struck a rare medal to Southern bravery. The victory vastly boosted morale in Western Rebel country.

548 **Union troops under General Frederick Steele marched from Helena, Arkansas, toward Little Rock on August 10, 1863,** and captured the state capital a month later. General Sterling Price's Confederates retired to Arkadelphia.

549 **On September 22, 1863, General Joseph O. (Jo) Shelby, sporting his**

Union Major General Frederick Steele.

black-plumed hat, started his Gray light-horse cavalry on a month's raid from Arkadelphia through Arkansas and Missouri.

550 And on September 26 a worried General Kirby Smith tried a proclamation to rouse western Rebels: "Your homes are in peril . . . You should contest the advance of the enemy, thicket, gully, and stream; harass his rear and cut off his supplies"—a dangerous game, since men on such missions were usually dispatched quickly.

551 Having failed to get a Texas foothold at Sabine Pass, General N. P. Banks took Brazos Island in early November 1863, moved to Brownsville on November 6, and went on to Corpus Christi by November 16. But he could not boast a solid invasion.

SEA BATTLES, 1863

552 The U.S.S. *Hatteras,* blockading Galveston, Texas, spotted a strange vessel approaching on January 11, 1863, and went to investigate. Rebel Admiral Raphael Semmes (q.v.) had brought the fabled C.S.S. *Alabama* into the gulf and ran it toward the *Hatteras.* A rare ship duel followed. The *Hatteras,* struck by a heavy shell, sank, and panic reigned briefly in the Gulf Blockading Squadron.

553 On Tuesday, January 13, 1863, General Joseph Wheeler's Gray cavalry cap-

tured the U.S.S. *Slidell* on the Cumberland River in Tennessee.

554 The C.S.S. *Florida,* under Captain John N. Maffitt, left Mobile on the night of February 19, 1863, on a shipping raid that captured twenty-five U.S. merchantmen.

555 A surprise foray by the Rebel gunboats *Chicora* and *Palmetto State* heavily damaged the Federal blockaders *Mercedita* and *Keystone State* in Charleston Harbor on January 31, 1863. The *Mercedita,* rammed and shelled, surrendered but later escaped; the *Keystone State* burned. Other Union ships were damaged. The Rebel gunboats, unscathed, gleefully announced

Captain John N. Maffit, C.S.N.

the blockade lifted. It was, however, only interrupted.

556 There were important naval actions around Vicksburg in February 1863. On February 2, the U.S.S. *Queen of the West* passed the Rebel batteries in daylight. Though it was hit a dozen times, the ship stayed on course and attacked the ram C.S.S. *City of Vicksburg* and took three other ships. On the night of February 13, the U.S.S. *Indianola,* towing two barges, passed unscathed under fire.

557 The British merchantman *Peterhoff,*

en route to Matamoros, Mexico, was seized by Union ships under the notorious Admiral Charles Wilkes on February 25, 1863. Britain claimed that the United States had no right to stop a neutral ship bound for a neutral port, even if some of the cargo might be destined for the Confederacy. Courts finally ratified that position. The United States avoided a breach with England because the precedent might later prove useful to British policy.

558 In a major defeat for the Confederate Navy, the ram C.S.S. *Atlanta*

Federal officers on the deck of the captured Confederate ram *Atlanta*.

surrendered to the U.S.S. *Weehawken* and *Nahant* on June 17, 1863, in Wassaw Sound, Georgia.

559 **A daring Confederate raider, though, caused major discomfort to Union shipping.** On June 12, 1863, Lieutenant Charles W. (Savez) Read, who had taken six prizes with the C.S.S. *Clarence,* captured the U.S. bark *Tacony,* transferred his crew, and continued capturing ships. He attracted forty-seven ships in pursuit, but managed to snare five fishing boats off New England on June 22. He sailed the prize *Archer* into Portland, Maine, on the afternoon of June 26 and took the revenue cutter 560 *Caleb Cushing.* Cut off and surrounded, Read blew up the *Cushing* and surrendered. In nineteen days he had taken twenty-one prizes.

561 **Naval warfare grew more technical as the war continued.** On August 5, 1863, an electric torpedo heavily damaged the U.S.S. *Commodore Barney* near Dutch Gap, Virginia.

562 **The C.S.S. *Alabama* captured the bark *Sea Bride* on August 6, 1863,** while crowds cheered at Table Bay, Cape of Good Hope. Admiral Semmes continued raids with the C.S.S. *Alabama* and took prizes on December 6, 1863, at the Straits of Malacca. On March 20, 1864, the raider arrived in Capetown, South Africa, and inspired an Afrikaner song, "Daar Kom Die *Alabama.*"

563 **At about 1 A.M. on August 21, 1863,** a steam torpedo boat sped from embattled Charleston Harbor and attacked the U.S.S. *New Ironsides.* The torpedo failed to explode, and the raider scuttled back under fire.

564 **Confederate Lieutenant John Taylor Wood's daring** at the mouth of the Rappahannock River in Virginia added embarrassment to the Union Navy. With ninety men (thirty of them army sharpshooters) in four small boats, Wood captured the gunboats *Reliance* and *Satellite* on August 23, 1863.

565 **In an unusual contact on September 13, 1863,** Confederate cavalrymen captured twenty of the U.S.S. *Rattler*'s crew at a church service in Rodney, Mississippi.

566 **John Y. Beall and other Southern sympathizers** captured a schooner in Chesapeake Bay on September 19, 1863, in the first of a series of attacks. A year later, to the day, Beall and other Confederate agents captured a steamer on Lake Erie. This was part of a plot to take another Yankee ship, and the two would cooperate in freeing Rebel prisoners of war on Johnson's Island.

567 **In a naval battle as important as the one between the *Monitor* and the *Virginia,*** a vessel, shaped like a cigar, powered by steam, and almost submerged,

made for the U.S.S. *New Ironsides* in Charleston Harbor on the night of October 5, 1863. Commander W. T. Glassell's four-man crew aboard the *David* rammed their spar torpedo into the big hull, and the explosion nearly swamped the *David*. Although the severely hurt *New Ironsides* did not sink, the attack marked a new era in naval warfare. Glassell and one man were captured; the other two got the *David* back to Charleston.

568 **The North lost a non-battle in Charleston Harbor on December 6, 1863,** when the U.S.S. *Weehawken* sank at anchor—a victim of poor design!

569 **Some Rebel sympathizers, led by James Braine,** captured the *Chesapeake* off Cape Cod on December 8, 1863, but the steamer was recaptured in Nova Scotia on December 17.

570 **One out of every four blockade runners was caught in 1863,** but the Confederate cotton trade with Matamoros, Mexico, flourished as that city's port remained open and protected by the Emperor Maximilian's French fleet.

DIPLOMACY

Both sides engaged in fierce diplomatic maneuvering in 1863. Confederate efforts still focused on foreign recognition as well as on commercial relations. The Union concentrated on foiling all Southern hopes abroad.

Lee's success at Chancellorsville, in May 1863, brought recognition close again. 571 In June, Napoleon III of France talked with pro-Confederates in the British Parliament about joint recognition of the Confederacy, but poor management of the discussion ended the venture, and the news of Gettysburg and Vicksburg extinguished all hopes of recognition for the South. The vigorous trading, however, continued.

572 **An adroit Southern agent named James D. Bulloch,** sent to Liverpool in 1861 to buy or build Rebel warships, did well. He arranged for the construction of both the C.S.S. *Sumter* and the *Alabama*. And, operating in a clandestine war against 573 U.S. Consul Thomas A. Dudley (both Bulloch and Dudley hired spies, paid informers, and may even have blinked at murders), Bulloch persuaded the Laird shipbuilding company to construct two powerful ironclad rams for use against Yankee blockaders. Knowing that the British were watching his every move, Bulloch shifted ownership of these vessels to a French company, which claimed to be making them for Egypt.

574 U.S. Ambassador Charles Francis Adams threatened war if the Laird rams escaped to the Rebels, and on September 6, 1863, the rams were detained and later

bought by the British. This was a major blow to Southern hopes abroad.

WAR GETS HARDER

575 Black troops, authorized as a Union South Carolina Volunteer Infantry on January 13, 1863, were commanded by Colonel Thomas W. Higginson, who had nursed the organization from unofficial to official status.

576 Lincoln's administration suppressed sedition. Newspapers were often censored or closed. On February 8, 1863, circulation of the Chicago *Times* was suspended by military order because of its Copperhead sympathies. General Grant rescinded the order a week later, but on June 1, General Burnside, commanding the Department of the Ohio, ordered that, "on account of the repeated expression of disloyal and incendiary statements, the publication of . . . the Chicago *Times* is hereby suspended." Outraged comments from prominent Chicagoans, including the mayor, caught Lincoln's attention. He discussed the problem of newspapers with Secretary of War Stanton, who revoked the suspension on June 4, 1863.

Disloyal sentiments bothered Lincoln. **577** Clement L. Vallandigham, the leader of Peace Democrats (the name of a group often disparaged as the Copperheads) and a former congressman, was arrested in Dayton, Ohio, for branding the war "wicked and cruel," merely a struggle to establish a Republican dictatorship. Tried by a Cincinnati military commission on May 6, 1863, he was convicted of treasonable remarks and was banished.

578 Frederick Douglass, ex-slave and marvelously articulate spokesman for *democracy*, called on blacks to fight. "This rebellion can be put down without your help," he said. "Slavery can be abolished by white men; but liberty so won for the black man, while it may leave him an object of pity, can never make him an object of respect."

579 On March 3, 1863, Lincoln signed the first national draft law of the United States. It called up all physically and mentally fit male citizens between twenty and forty-five, but exempted some with dependents, also criminals, and high state and Federal officers. Weakened by the provisions allowing men to hire substitutes or to purchase exemption for $300, the law nonetheless stimulated volunteering. For the war some 162,500 men were drafted, about 47,000 served, 116,000 hired substitutes; 87,000 paid their way out.

580 It was Friday, March 13, 1863—a day to confirm superstitions—and Mary Ryan, working on friction primers in the Confederate Ordnance Laboratory on Brown's Island, made a mistake. When her primer stuck, she hit the table three times and flew up in the air. When she came

The Richmond Arsenal, a laboratory for small ammunition.

down, she flew up again. Richmond mourned the loss, to death and wounds, of almost seventy people, sixty-two of whom were indigent women and girls who worked in the plant. Safety precautions were lax, and the losses shocked the Confederate capital.

581 On Wednesday, May 27, 1863, the C.S.S. *Chattahooche* accidentally blew up on the Chattahooche River in Georgia, with a loss of eighteen crewmen.

582 A Union powder magazine near Alexandria, Virginia, exploded on June 9, 1863. Twenty were killed and fourteen wounded.

583 On March 26, 1863, the Confederate Congress passed an Act to Regulate Impressments, which legitimated a longstanding military practice of "impressing"

(commandeering) supplies. Impressment irritated everyone who was forced to yield property and did much to dim faith in the government, but without it, the war could not have been sustained.

584 Particularly unpopular were the government price schedules for impressment. State impressment commissioners issued periodic lists of prices to be paid for impressed items, most of them ludicrously low when compared with the open markets.

585 On April 24, 1863, the Confederate Congress tried again to sustain the military commissary by passing a national "tax in kind," a levy of a tenth of all agricultural produce for 1863.

586 President Lincoln, on June 20, 1863, proclaimed West Virginia a state.

Carved out of the Old Dominion, the area had deep Union sympathies, and many of its citizens resisted the Confederacy.

587 General Truman Seymour's 6000 Federals failed in a second attack on Battery Wagner in Charleston Harbor. Heading the fierce assault, on July 18, 1863, was the 54th Massachusetts Colored Infantry, which took 1515 losses, more than 25 percent of its men, including the regiment's organizer, Colonel Robert Gould Shaw.

588 An era shifted as three stalwarts of an older time passed from the scene on July 26, 1863. General Sam Houston, giant of Texas and American history, died in Huntsville, Texas. Originally a Unionist, he had finally supported the Confederacy; one of his sons was in the Confederate Army. On the same day, John J. Crittenden of Kentucky died. A veteran member of Congress, defender of the Union, although he opposed emancipation, he had sons in both armies. And William L. Yancey, once considered for the presidency of the Confederacy, died in Montgomery, Alabama.

589 One of the war's worst massacres took place in Lawrence, Kansas, on Friday, August 21, 1863. About 450 Southern raiders, under William Clarke Quantrill, sacked, wrecked, and burned the town. A ruthless bushwacker, Quantrill

held a captain's commission in the Confederate Partisan Rangers, but he ignored the laws of war at Lawrence. His men killed 150 men and boys—they spared only women and small children. Lawrence's smoky ruins became a symbol of the outrage of war. Quantrill, discredited, was denied another Confederate command and was killed in Kentucky in 1865. Partisans were generally unruly and made more enemies than friends. The best of these units was Colonel John S. Mosby's 43rd Virginia Battalion, which efficiently patrolled northern Virginia so that it became known as **590** "Mosby's Confederacy."

591 An indication of change came from the Alabama legislature on September 2, 1863, when a joint committee approved the use of slaves in the Confederate armies, and the House adopted the resolution. The idea grew.

592 At Gettysburg, Pennsylvania, on November 19, 1863, a crowd gathered to dedicate a military cemetery and commemorate the battle that had been fought in July. The Noted orator **593** Edward Everett talked for two hours. Then Lincoln took the podium and, in about two minutes, gave the Gettysburg Address. A few people seemed impressed, but most did not hear him in the restlessness following Everett. Several newspapers commented favorably on what Lincoln said; most merely mentioned that he spoke. His

Crowd at Gettysburg, gathered to hear President Lincoln dedicate the National Cemetery.

short speech enshrined the hope of democracy, the valor of those who defended it, and lifted his vision of freedom beyond the conflict to a promise for the future. The Gettysburg Address belied one of its premises: "the world will little note, nor long remember what we say here."

594 **Lincoln's own optimism grew as Northern morale rose,** and on December 8, 1863, he outlined a policy for Reconstruction, in an attempt to save that issue from complete Radical Republican domination. His "10 percent plan" provided that if 10 percent of a state's prewar population proposed it, a national government would be organized in any seceded state. This mild program flew in the face of Radical Republican wishes.

595 **Confederate morale sank as 1863 ended.** The Richmond *Dispatch,* on December 18, urged an end to criticism of the government at "this decisive crisis in the national affairs." On December 31, the Richmond *Examiner* lamented that "to-day closes the gloomiest year of our struggle."

1864 AND 1865

THE LAST
YEAR OF
THE WAR

Both sides hoped for good things in 1864. Major fighting subsided while the major armies girded.

596 President Lincoln spent much time planning Reconstruction in parts of states under Federal occupation. He hoped these activities would shore up his chances for re-election in November. As campaigning progressed well, the administration's anxiety lifted a little, but the President skirmished with the Radicals about Reconstruction and tried to improve military command so that all Northern operations were coordinated against Rebel armies.

597 President Davis's woes were heavier, but prospects cheered. His two main field armies were refitting well; supplies and some reinforcements had strengthened both Lee and Joe Johnston. Forces around Mobile, in the Deep South, and in the Trans-Mississippi were improving. There seemed every chance for his offensive-defensive strategy to enter an offensive phase and for the South to wrest the initiative from the enemy and encourage Rebel morale.

598 The weather stayed harsh. On New Year's Day, 1864, Memphis, Tennessee, and Cairo, Illinois, shivered in below-zero temperatures.

599 Financial weather in the North looked unstable as gold rose steadily on the New York market.

But, reflecting the mood of respite, both Presidents showed mercy. **600** On January 6, 1864, Jefferson Davis stayed a military execution, and on January 7 **601** Lincoln spared a deserter, "because I am trying to evade the butchering business lately."

602 President Davis took stock of political realities and wrote to North Carolina's governor, Zebulon Vance, on January 8, 1864, about the discontent in that state. He still thought that peace could come only when the enemy abandoned "his vain confidence in our subjugation." At the same time, he recognized a dangerous trend against his administration and against the war. **603** Heavy opposition to the Confederate draft was exemplified by protest meetings in western North Carolina. In occupied New Orleans, a pro-

Union convention met on January 8, 1864, to consider Reconstruction of Louisiana—one of Lincoln's long-held desires—and some sentiment developed for Reconstruction in Florida. On January 19, a pro-Union Constitutional Convention in Arkansas adopted an antislavery constitution and chose a provisional governor; President Lincoln urged a quick election. (By mid-April a pro-Union government was installed at Little Rock.) **604** And on January 21, 1864, Arkansas pro-Unionists proposed an end to slavery. **605** On March 4, 1864, the Unionist Andrew Johnson became U.S. Military Governor of Tennessee.

606 A pro-Union Louisiana government, led by Governor Michael Hahn,

Brigadier General Andrew Johnson, later seventeenth President of the United States.

began functioning in New Orleans on March 4.

607 Lincoln, hoping to encourage Southern defection, approved, on January 23, 1864, a plan for plantation owners to free their slaves and hire them as free labor.

608 On January 11, 1864, U.S. Senator John Henderson of Missouri proposed a joint resolution to abolish slavery in the United States by amendment. This historic action resulted in the Thirteenth Amendment.

There were other anxieties. **609** President Davis lamented to General Lee on January 4, 1864, that the food emergency in the Army of Northern Virginia "justifies impressment," and on January 9 he warned commanders of a pending attack on Mobile. On January 13 he cautioned General J. E. Johnston about the military and political complications of retreat. **610** In early February 1864, President Davis told the Confederate Congress about the "discontent, disaffection, and disloyalty" affecting the morale in the Deep South. He called for the suspension of habeas corpus to curtail spying, desertion, and sedition. **611** On January 5, 1864, Lincoln urged continuation of the $300 bounty for each U.S. volunteer. And on February 1, Lincoln ordered 500,000 men drafted on March 10 for three years or the duration. In March, he called up 200,000 men for the Navy and general reserve.

RAIDERS AND PARTISANS

612 The early months of 1864 saw a sharp increase in partisan activities, small expeditions, riverine attacks, and angry patrols. Scattered operations offered both sides minor successes. A January Federal expedition under Kit Carson rounded up Navajo Indians in New Mexico Territory and sent many to the Bosque Redondo Reservation. **613** Early in the month, a lieutenant and private of the 21st Georgia Cavalry captured twenty-five Union soldiers near Charleston. **614** General Bedford Forrest turned back General William Sooy Smith's raid from Memphis to Meridian, Mississippi, on January 25, 1864. **615** A fierce cavalry fight raged at Dandridge, Tennessee, from January 16 to 17; finally the Federals retreated.

616 On February 3, 1864, General William T. Sherman, aided by General William Sooy Smith's 7600 horsemen, began another campaign to take Meridian, Mississippi, an important Southern rail and supply center. It was ineptly defended by cavalry forces under General Leonidas Polk, and Sherman took Meridian on February 14. He described what happened then: "For five days 10,000 men worked hard and with a will in . . . destruction . . . Meridian, with its depots, store-houses, arsenals, hospitals, offices, hotels and cantonments, no longer exists." The expedition had wrecked over a hundred miles of track, sixty-one bridges, and twenty locomotives in what Confederates feared was a move toward Mobile.

617 While Sherman took Meridian, General W. Sooy Smith's troops were attacked by Bedford Forrest's cavalry, on February 22, 1864, at Okolona, Mississippi. In one of Forrest's greatest victories, his 2500 men routed Smith's 7000 and pursued them back to Memphis.

618 Meanwhile, another Union expedition worried Confederates. A force under General Truman Seymour occupied Jacksonville, Florida, on February 7, 1864, and moved inland toward Lake City. Seymour's 5500 men ran into some 5000 Rebels at Olustee (Ocean Pond), not far from Lake City, on Saturday, February 20. In what became Florida's major battle of the war, Confederate General Joseph Finegan's men attacked and drove the Federals back. Hard fighting continued through the day; the Federals finally broke and retreated to Jacksonville. Union losses were 1861 against the Rebels' 934.

619 On February 28, 1864, General Judson Kilpatrick led 3500 men from the Rapidan River on a raid to release Union prisoners in exposed Richmond. On February 29, Kilpatrick detached 500 men under Colonel Ulric Dahlgren on a separate road to Richmond; both columns were to attack different points of the capital's defenses. Kilpatrick veered off but

Dahlgren got within two miles of Richmond before encountering heavy resistance by a force under General Custis Lee. Then Dahlgren, too, shied off. In an interesting aftermath, Dahlgren was ambushed and killed on March 2. Papers, whose authenticity is in doubt, were apparently found on his body that revealed a scandalous assassination plot against President Davis. The raid fizzled amidst the furor.

620 **Fresh from defeating General W. S. Smith's men at Okolona, Mississippi, "that Devil Forrest," on March 16, 1864, launched an expedition into west Tennessee and Kentucky.** It lasted until April 14, by which time he had reached and ranged along the Ohio River. Although he did not capture Paducah or Cincinnati, he did alarm the whole Ohio Valley and enhance his reputation.

REORGANIZATIONS

621 **Lincoln's Cabinet was shaken by the so-called Pomeroy Circular on February 22, 1864, when Secretary of the Treasury Salmon P. Chase offered to resign.** A group of dissident Radical Republicans and abolitionists, led by Senator Samuel C. Pomeroy of Kansas, issued a circular suggesting Chase for President. Although Chase denied knowledge of the circular, evidence indicates that he had approved it. Despite this indication of Chase's maleficence, Lincoln, after talking with him,

refused his resignation and kept the Cabinet together. **622** When, however Chase resigned again, on June 30, 1864, Lincoln accepted the resignation with one of his homilies: "You and I have reached a point of mutual embarrassment in our official relation which . . . can not be . . . longer sustained."

623 **The U.S. Senate, on February 24, passed a bill reviving the rank of lieutenant general,** last held by George Washington. Grant was the obvious candidate. Lincoln approved the bill on February 29. **624** The Senate confirmed Grant's nomination on March 2.

625 **On March 12 a major shake-up of the Union command** put Grant in charge of the Union's armies; General Henry Halleck became chief of staff; General Sherman took over the Military Division of the Mississippi, including the Departments of the Cumberland, the Tennessee, the Arkansas, and the Ohio; General J. B. McPherson commanded both the Department and the Army of the Tennessee.

626 **On February 24, President Davis appointed General Braxton Bragg virtual chief of staff** by charging him with conducting the military operations of the Confederate armies. He had been relieved after Missionary Ridge, but Davis maintained confidence in his strategic sense. **627** General John C. Breckinridge took command of the Confederate Department of Western Virginia on March 5, in place of General Samuel Jones. Lead and salt mines in that area were vital to the Confederacy. 628 In a popular move, Major General Sterling Price was named to relieve Lieutenant General Theophilus Holmes as commander of the Confederate District of Arkansas on March 16. 629 And on April 18, General P. G. T. Beauregard left his well-held post at Charleston to command the Department of North Carolina and Southern Virginia. His task was to defend that sector, including Richmond, against possible coastal attacks.

Sea Actions, 1864

Blockade runners had trouble in January 1864. 630 On January 11, 1864, two runners were captured off the Florida coast and two others were grounded and burned at Lockwood's Folly Inlet, North Carolina, but Rebels continued to harass Union ships.

631 The U.S.S. *Florida* destroyed two other blockade runners near Masonborough Inlet, North Carolina, on February 10 as the Union noose grew tighter.

632 **On January 10, the U.S.S.** *Iron Age* **was lost at Lockwood's,** and on January 29, Rebels on the Mississippi hit the *Sir William Wallace.* Also on that date, 633 the new ironclad *Charleston* joined Confederate defenders of its eponymous city. 634 On February 2, a Rebel small-boat flotilla

captured the U.S. gunboat *Underwriter* near New Berne, North Carolina, but pursuers forced them to burn the prize. 635 Meanwhile, on February 10, the Rebel cruiser *Florida,* having been refitted at Brest, in France, escaped the U.S.S. *Kearsarge* and resumed raiding under a new captain, Charles Manigault Morris. On October 4, 1864, Morris entered the Brazilian port of Bahia for repairs and supplies; the *Florida* had been at sea for sixty-four straight days. Unfortunately for Morris, the U.S.S. *Wachusett* was in port and, utterly against international law, rammed and captured the *Florida* on the night of October 7.

636 The transport U.S.S. *Maple Leaf* struck a mine and sank in Florida's St. John's River on April 1, and the transport *General Hunter* met a similar fate on April 16.

637 **February greeted a new kind of sea warfare.** On February 17, the cigar-shaped Confederate submarine *H. L. Hunley* sank the U.S.S. *Housatonic* on blockade duty off Charleston; this was the first victory for a submersible. The *Hunley* was the product of two years of experiments, beginning in New Orleans, that produced several prototypes. H. L. Hunley was one of the original five partners who hatched the idea of underwater war. An early version of the ship, the *American Diver,* sank in rough seas off Fort Morgan in Mobile Bay while attempting an attack on blockaders. Hunley built another boat, which he tested in Mobile and then moved to Charleston.

Eleven-inch pivot gun on the U.S.S. *Kearsarge.*

The *H. L. Hunley* sank twice during unsuccessful attacks on the Union fleet off Charleston. Raised and refitted, the submarine enjoyed the patronage of General Beauregard, and, armed with a spar torpedo, rammed the *Housatonic,* which sank rapidly. So, apparently, did the *Hunley.*

638 When Admiral Raphael Semmes, in the *Alabama,* challenged the U.S.S. *Kearsarge* in a classic battle off Cherbourg, France, on June 19, 1864, the nearly legendary C.S.S. *Alabama* had already sailed all the Atlantic, adjoining oceans, the Indian Ocean, had sunk the U.S.S. *Hatteras,* and captured sixty-two ships valued at over $10 million. The fight between the *Alabama* and *Kearsarge* was the biggest open-sea battle of the war. Rumor had it that the *Kearsarge* carried a coat of chain mail along her hull and hence should have been considered ironclad. Admiral Semmes maintained always that he did not know about the mail. Whether he did or did not know, he had to fight—and he lost a gallant challenge.

639 Survivors of the encounter between the *Alabama* and the *Kearsarge,* including Raphael Semmes, were picked up by the English yacht *Deerhound.*

640 An observer of the duel between the *Alabama* and the *Kearsarge* was the French painter Edouard Manet. Fascinated, he captured the scene on canvas, and his painting hangs in a Philadelphia museum.

641 Prizes taken by the *Alabama* gave rise to the postwar *Alabama* Claims litigation between the United States and Great Britain.

642 **Admiral David G. Farragut led his four ironclads and fourteen wooden ships against Mobile Bay at 5:30 A.M. on August 5, 1864.** Against him stood the heavily armed Fort Gaines and Fort Morgan and lightly armed Fort Powell, plus Admiral Franklin Buchanan's C.S.S. *Tennessee* (rumored to be the strongest ironclad in the world) and three small gunboats. A narrow channel between the inner and outer harbor was partly blocked by obstructions and mines, then called torpedoes. Battle was joined about six-thirty, and soon the U.S.S. *Tecumseh,* heading for

U.S.S. *Farragut,* commanded by Captain Percival Drayton, shortly after the Battle of Mobile Bay, August 1864.

the *Tennessee,* hit a torpedo and swiftly sank. At this point, legend has it, Farragut, aloft in the U.S.S. *Hartford's* rigging, yelled, "Damn the torpedoes, full speed ahead." Onward charged his fleet, passing the forts with minor damage, and the three ships rammed the poorly powered *Tennessee.* Buchanan's little fleet poured murderous fire at the Union ships, disabling several while slowly being chopped up. Only one survived the day. The *Tennessee* put up a terrific fight and damaged several wooden and iron ships, but finally, hit by several 11-inch shots, its armor cracked, funnel smashed, steering gone, and Admiral Buchanan wounded, the great ram struck its flag at 10 A.M.

643 Farragut had won a big but costly victory. Mobile's outer harbor was closed to blockade runners at last. **644** One out of three blockade runners was captured in 1864.

645 The C.S.S. *Tallahassee* left Wilmington, North Carolina, on August 6, 1864. During a three-week rampage, the Rebel raider took thirty-three merchantmen, destroying twenty-six, releasing two, and bonding five. This ship represented a change in Confederate naval strategy.

646 Confederate Navy Secretary Malloy had, by 1864, new ideas about destroying commerce. Now he sought light-draft, fast steamers to hit enemy coastal waters and perhaps pull some blockading ships off station. The *Tallahassee* was one of

these, and it did so well that New York City and much of the New England coast trembled in alarm at its name.

647 Confederate river forces were called on frequently as Sherman marched inexorably to the sea. The C.S.S. *Savannah* was summoned to help hold the city of that name in November 1864. The *Savannah* was one of the best ironclads produced by Secretary Mallory's riverine strategy; it was 150 feet long with a 22-foot draft, four 6.4-inch Brooke guns, and four air blowers to make life bearable below deck. The *Savannah* had unusually good engines and could make a steady 6.5 knots. Where General William J. Hardee was trying to cobble together a defense against Sherman, he called on the Confederate Navy for help. The *Savannah* did important service in protecting Rebel troops as they evacuated the city in December 1864. Unable to reach the sea, this superior ironclad was burned on December 21, 1864.

648 In the waning months of the war, Confederate naval support installations were threatened. The Naval Cannon Foundry in Selma, Alabama, was destroyed by Union cavalry raiders; the Columbus, Georgia, Naval Iron Works, like army ordnance plants in that state, soon became targets of Federal expeditions. Effective in sustaining small naval squadrons that did great service in sealing many Southern rivers, these key plants were taken from the

Fort Fisher, which guarded the North Carolina coast near Wilmington.

land side—small consolation for the naval officers.

649 On December 23, 1864, a combined Union Army and Navy expedition made an attempt to take Fort Fisher, which guarded the harbor of Wilmington, North Carolina, the last surviving Confederate blockade-running port. General Benjamin F. Butler, of New Orleans infamy, exploded a hulk containing 215 tons of powder near the fort—without result. On December 24, Butler's two army divisions supported Admiral David D. Porter's sixty-ship fleet in a general attack, which began with what the best historian of the Confederate Navy,

Raimondo Luraghi, has called "one of the most fearful bombardments in history." Fisher's 1900 defenders were buffeted by 627 naval guns, suffered slight casualties, and the next day warded off a land attack with its artillery and Rebel reinforcements. The whole expedition fizzled in anger and recriminations. Renewed attacks under General Alfred H. Terry and Admiral Porter continued on January 14, with trenches erected against possible Confederate reinforcements commanded by General Bragg.

650 Terry and Porter tried again on January 15, 1865—a two-pronged attack from the sea and land hit the thinly held fort. Heroic fighting by the fort's outmanned defenders inflicted over 1400 casualties against some 500, but the fort was lost. President Davis and many others blamed General Bragg's timidity in committing 6000 Confederate reserves against some 5000 Yankees. The last blockade-running port was closed.

651 With all important Confederate ports on the Atlantic closed in 1865, one out of every two blockade runners was captured.

SEA ACTIONS, 1865

652 **The Confederate agent James Bulloch, on January 7, 1865, acquired one of the huge ironclads that had been built in France and sold to Denmark.** Christened the C.S.S. *Stonewall,* and commanded by the able Captain T. J. Page, the ironclad did more frightening than sinking; her rumored invincibility and range panicked much of the Atlantic coast. Hearing of the

C.S.S. *Stonewall* in drydock, Port Royal, Georgia.

Confederacy's collapse, Page turned his ship over to Spain on May 19, 1865.

653 **On October 19, 1864, the C.S.S. *Shenandoah* went into commission at Madeira, with Captain James I. Waddell commanding.** Purchased in England by James Bulloch, the *Shenandoah* had the sleek swiftness for a successful commerce raider—and enjoyed an unusual and lengthy career. Waddel would surrender his ship to British officials at Liverpool on August 2, 1865, after a world cruise and after nearly finishing off the Union whaling fleet in the northern Pacific.

PRISONERS

654 **The most famous prison escape of the Civil War took place on Tuesday, February 9, 1864, in Richmond, Virginia.** Colonel Thomas E. Rose and Colonel Abel D. Streight, with 107 other Union officers, tunneled their way out of the notorious Libby Prison. Forty-eight were recaptured, two drowned, and fifty-nine reached Union lines.

655 **The first black prisoners of war reached Richmond on March 7, 1864.**

656 **Federal prisoners were ushered into a place called Camp Sumter, near Americus, Georgia, on February 27, 1864.** This isolated and unfinished camp was designed to hold about 10,000 men—

Libby Prison, Richmond, showing provisions delivered by boat on the James River.

and ended up holding 33,000. It was to become infamous under the name Andersonville, the most hated prisoner-of-war site of the Civil War. Short rations, unsanitary conditions, scant drinking water, diseases—all contributed to the high death rate: nearly 13,000 prisoners died during Andersonville's short existence. 657 Survivors blamed Captain Henry Wirz, in charge of interior conditions, for their ills. Despite his efforts to aid prisoners, he was the only military official hanged after the war.

658 **Prisoners of both sides were subject to the whims of captors and to local conditions.** Some fared badly, indeed, such as those at Andersonville in Georgia or the equally overcrowded and deadly facility in Elmira, New York. 659 Often they were pawns in a hectic bargaining game: some were held as hostages against threatened enemy atrocities. Generally each side made efforts to treat its prisoners humanely, but deteriorating conditions eroded the Confederates' capacity to keep up rations and other

Andersonville, Georgia, the Confederate prison, as it appeared on August 17, 1864.

supplies. Northern efforts were fairly well coordinated under a commissary general of prisoners; less well coordinated Confederate efforts were largely the responsibility of 660 Brigadier General John H. Winder. As provost marshal of Richmond, Winder aroused public anger by his harsh policies, but he took his duties seriously, even though he concentrated too much on security. His death, in February 1865, relieved the Union prisoners and did lead to better conditions.

661 **Both sides tried to ameliorate prisoner life.** Mail was often allowed, and prisoners with money (usually officers)

Left: Evening roll call at the Union prison in Elmira, New York, 1864.

Brigadier General John H. Winder, C.S.A., provost marshal of Richmond and commissary general of prisoners east of the Mississippi, from November 1864 until his death, on February 7, 1865.

could buy additional food or clothing (the South issued no clothes to prisoners). Civilian gifts were often permitted. But the hastily constructed Northern camps were never warm enough in winter, and the Southern ones were hot and unhealthy. Nothing could make prison life more than barely endurable.

662 On July 22, 1862, both sides concluded an exchange agreement for swift repatriation of captives. This held until December 1862, when the Confederates' refusal to treat former slaves as prisoners of war ended formal exchanges. Informal transfers continued until mid-1863, and the two navies exchanged prisoners without quibbling.

663 General Grant, who realized that exchanges would help to sustain the Rebel armies, finally ordered a complete halt in April 1864. The process resumed in January 1865, too late to help the crumbling Gray legions.

664 Statistics tell the hard story of prison conditions. Of an estimated 211,411 Union soldiers captured, 16,668 were paroled immediately and 30,218 died in prison. Of an estimated 462,634 Confederates captured, 247,769 were paroled immediately and 25,976 died in prison. In other terms, 12 percent of Confederate prisoners died in the North, and 15.5 percent of Federal prisoners died in the South—close numbers for a tough war.

SOME DEFINING OF THE WAR

665 On April 22, 1864, in accord with an act of Congress, the words "In God We Trust" were first stamped on U.S. coins.

666 Lincoln understood more about Americans than most people realized.

He said, in April 1864, "We all declare for liberty; but in using the same word we do not all mean the same thing."

667 Grappling with the problem of the Union's black troops, President Davis, in April 1864, ordered Confederate officers to return captured former slaves to their owners; he would deal with the free black prisoners.

668 In the heat of Grant's Spotsylvania fighting, Lincoln was hurt by what struck him as treasonable articles published in the *New York World* and the *Journal of Commerce* on May 18, 1864. The papers printed a false presidential proclamation calling for 300,000 more soldiers. Overreacting, Lincoln ordered the editors and others arrested and the papers shut down. He soon relented, and the papers resumed publication. Clearly, the war was now testing everyone's nerves.

669 Hard war hastened the centralization of the North's financial system. On May 17, 1864, the U.S. Congress initiated a postal money-order system. And on the awful day of Cold Harbor, June 3, 1864, President Lincoln signed **670** an act of Congress establishing the Bureau of Currency and the office of the Comptroller of the Currency.

671 Once Grant took charge of the Union's war, he stuck grimly to his strategy of pressure. Despite criticisms

and casualties, he announced to General Halleck on May 11 that he proposed "to fight it out on this line if it takes all summer." It took more than all summer, but his purpose did not flag.

672 War's winnowing of men heightened the Southern personalization of the conflict, especially when heroes like Jeb Stuart fell. When President Davis heard how Lee had gone to the front in the Wilderness and Spotsylvania, he urged caution; "The country could not bear the loss of you." Davis, by mid-1864, came to rely completely on Lee and lamented that he had such scarce resources to help "in your unequal struggle so long and nobly maintained." He gave Lee complete discretion in Virginia.

673 Trading with the enemy became a big problem. Northerners sought profits, but Southerners wanted sustenance. On May 20, 1864, Lincoln ordered protection for anyone trading within Treasury Department guidelines, and on September 24, Lincoln approved legalization of such trading. Davis, too, accepted the trade as essential.

674 War worked its changes. On June 28, 1864, President Lincoln approved a bill that repealed the old Fugitive Slave Acts.

675 The Union's rising strength could be seen in Lincoln's signing a bill, on

July 2, 1864, that granted public lands for railroad construction in the Northwest and that chartered the Northern Pacific Railroad.

676 **Still, the war's costs hurt the North.** Late in June 1864, Lincoln approved bills increasing assorted revenues as well as the income tax.

677 **In the wreckage of Confederate finances,** President Davis yielded to public pressure and appointed a new Treasury Secretary on July 18, 1864. George A. Trenholm, a wealthy South Carolina businessman, who had done well in blockade trading, took the job reluctantly. He was popular, and he worked to restore confidence in Southern money—with some small success. According to a student of Confederate funding, "Trenholm wondered . . . why the people could never see and think of the Confederacy as part of themselves—not something far away—and why they as one great family did not come to the rescue."

678 **The famous Rebel raider Brigadier General John Hunt Morgan,** commanding the Department of Western Virginia and Eastern Tennessee, was caught by surprise and killed by Yankee raiders on September 4, 1864. His heroic cavalry escapades were not forgotten.

679 **Citizens of Louisiana who had taken the loyalty oath went further.** On September 5, 1864, they ratified a new state constitution that abolished slavery.

680 In Maryland, on September 6, 1864, a state convention also adopted a new constitution that abolished slavery; it was narrowly ratified by voters in October.

681 **President Lincoln, on October 31, 1864, proclaimed the admission of Nevada as the thirty-sixth state of the Union.**

682 **General McClellan said, after Lincoln's re-election on November 8, that he deplored "the result" for "my country's sake."** Lincoln took a longer view. On November 10, 1864, he said, "We cannot have free government without elections; and if the rebellion could force us to forgo or postpone a national election, it might fairly claim to have already conquered and ruined us."

683 **Lincoln's compassion swelled as the war cut down so many.** On November 21, 1864, he wrote one of his most famous letters to a bereaved mother, Mrs. Lydia Bixby, who, he heard, had lost five sons in the war: "I feel how weak and fruitless must be any words of mine which should attempt to beguile you from the grief of a loss so overwhelming. But I cannot refrain from tendering to you the consolation that may be found in the thanks of the Republic they died to save." He mentioned "the solemn pride that must be yours, to have laid so costly a sacrifice on the altar of Freedom."

Mrs. Bixby did have five sons, but two of them were killed in action, one received a discharge, and the other two may have deserted.

684 Tennessee's Constitutional Convention abolished slavery in a constitutional amendment of January 9, 1865, ratified by popular vote on February 22.

685 In St. Louis, on January 11, 1865, Missouri's Constitutional Convention adopted an ordinance abolishing slavery.

686 In early January 1865, the United States Congress debated the pending Thirteenth Amendment. In bringing up the amendment, which had already been passed by the Senate, Ohio Republican Representative J. M. Ashly argued that "if slavery is wrong and criminal, as the great body of enlightened men admit, it is certainly our duty to abolish it." That set off arguments. New York's Fernando Wood replied: "The Almighty has fixed the distinction of the races; the Almighty has made the black man inferior; and, sir, by no legislation, by no partisan success, by no revolution, by no military power, can you wipe out this distinction. You may make the black man free, but when you have done that, what have you done?" A bandwagon rolled for the amendment, with Maine and Kansas aboard in early February. That month, though, Delaware

rejected it, followed by Kentucky and, in March, by New Jersey. The amendment became effective in December 1865.

687 As Confederate military fortunes crumbled in the wake of Hood's debacle and Sherman's incursions, Southern public opinion turned against President Davis. A frustrated Congress took away some of his powers, and on January 23, 1865, it passed "An Act to provide for the appointment of a General-in-Chief of the Armies of the Confederate States." The appointee would be "the ranking officer of the Army, and, as such, shall have command of the military forces of the Confederate States." Davis got the point and appointed Lee to a job now beyond even his magic, though he pledged to fight on.

688 On February 17, 1865, both Columbia and Charleston, South Carolina, fell. Who burned Columbia remains an issue but the loss of Charleston, the cradle of secession, was a grave blow to the people of the South. A Yankee newsman saw it as "a city of ruins."

689 Lincoln hoped that some of the war's emotional wounds might be healed by the implementation of his old scheme for compensated emancipation. His Cabinet wholly disapproved, when the members heard, on February 5, 1865, a proposal to pay $400 million to the states that gave up the war before April 1, 1865. They were sure it would never get through Congress.

Columbia, South Carolina, after capture by the Federals in February 1865.

690 Lincoln's Reconstruction plans were not acceptable to the Radicals. On February 18, 1865, the U.S. Senate postponed a vote on the admission of Louisiana to the Union under Lincoln's 10 percent scheme.

691 **President Davis came to the conclusion, in mid-February 1865, that "we are reduced to choosing whether the Negroes shall fight for us or against us."** The Confederate Senate dragged its feet on admitting blacks into Rebel ranks.

692 **General Lee saw the future all too clearly.** On February 21, 1865, he outlined a realist's plan to abandon the lines north of the James, fall back, and try to reach General Johnston's army.

693 **Conscription proved a constant problem for Kirby Smith,** as his vast western domain resisted discipline. The governors of Texas and Arkansas continued to raise objections to the conscription of men from their states, and Kirby Smith found himself embroiled in bitter arguments, which he usually lost.

694 **Another problem dogging Kirby Smith was the Texas Cotton Bureau.** An outgrowth of an early state agency, the Cotton Bureau, under Colonel W. A. Broadwell, confiscated bales by outright

theft, badgered growers, and tried commandeering transportation for Mexican shipments. So outrageous did the bureau become that Broadwell was finally tried for fraud.

695 **In an attempt to shore up crumbling fortunes, the Confederate Senate, on March 8, 1865, approved allowing slaves, long used in noncombatant roles, to serve as soldiers.** Talk about this radical social shift had been heard in the army since early 1864. Finally, General Lee urged the measure, as did President Davis and a reluctant Congress. On March 13, a law was passed putting blacks in the Confederate Army. Although the law did not say so, the idea was that blacks who served would be granted freedom. A few black units were formed in Richmond. Free and slave blacks had already been conscripted, in late February 1865, for duties behind the fighting lines. Many blacks had served with their owners in action, and some explained that they were fighting for their homeland.

DIPLOMACY, 1864

696 **In early April, the U.S. House of Representatives approved a joint resolution rejecting the creation of a Mexican monarchy,** an action aimed against Maximilian's pretensions.

697 Whether he was aware of U.S. Congressional objections or not, Maximil-

ian of Hapsburg landed at Vera Cruz on May 28, 1864, to become Emperor of Mexico.

698 **On April 27, 1864, President Davis dispatched Jacob Thompson, aided by C. C. Clay, Jr., on a secret mission to Canada.** He apparently hoped to obtain Canadian aid in working on peace efforts.

699 **On June 14, 1864, the Confederate Congress issued a manifesto to the world,** outlining the Southern concept of the old Union and declaring its continuing determination to win independence. The manifesto also recalled the long-standing Confederate wish for peace and amity with the Union. This "peace feeler" stemmed, it stated, from a feeling of strength, which "enables us to profess this desire of peace in the interests of civilization and humanity without danger of having our motives misinterpreted, or of the declaration being ascribed to any unmanly sentiment, or any distrust of our ability fully to maintain our cause . . . The wildest picture ever drawn of a disordered imagination comes short of the extravagance which could dream of the conquest of eight millions of people resolved with one mind 'to die freemen rather than live slaves.' "

700 **Peace was in the minds of both sides,** and contacts between private citizens grew more frequent. Influential Frank Blair, Sr., journeyed to Richmond and suggested talks. A skeptical President Davis, on January 28, 1865, at last named as delegates Vice-President Alex Stephens; Virginia's R. M. T. Hunter, who was president pro tem of the Confederate Senate; and former U.S. Supreme Court Justice John A. Campbell. On January 30, President Lincoln issued passes for the Rebel delegates to Fort Monroe and, on January 31, instructed Secretary of State Seward to meet them. Lincoln let it be known that, though he might yield on certain matters, the preservation of the Union was essential—a point not acceptable to the Confederates.

Lincoln joined the group, which met aboard the *River Queen* at Hampton Roads, on February 3, 1865. He reiterated his determination to preserve the Union. The Southerners suggested that Union and Confederate troops join together against French intervention in Mexico, but Lincoln said there could be no alliance with the Confederate states, since they were not a country. An armistice was mentioned, and Lincoln said it could not be effected until the Union was restored. The Southerners felt that total submission was required of them; Lincoln noted that if he had control of things, he would be liberal in Reconstruction but could not speak for Congress. Since there were no bases of negotiation, the meeting ended and the war continued.

701 The Confederate Congress tried again for foreign sympathy. A Joint Resolution of March 14, 1865, reaffirmed congressional commitment to continued war, thanked many army units for pledges of constancy for independence, and asked God's blessing for the cause and for the soldiers and people who cherished it.

702 On March 18, 1865, the Confederate Congress adjourned *sine die.* Its last session had been less than fruitful; much important legislation was unpassed and much time wasted in arguments with President Davis about who was to blame for the sad state of affairs. The Congress never met again.

POLITICS, 1863

Political activity, always important to Americans, affected the Confederacy in 1863. Union affairs remained fairly settled until the 1864 elections. **703** For President Davis, though, 1863 offered serious political problems. The South's congressional elections came that year, and lack of party partisanship hampered Davis in winning support for an administration constitutionally prohibited from being re-elected. Unable to focus on party issues, opposition focused on Davis's poor handling of the war. He failed to boast enough that there would be elections in that hard year. When the counting ended, the administration had taken a beating; it held a majority of fifteen in the House and of two in the Senate. Without party discipline, though, Davis could not count on a majority. And since many of the states canvassed were at least partly occupied by the enemy, there was evident doubt about total support for the Confederate government. For the moment, though, Davis's was the South's war program. And still he offered centralization, hard war, and sacrifice for independence.

FAR WESTERN ACTIVITIES

704 In a major delegation of authority, on April 28, 1864, President Davis wrote to General E. Kirby Smith, commanding the Trans-Mississippi Department, that "as far as the constitution permits, full authority has been given to you to administer to the wants of your Dept., civil as well as military." Shadow offices of the Treasury, State, and War Departments were established in Shreveport and other cities beyond the river.

705 From May 9 to June 22, 1864, Union troops pursued Indians from the Utah Territory to the Arizona Territory and from Gila, Arizona, to Cedar Bluffs, in the Colorado Territory. **706** U.S. troops fought Indians in the Colorado Territory in August 1864 and in the Nebraska Territory from August until October.

707 Major General Sterling Price began a huge raid from Camden, Arkansas, toward St. Louis, Missouri, on August 28, 1864. Lured by promises of heavy

reinforcements awaiting him in Missouri, and eager to return to scenes of earlier triumphs, Price led 12,000 cavalrymen (4000 of them unarmed) against scattered but strong Union units. Troops under Major General W. S. Rosecrans and Major General Samuel Curtis plotted to trap Price. His subordinates, including Major General J. S. Marmaduke and Major General James Fagan, were not outstanding, but Brigadier General Joseph S. Shelby and Stand Watie had real talent. As the Rebels moved toward Ironton, Major General A. J. Smith's corps left Sherman's area to help Rosecrans.

Skirmishing at Fredericktown and Ironton, **708** Price launched an unneces-

Major General Sterling Price, C.S.A. who fought on both sides of the Mississippi River.

sary frontal attack at Pilot Knob and took a thousand casualties. He moved westward along the Missouri River, hoping to get men and supplies, and perhaps have an effect on the Federal November election. He collected about 2000 more men and zuch booty, which tied him to a huge wagon train. Pursued diligently, Price barely escaped capture several times and at last returned to Laynesport, Arkansas, on December 2, 1864. His men had marched 1488 miles, destroyed miles of Missouri railroads, diverted Union corps, and brought back valuable supplies. But the raid had failed in its main objectives and had lost 4000 men.

QUARRELING
BEFORE THE STORM

709 **For both the Union and the Confederacy,** the year 1864 promised much. Grant planned to put all the Union armies into action and pin down the Rebel forces. **710** The Army of the Potomac, under General Meade, was to stick to Lee's army ("Wherever Lee goes, there you will go also"), while smaller forces were to threaten Richmond from the James River and the Shenandoah Valley. General Sherman, commanding a big western army, would press the Army of Tennessee into Atlanta and destroy Southern war resources in Georgia. General N. P. Banks's army was to march from New Orleans to Mobile, where it was expected

to link up with Sherman and secure the Chattanooga-Mobile line.

711 Aware of these threats, President Davis diligently reinforced his two main armies—Lee had almost 70,000 men and Joe Johnston nearly 60,000—as well as conditions allowed. If Meade and Sherman could be checked, the upcoming Northern election might change the nature of the war.

712 General Banks ruined Grant's plans by launching an expedition up the Red River in mid-March 1864. With a strong force, and aided by gunboats, Banks planned to capture Shreveport, Confederate headquarters in the Trans-Mississippi Department, and make war in Texas. But when Banks advanced late in the month, he encountered low water, difficult geography, and Rebels under General Richard Taylor. **713** On April 8, Banks's column—a jumble of men, guns, and wagons distant from Union gunboats—was attacked by Taylor's troops near Mansfield, Louisiana. This proved to be the major battle west of the Mississippi. Doubly outflanked, the Yankees fled in confusion and finally rallied near Pleasant Hill. Rebel casualties were 1000 of 8800 engaged; Banks lost 2235 out of 12,000.

714 **Taylor struck again late on April 9,** but the Federals counterattacked and held the field. Blue losses were 1369 out of 12,000; Gray were about 1600 out of 12,500. Banks's expedition ended in a humiliating scurry to gunboats.

715 Grant, frustrated in his plans, had to adjust the offensive while Banks's force straggled back toward Grand Ecore, under constant harassment from artillery and small arms. Admiral Porter feared his gunboats might be stranded as the Red River and tributaries thinned. Banks's expedition was a complete failure.

716 On April 12, 1864, Nathan Bedford Forrest, operating near Union communications in Tennessee, attacked Fort Pillow. The earthwork fort held about 560 white troops and black troops who guarded supply lines. Forrest's 1500 struck early on the morning, and at 3 P.M., with the fort under a circle of fire, Forrest demanded unconditional surrender. "Should my demand be refused," Forrest wrote, "I cannot be responsible for the fate of your command." Union commander Major William F. Bradford refused.

Rebels stormed the fort. Some Yankees fought, some ran, others tried to surrender and were shot down—especially black soldiers. A killing frenzy raged. Rebel losses of 14 killed and 86 wounded compare with 231 Union killed (a disproportionate number of them black), 100 wounded, and 226 captured.

The Fort Pillow Massacre remains a highly controversial episode in Forrest's career and Civil War history.

717 A rare Confederate seaboard victory came in April 1864, when Brigadier General Robert Hoke attacked and recap-

C.S.S. *Albemarle,* launched April 18, 1864, with forges and workmen aboard to complete her armor. The following day she sank the U.S.S. *Southfield.*

tured Plymouth, North Carolina. Aided by the powerful new ram *Albemarle* (which sank the U.S.S. *Southfield* and damaged another gunboat), Hoke's men took the town on April 19, along with 2800 Yankee prisoners and vast amounts of supplies, thereby raising Rebel morale. **718** So fearsome was the *Albemarle* that a special attack was made to sink it. Commander William B. Cushing, U.S.N., copied Rebel torpedo boat tactics by getting two steam barges fitted with spar torpedoes, or rams. On the black and foggy night of October 27, 1864, he and seven others exploded one barge close enough to sink the *Albemarle*. Without the ram's protection, Plymouth was recaptured by the Yankees on October 31.

719 The Nebraska Territory was admitted to the Union on April 19, 1864.

720 In Richmond, uncertainty greeted

the approach of a new campaign season in April. A newspaper, the *Examiner,* wrote that "so far, we feel sure of the issue. All else is mystery . . . Where the first blow will fall, when the two armies of Northern Virginia will meet face to face; how Grant will try to hold his own against the master spirit of Lee, we cannot even surmise."

721 **A tragedy struck the Davis family on April 30, 1864.** Their five-year-old son, Joe, fell off the verandah of the Confederate White House and died. Each of the Presidents had lost a son.

FIGHTING IN THE EASTERN THEATER

Finally the skirmishing and quarreling on the peripheries shrank, and attention focused on Grant and Lee, on their armies, and on the campaign of 1864.

722 **Grant's "crusher" strategy called for multiple points of pressure on the Rebels to deny them the advantage of inner lines.** His campaign began with an order to General George G. Meade on May 3: the Army of the Potomac, counting some 122,000 men, would turn Lee's right, and head, one more time, for Richmond. General Ben Butler's Army of the James would move up that river against Richmond.

723 Sherman, with 98,000 men, would attack Joe Johnston's Army of Tennessee, which had 60,000, and prevent detachments to Lee.

724 **Fighting erupted in the Wilderness on Thursday, May 5, 1864.** Lee's army, 66,000 men strong, engaged a large portion of Meade's army in heavy but indecisive fighting; then both armies entrenched for the night. Bloody engagements continued on May 6, with slight advantage to Lee. "Lee to the rear," his troops called, as Lee's emotions led him toward the front. Heavy casualties continued to mark Grant's grinding war: of some 100,000 Yankees, 17,666 were killed, wounded, or missing. Lee lost 7500.

725 **Butler's 30,000 men landed on the south side of the James River,** near Bermuda Hundred, on the same day, May 6, and inched toward Petersburg, but the venture came to nothing. Butler's force, which probably could have taken Petersburg and threatened Lee from two sides, was at first opposed by only 2700 old men and boys under General Beauregard, who quickly gathered reinforcements. Butler advanced and retreated several times during the next two weeks; but ineptitude dogged his campaign, and General Beauregard at last launched 18,000 hastily gathered Grays against Butler's 16,000 men at Drewry's Bluff on May 16 and shook the Union right. There were 4160 Union casualties and 2506 Confederate losses. Confusion and uncertainty made Butler retreat to Bermuda Hundred Neck, where the Rebels bottled him up for months.

726 Fighting focused at Spotsylvania Court House from May 8 to 21, with Grant trying to turn Lee's right and running against entrenched positions. Lee's army was hurt by the loss of two veteran corps commanders—Longstreet to wounds and A. P. Hill to temporary illness. Still, the Rebel defenses held in fierce fighting on May 8. Grant's army lost a fine corps commander on May 9—Major General John Sedgwick. Both sides adjusted their lines during most of that day. Heavy Union attacks on May 10 gained little, but Grant struck an exposed Confederate salient called the Muleshoe on May 12. General Winfield Scott Hancock's corps

Spotsylvania Court House, with village pump in foreground.

hit the Muleshoe at 4:30 A.M., drove into General Richard Stoddert Ewell's men, and took almost 4000 prisoners, including two generals. Ewell's line held, but other Union attacks continued long into the night at the **727** Bloody Angle. Again during that day, "Lee to the rear" was heard close to the front. Grant lost nearly 7000 men to Lee's 5000.

Although many Northerners were calling Grant a butcher as his grinding continued, he tried to divert some of Lee's limited strength from the Wilderness. **728** Cavalry under General Philip Sheridan approached Richmond from the east along the Chickhominy River, and another force struck at the vital Richmond and Danville Railroad. Butler tried to break out of the Bermuda Hundred snare, but succeeded only in worrying President Davis about the capital's safety. **729** At Yellow Tavern, some five miles north of Richmond, on May 11, Sheridan encountered General Jeb Stuart's cavalry, and, in hard fighting, Stuart was mortally wounded. Richmond was saved; Stuart died on May 12. The Confederacy's great Paladin was gone.

Grant, instead of retreating after his failure to break Lee's front at Spotsylvania, moved by his left to the south and east of Lee's army. **730** Convinced that constant pressure on all Rebel forces was the key to victory, Grant sent a force of 7000 men, under the overrated General Franz Sigel, into the Shenandoah Valley. Opposition built against Sigel, and on May 15, 1864, he met General John C. Breckinridge's Confederates. Two hundred forty-seven young cadets from the Virginia Military Institute formed part of the army, and they fought heroically at **731** New Market, Virginia. Ten cadets were killed and forty-seven wounded in the victorious action. (Sigel had 800 casualties among his 5500 men, and Breckinridge lost 550 of his 5000). For a moment, Lee's Shenandoah granary was safe. Every year, on the anniversary of New Market, the roll of fallen cadets is still called at a VMI review. Each time a name is called, a cadet answers, "Killed on the field of honor."

732 General Butler tried to get his army out of the trap in the Bermuda Hundred and into action. But on May 13, his men failed against Beauregard's men at Drewry's Bluff, and on May 16 his muddled efforts could not withstand the Rebels, who attacked and drove him ignominiously back to his old lines. Union losses were over 4000; the Rebels lost about 2000. It was a dismal end to what had promised to be a major blow against Richmond and against Lee's rear.

733 At Spotsylvania on May 18, heavy Union attacks against firm entrenchments were bloodily repulsed. Grant moved again by his left, still trying to turn Lee's right. A reconnaissance by Ewell's Corps confirmed the move, and Lee followed inner lines for interception.

These actions ended the Spotsylvania

Dead Confederate soldiers, members of Ewell's Corps, who fell during attack on Federal lines at Spotsylvania, May 18, 1864.

campaign, which had cost Grant nearly 18,000 men. Combined with the losses in the Wilderness, Grant's indecisive fighting produced more than 30,000 casualties. Confederate losses, although far fewer, could not be replaced.

Despite casualties and indecision, Grant kept moving to his left, skirmishing heavily with Lee's men, sometimes fighting fiercely. By the end of May, his army was north of the Chickahominy River, close to the site of the Seven Days' Battles, almost in sight of the Confederate capital, and moving toward a place called Cold Harbor.

734 One of the bloodiest battles of the war—perhaps of military experience, considering the time involved—raged at Cold Harbor in Virginia on June 3, 1864. Grant's and Meade's men deployed near the old battleground of 1862, only to find

Lee's legions waiting in formidable trenches. Foolishly, Grant ordered an attack—he would later admit his mistake—for 4:30 A.M. Into a freshly drenched, dank woodland, cheering Yankee soldiers charged Lee's daunting defenses. Bluecoats were realists by now, and many had fashioned paper name tags they pinned on their backs so that they would be known when they were hit. When they saw the enemy lines, they remembered that 5000 of them had fallen in the past forty-eight hours. **735** One Union soldier wrote in his diary that night, "June 3. Cold Harbor. I was killed." He was right. In approximately thirty minutes, 7000 Union men were killed or wounded. Confederate lines flamed with a rifle fire so fearsome that Lee heard a sound like "wet sheets tearing in the wind." Fifteen hundred Rebels were killed and wounded between June 4 and 6, at **736** what old war hands called Second Cold Harbor.

737 Charles Francis Adams, Jr., a Union cavalryman, in assessing Grant's campaign after the massacre of June 3, 1864, said that the Army of the Potomac "has literally marched in blood from the Rapidan to the James." But his faith in Grant remained strong.

Despite telling Lee in May that "your dispatches have cheered us in the anxiety of a critical position," President Davis shared his general's anxiety about the enemy advance toward Richmond. Grant had been balked, but he did not retreat. There were problems with the wounded between the lines. **738** Grant wanted to help them, but he did not want to ask for a truce, lest that indicate a Confederate victory. Lee understood this clearly enough and held out; Grant finally accepted a truce.

739 Grant had intended, from the beginning of the summer, to force Lee's smaller army into unequal battle with the Army of the Potomac. Lee's switch from his usual daring to strategic defense foiled Union plans. Now Grant adopted the offensive, to high cost. Ancillary battles had not diverted enough men from Lee nor disrupted his communications. Frustrated by Lee's tactics, Grant continued moving southeastward, closer to Richmond. **740** At last he fooled Lee. To screen his major move south across the James River, Grant moved away from Lee, who did not, for several days, believe that the Federals had left the Cold Harbor sector.

Worried about another invasion of his Shenandoah granary by a force under General David Hunter, 741 Lee, on June 7, detached 2100 men under General John Breckinridge to meet the new threat near Lynchburg. At almost the moment Breckinridge departed, Lee heard of another Union diversion. **742** General Philip Sheridan, with 9000 troops, left Meade's ranks on a raid to wreck railroads and link up with Hunter. Lee ordered General

Wade Hampton's horsemen in pursuit, and a huge and wild cavalry battle followed at 743 Trevilian Station, Virginia, on June 11 to 12, 1864. The Rebels contrived not to lose it, despite their inferior numbers. Sheridan returned to Grant's lines, ending one threat to Lee. Breckinridge had disposed of Sigel at New Market, but when 744 Hunter ravaged the Shenandoah Valley and burned the Virginia Military Institute in Lexington, on June 11, 1864, Breckinridge's small force could not stop him.

To deal with Hunter's growing threat to his communications, Lee detached his Second Corps under General Jubal Early, on June 13, 1864. By June 17, Early joined

Railroad bridge over the North Anna River, Virginia, ruined by Sheridan's raiders.

Ruins of the Virginia Military Institute, burned by Hunter's men, June 11, 1864. Before the war, Stonewall Jackson had taught here.

Breckinridge at Lynchburg and, on June 18, attacked Hunter and drove him westward out of the Shenandoah. General Early pressed northward and reached Lexington on June 24, 1864—his Second Corps had once been **745** Stonewall Jackson's Army of the Valley—and Early led them past their revered general's grave, not far from the Virginia Military Institute. Henry Kyd Douglas, once a member of Jackson's staff, felt the emotion of the visit as some lines of Tennyson came to him:

> *They are here my own, my own;*
> *Were it ever so airy a tread,*
> *My heart would hear them and beat,*
> *Were it earth in an earthy bed:*
> *My dust would hear them and beat*
> *Had I lain for a century dead!*

General Jubal A. Early, whom Lee called "my bad old man" because of his profane and caustic wit.

Although he needed Early's rifles, Lee hoped that if the Second Corps pressed on, it might threaten Washington and divert some of Grant's troops from the Richmond front.

Early was no Jackson, but he had learned from his old leader a sense of urgency and the value of attack. Swiftly, he moved *down* the Shenandoah Valley (the river flows *north*)—sparing the harvest as he went—and as he attacked several small Union units, word of his coming reached Washington.

746 Early invaded the North with scarcely 10,000 infantry and 4000 cavalrymen. Inept Union leadership let Early seize the lower Valley, with its vast stores of supplies, and his rejuvenated Army of the Valley crossed the Potomac on July 5 and 6, 1864.

747 Early took advantage of the Yankee disarray to move against Washington, D.C. Although he did not hope to capture the enemy capital, he thought he might divert enough of Grant's men from Richmond to help Lee. By pushing hard, he forced Grant to send some of his men to reinforce the city's ring of forts. And that gave Early the chance—though it was a small one—to get into Washington, since the city's defenders were few and untried. But at the Monocacy River, near Frederick, Maryland, he ran into stiff resistance.

On the eastern side, barring two main roads toward Washington and Baltimore, Major General Lew Wallace deployed some militia and other ragtag troops—hardly 2000. A big division from Grant's army came to help him, so part of Early's hopes of diverting troops were realized.

748 For all of Saturday, July 9, 1864, Wallace held Early at the Monocacy, and that delay probably spared Washington at least a temporary Rebel capture, which might have won foreign recognition of the Confederacy.

749 Pressing on, Early did get to the outskirts of the capital on July 11. A frightened citizenry prepared to skedaddle; the dollar fell to its lowest value—only

Major General Lew Wallace, C.S.N., later author of *Ben-Hur: A Tale of Christ* and governor of the New Mexico Territory, 1878–1881.

thirty-nine cents—and President and Mrs. Lincoln visited embattled Fort Stevens out on Seventh Street Road and saw some fighting. On the next day, Lincoln again went to Fort Stevens, climbed up on the parapet, and attracted some Rebel snipers. Facing growing odds, Early retreated back across the Potomac.

750 **What about Jubal's Raid?** It failed to capture Washington or to drain enough men from Richmond to relieve Lee. Southern opinion turned against him; so much had been expected, so little achieved. But Early brought Confederate soldiers more boldly into the consciousness of Northerners than they had been; he laid brief siege to the enemy's capital; drew closer to the defenses than Federal forces had yet come to Richmond; paralyzed the Union high command for almost two weeks; brought vast, invaluable stocks of horses, cattle, food, and forage from Maryland; cleared the Shenandoah Valley at harvest time, which fed Lee's men through the winter—and he took a shot at Abraham Lincoln. **751** On July 25, 1864, the London *Times* summed up Early's campaign: "The Confederacy is more formidable as an enemy than ever."

Early stayed in the Valley. **752** Grant decided to oust him and, in August 1864, sent General Philip Sheridan, with some 30,000 men, to do the job. So began the last Valley campaign.

Sheridan and Early skirmished, fought, and maneuvered through the last of the summer, as Rebels crossed and recrossed the Potomac. 753 On the morning of July 30, 1864, some of Early's cavalry, under General John McCausland, occupied Chambersburg, Pennsylvania. McCausland demanded $500,000 in cash or $100,000 in gold as reparation for Hunter's scorching of the valley. The citizens could not raise the money, and the town was burned. 754 On October 19, 1864, Early surprised Sheridan's army at Cedar Creek. Sheridan was in Washington, and his army was under General Horatio Wright. Jubal Early stopped his attack too soon, and Sheridan raced to the field, rallied his men, and counterattacked, achieving a smashing victory. Rebel losses were about 3000 out of a force estimated at 10,000; Yankee losses were 5665 out of 30,000 engaged. Although Early's small force hung on, the Valley was now Yankee territory. 755 At Waynesborough, Virginia, on March 2, 1865, Sheridan's army smashed the fragments of Early's forces, captured most of the men, and rode on toward Charlottesville. Early escaped, scorched by "the mortification of seeing the greater part of my command being carried off as prisoners," and the Army of the Valley disappeared.

756 **General Pierre Gustave Toutant Beauregard had uncommon battle sense.** Flamboyant, yes, boastful sometimes, a reckless strategist, he was at his best in battle. On June 15, 1864, he met his fiercest test at Petersburg, Virginia. That day his 3000 men faced the coming of the Army of the Potomac, which had threatened Richmond for days and pinned down Lee's army north of the James River. Beauregard knew the fullness of the threat and asked for help against the 16,000-man van of Meade's full force. As one historian noted, "On this day Petersburg, the back door to Richmond, might well have fallen." That it did not fall is the result of a collection of Union errors in logistics, geography, confused orders, and general bedlam, as well as Beauregard's heroic defense. When Beauregard again called for help, Lee vacillated. 757 Lincoln telegraphed Grant a vision: "I begin to see it. You will succeed. God bless you all."

758 Jefferson Davis had warned Lee that "Grant, despairing of a direct attack, is now seeking to embarrass you by flank movements."

759 Stripping all parts of his front to the bone, Beauregard had collected almost 14,000 men by June 16, the day that most of Meade's army arrived. The hard-fighting Confederates lost a redan and some trenches that day, and took up shorter lines around Petersburg. Lee, at last convinced of Grant's movements, the next day sent two corps to Beauregard, who held on and even counterattacked.

760 The Siege of Petersburg really began on June 18, 1864. Beauregard's growing force repulsed two Union attacks that day, and both sides settled into digging trenches. Beauregard's tough stands had cost about 8000 Union casualties during

Fort Sedgwick, called "Fort Hell," from which Grant's soldiers besieged Petersburg.

his isolated four days. Confederate losses are unknown. This much was clear: Lee would hold his lines with about 60,000 Grayclads against Grant's 110,000 Bluecoats in a seesaw ditch and artillery war—that was to last for eleven months.

761 Lee dreaded a siege—it denied him mobility and the chance to detach troops to other armies. The Petersburg siege marked the success of the eastern phase of Grant's "crusher" strategy: to pin Rebel armies into campaigns of attrition they could not win.

762 Meade's Army of the Potomac tried several direct assaults on Lee's trench-lines, was repulsed each time, and finally settled into a slow extension of the siege westward, along the Appomattox River.

The elongation of the line stretched Rebel defenders thin. **763** Although efforts were made to cut the Petersburg and Weldon Railroad and other arteries into the Confederate capital, Lee's men clung grimly to their lines. The trenches developed in engineering ingenuity and complexity; they presaged those in France during World War I. Sometimes there were local actions, as at the Crater in July 1864, but mostly the lines grew stronger and deadlier—and those who manned them became more anxious. **764** All this time, the artillery dueling grew into a staccato overtone of war. The Confederate Ordnance Chief, General Gorgas, noted, of the recent fighting, "an apparent nervousness on the part of our men and of the enemy, causing an unusual rapidity of fire . . . The expenditure of Artillery ammunition, especially of Napoleon[s], has been very great."

765 The sniping, bombardments, and raiding took a daily toll of men, equipment, and supplies. Union losses were replaced; Confederate losses accumulated.

766 **Grant tried a two-pronged direct attack on Lee's lines in September 1864.** In an attempt to cut off Rebel reinforcements to the Valley and also to encircle Richmond, elements of the Army of the Potomac stormed Fort Harrison, north of the James River, on September 29, took it, but failed to breach Richmond's defenses. Both Lee and Grant were in command during the battle. On the next day, a worried Lee ordered a strong counterattack at Fort Harrison. It failed.

767 At Peeble's Farm, southwest of Petersburg, a strong Union effort to break the Weldon and South Side Railroads began on September 29, 1864, and raged for almost five days. This stretching of Rebel lines heavily stressed the defenders. Although they did at last contain the Yankee drive from Peeble's Farm to Poplar Spring Church at the Squirrel Level Road, the Confederates were forced to shift troops quickly from point to point. They knew that if the Union forces continued to move westward along the Appomattox, Lee's numbers would fail.

768 Aware that Lee's numbers limited Confederate options, Grant tried another major extension of the lines southwest of

Petersburg. Probes at Hatcher's Run on October 27, 1864, failed to take the South Side Railroad, and the Yankee effort cost more than 1500 men.

769 A Union diversion at about the same time attacked Rebel positions north of the James River near the old battlefield of Fair Oaks (Seven Pines). Simultaneous Federal probes on the Petersburg front failed, and winter halted the main operations.

770 **During Virginia's fiercest winter of the war,** Lee's remaining 45,000 men held about thirty-five miles of entrenchments, running from the Williamsburg Road to Hatcher's Run. Odds were worsening for the Rebels; the Yankees in the Richmond theater outnumbered them by more than two to one.

771 He was never an alarmist, yet Lee told President Davis, in the last months of 1864, that without reinforcements he felt "a great calamity will befall us."

772 **The South took some comfort from noting that the new Northern bounty soldiers and substitutes showed poor morale.** In close fighting, they tended to surrender quickly, which both Meade and Grant noticed. Although attention fastened on the stressed Rebels, their Yankee enemies were also suffering attrition and stress. Lincoln could, and did, call out more men, but the terrible killing rankled the Union. Grant called Sheridan's troopers from the ravaged Valley, along with the veteran 6th Corps, to bolster Federal hitting power.

773 **When spring arrived, in 1865, campaigning began again.** Prospects were far dimmer than before for the South, but Lee clung grimly to his ditches around Petersburg. Sherman's march into the Carolinas met only a trickle of resistance. The Shenandoah Valley was virtually a Union camp now, and Confederate efforts to hold the coastline wobbled.

774 Aware that he was unlikely to get reinforcements, Lee took a desperate gamble. In an attempt to free his army from a siege, to break out and join Johnston in North Carolina, Lee ordered General John B. Gordon to attack the Union right, east of Petersburg. He would strike Fort Stedman and break through to hit Federal communications at City Point. Success might force Grant to pull his lines in,

which would give Lee's men a chance to move southwest, toward North Carolina. This last offensive of the Army of Northern Virginia was carefully planned. At 4 A.M. on March 25, 1865, Gordon's big attack jumped off and stormed into the fort, swept defenders aside, and soon controlled nearly a mile of enemy works. Small probes moved toward City Point, but they were soon pinched off. By 8 A.M., Gordon's attack had failed, at a cost of 5000 men. President Lincoln, along with General Grant, watched the attack. Lee watched, too, bitterly disappointed.

775 **Lee had been preparing an evacuation of Richmond whenever he could arrange it, but now the enemy dictated the timing.** Grant's men pushed hard on

Richmond in ruins, occupied by the Federals.

Lee's right in a general movement of the Army of the Potomac. On March 29, 1865, Lee sent Generals George Pickett and Fitzhugh Lee to the Five Forks area to hold the flank, but the move thinned Lee's ranks in front of Petersburg almost to skirmish lines, leaving only 12,000 Rebels against 50,000 Bluecoats. Lee issued peremptory orders to Pickett: "Hold Five Forks at all hazards."

On that position hung Lee's last escape route. On April 1, as fighting flickered along the lines, Lee advised President Davis that preparations should be made to evacuate Petersburg and Richmond. Later that day, a major Federal attack on Five Forks crushed Pickett's men. (Pickett himself was absent from the field, attending a shad bake, and Lee was so infuriated that he relieved Pickett of command.) Lee's army was nearly cut off; on Sunday, April 2, he telegraphed President Davis that Richmond should be evacuated that night. By midafternoon the retreat toward Amelia Court House began. On April 3, Union troops entered Richmond and Petersburg while President Davis, with some officials and records, were escaping by train toward Danville, Virginia.

776 For a long, agonizing week the Army of Northern Virginia retreated and clung together. Misfortune dogged the march as the Bluecoats got between Lee and Johnston. Supplies failed to arrive at Amelia Court House, and a nearly starving army trudged on while stragglers grew

in number. On April 6, a major fight took place at Sayler's Creek when elements of Lee's army got separated from one another, and by day's end 8000 Rebels had surrendered—almost a third of Lee's strength. On Friday, April 7, Grant opened correspondence with Lee, suggesting the surrender of his army. Lee demurred but asked to hear Grant's terms. Grant said that surrendered troops could not take up arms again until exchanged. As the Federals closed in around the Confederates, and Lee's options narrowed, some of his generals urged surrender.

777 Palm Sunday, April 9, 1865, began ominously for the Rebels. General Gordon tried to open a road to Lynchburg but ran into Blue masses. When he reported this to Lee, his commander said, solemnly, "Then there is nothing left for me to do but to go and see General Grant, and I would rather die a thousand deaths!" The soldiers could see their general's sorrow and nearly mobbed him in anguish. He had brushed aside one general's suggestion of dispersing the army as partisans with the calm assertion that his men would be reduced to marauders and would disgrace the South. So he went up to Appomattox Court House and waited for Grant.

They met in the parlor of the McLean House. The meeting was amiable, with old army reminiscences starting it off, and then proceeded to business. Officers and men would be paroled, Grant said, after they surrendered their arms, ammunition, and

Appomattox Court House, April 9, 1865.

supplies. As the terms were being written out, Lee mentioned that his men owned their horses. Could they keep them? Grant conceded at once, and a grateful Lee said that the agreement "will do much toward conciliating our people." Both men signed the terms, Lee arose, shook hands with Grant, and walked out.

Back among his weeping men, Lee urged them to be as good citizens as they had been soldiers. He expressed his admiration for them in his eloquent General Order No. 9, on April 10, and then went back to Richmond. For all intents and purposes the war was over, although Johnston's army and other Southern scatterings remained in the field until late May 1865.

778 The house where the surrender took place belonged to one of the most war-bedeviled individuals in America. Wilmer McLean owned the house near Manassas that had been used by General Beauregard as temporary headquarters at First Manassas. After that battle, McLean moved his family to the less violent surroundings of Appomattox Court House, Virginia. Once Lee and Grant had used the house to arrange surrender terms, most of the furnishings were "purchased" or "expropriated" by those who witnessed the end of the Civil War. The U.S. government rebuilt the house in 1948 according to exact early drawings, some of the furnishings were returned by families who found them among their treasures, and some were replicated.

The Election of 1864

779 The National Union Convention opened in Baltimore on June 7, 1864. Its purpose was to nominate a presidential candidate. Republicans dominated the convention, even though some War Democrats appeared. Lincoln remained the favorite, despite Radical opposition. Wisely, he left the choice of vice presidential candidate to the delegates. Hannibal Hamlin, dumped as vice president, worked loyally for Lincoln and for his own successor as the President maneuvered to contain radicalism and keep to the center.

For Lincoln, the convention came at an odd time and amid confusing events. **780** Radicalism haunted the president. Well he knew that an important segment of his party wanted harder war and harder policies for peace, but he knew, too, that generosity would make peace easier to achieve. He had to hold together both ends of the party. Leaving the vice presidential nomination to the convention proved a stroke of genius. Once Andrew Johnson, a Tennessee War Democrat, was selected, both hard-war advocates and peace Democrats took solace. War had pulled the Republicans toward the center. **781** But the opposition, rallying around General John C. Frémont, formed a party called the Radical Democracy. Frémont

had been the Republican candidate in 1856 and the darling of the militant anti-slavery element since his 1861 emancipation proclamation. He also enjoyed some support from German-Americans and from die-hard Salmon Chase people. Frémonters pushed a radical platform urging confiscation of Rebel land, amendments guaranteeing "all men absolute equality before the law," a one-term presidency, and abolition of the electoral college. No prominent Republicans endorsed Frémont, but **782** Susan B. Anthony and Elizabeth Cady Stanton, leaders of the women's movement, joined him. Frémont's support finally dwindled. The only item from his platform to be incorporated into the final Republican platform was the Antislavery Amendment.

Part of Frémont's failure was a matter of appearances. Republicans said that conniving Democrats were trying to infiltrate his movement. **783** Since Copperheads were spoken of as part of the Radical Democracy, some Republicans who might have joined Frémont were alienated. Even abolitionists moved to the right to save their power in the Union.

The Democrats had high hopes for the 1864 election; the war seemed stagnant, and Lincoln's popularity had dwindled in the Wilderness and in the reaches of Georgia. Northerners were tired of stringent government regulation, tired of war. For the disillusioned, there was an obvious candidate. **784** General George B.

McClellan, an old-line Democrat, a renowned leader of Union armies, met all the requirements. He was a national figure whose candidacy would strengthen the notion of Democrats being in favor of the war. It was thought that Little Mac's personal charm would wear well on the hustings. Then, too, his candidacy would symbolize the conservatism of a time before Lincoln, before his war had brutalized the Union. Like Frémont's party, the Democrats were divided into war and peace factions. George Pendleton of Ohio was chosen as vice presidential candidate, and the convention adopted a platform critical of emancipation and dictatorial government; it demanded that "immediate efforts be made for a cessation of hostilities." McClellan somehow had to tie together a party separated over peace. In his acceptance speech he said the Union "must be preserved at all hazards." This almost sundered his party, but, like the Republicans, it came together and moved toward the center.

As it worked out, the 785 1864 election resolved many problems. Frémont resigned from the campaign in September and gave his support to Lincoln. Sherman conquered Atlanta on September 2, and the war brightened. 786 Lincoln squarely met the issue of Reconstruction in July 1864, when he pocket-vetoed the plan Congressman Henry Winter Davis and Senator Ben Wade had offered in February. These Radicals, though they agreed with much of Lincoln's so-called 10 percent plan for readmitting Rebel states, wanted 50 percent of each state's citizens to take an oath of loyalty. They also wanted protection for the freedmen. Lincoln's veto rested on his determination to keep Reconstruction policy in his own hands, and most Republicans agreed. In August, his veto gave rise to the Wade-Davis Manifesto and rallied some Radical support, but this opposition collapsed when evidence of Copperhead influence was dis-

Major General George B. McClellan (of whom Meade said, "Had there been no McClellan, there could have been no Grant") and his wife.

closed. Lincoln mended fences with the Radicals.

787 Obviously concerned about the election, Lincoln asked General Sherman to furlough his Indiana soldiers so that they could vote. Indiana had no provision for voting in the field, and the state was crucial to the Republicans.

788 On September 13, Lincoln asked Postmaster General Montgomery Blair to resign; this was a concession to the Radicals, who had long disliked Blair.

789 Lincoln won the election on November 8, 1864, with 2,330,552 votes to McClellan's 1,835,985 and an Electoral College avalanche of 212 to 21. His coattails swept in heavy congressional and gubernatorial majorities and won control of most state legislatures. Lincoln, who had feared he would lose, now had a Union mandate.

The Strength of the Union could be seen not only in its ability to hold wartime elections, but also in its westward expansion. **790** On May 26, 1864, the Montana Territory was carved out of the Dakota Territory.

FIGHTING IN THE CRUCIAL CENTER

791 Sherman's three armies, totaling about 100,000 men and representing the main western sweep of Grant's "crusher" strategy, advanced against Joe Johnston's 60,000 entrenched Rebels near Dalton, Georgia, on May 7, 1864. General James B. McPherson, leading the Army of the Tennessee, tried turning Johnston's left flank toward Atlanta, but he halted at Snake Creek Gap on May 9, much to Sherman's irritation. He concentrated on his right flank, however, trying to exploit easier terrain.

792 Johnston evacuated Dalton on the night of May 12. He guessed correctly where Sherman was headed, and put his men in front of Sherman at Resaca, Georgia, the next day. Reinforced by a new corps under General Leonidas Polk, Johnston held strong lines. Sherman wanted to take Resaca, but his advance was delayed. General John B. Hood's Confederate corps engaged General Joseph Hooker's corps in heavy fighting on Sunday, May 15, 1864, with Hooker getting the best of it. **793** Johnston again avoided being outflanked by retiring from Resaca on the night of May 15, burning the Oostenaula River bridge as he pulled out, and falling back toward Adairsville.

794 With General George Thomas's Army of the Cumberland in front and Schofield's and McPherson's armies on his flanks, Johnston pulled back toward Cassville and Kingston on the night of May 17. President Davis complained of the retreats; they hurt morale. But Johnston's delaying tactics had yielded ground, not victory, and had saved his army. At last he found a place from which to launch an

General William Tecumseh Sherman (leaning on the gun's breach) and his staff toward the end of the war.

attack. 795 With Sherman's armies separated, Johnston ordered action on May 19. General John Bell Hood's corps would start. In one of the great lapses of the campaign, Hood—whose motives may be suspect, since he wanted Johnston's command—conjured up visions of enemies on his flank and, instead of attacking, retreated. By evening, Generals Hood and Polk advised withdrawal from the exposed positions; Johnston's Third Corps commander, General William J. Hardee, advised staying put. Johnston, angry, reluctantly retired across the Etowah River on May 20, 1864.

796 Clearly, trouble still dogged the high command of the Army of Tennessee. The question was whether Joseph E. Johnston was tough enough to dominate a group of prima donnas. Or it may have been that Johnston felt that President Davis might not support him if he relieved any of the corps commanders; after all, the Bragg precedent was cause for worry.

While the fighting ebbed at Spotsylvania, Johnston took a strong position at Allatoona Pass on the Western and Atlantic Railroad and forced Sherman to face him. 797 Lincoln, on May 21, 1864, asked the governors of the Western states to hurry troops to Sherman because of his "lengthening lines."

Confederate entrenchments at New Hope Church, Georgia.

Sherman maneuvered again by Johnston's left, trying to get between him and Atlanta. Johnston fell back, on May 24, toward New Hope Church and Dallas, barely twenty-five miles from Atlanta, again causing worry to beleaguered President Davis. **798** On May 25, Johnston's men repulsed several attacks around New Hope with heavy casualties on both sides. That action briefly checked Sherman's advance.

799 By the end of May, Sherman and Johnston had each lost about 9000 men in the Georgia fighting. Johnston conducted one of history's great retreats; preserved his army in fine condition; retired on his Atlanta base; stretched Sherman's supply lines (250 miles to Nashville and 90 to Chattanooga); and fought where he had a chance for success. He planned a further fight from the dominating ground at Kennesaw Mountain.

800 Johnston also sought to disrupt Sherman's advance by sending Forrest's cavalry against Union supply lines. A Federal column under General S. D. Sturgis set out from Memphis to catch "that devil Forrest."

801 On Friday, June 10, 1864, Forrest won probably his most brilliant victory at Brice's Cross Roads (also called Guntown and Tishomingo Creek), Mississippi. Taking advantage of the weather and road conditions, temperature, enemy dispositions, and ground, Forrest forced Sturgis to race his infantry forward in deadly heat, over muddy roads, and into a trap of Confederate brigades spread in an arc at the Cross Roads. Sturgis was badly beaten, and his disorganized troops struggled back toward Memphis with Forrest harassing them all the way. Union losses were 2240 of 8000 engaged; Forrest lost fewer than 500 of his 3500 men.

802 **Sherman should have avoided attacking Big and Little Kennesaw,** but, like Grant at Cold Harbor, frustration drove him to a frontal assault. The drive, made against Johnston's careful entrenchments on a searingly hot Monday, June 27, 1864, stalled quickly. Many of the attackers fainted from the heat; clumps of men reached close to Rebel lines; most fell far down the slopes. The woods caught fire; some of the wounded were burned; and Sherman lost his biggest gamble of the campaign and more than 2000 men. Johnston lost perhaps 500 and held his lines. Sherman, though, made a flank move closer to Atlanta, and Johnston took up position near Marietta, Georgia.

803 Georgia Governor Joseph E. Brown, who kept a constant eye to state rights, almost panicked and demanded assurances from President Davis that he would stop Sherman. Davis, on June 29,

Federal entrenchments at the foot of Kennesaw Mountain, Georgia.

1864, answered that he had sent troops to reinforce the Army of Tennessee from "points that remain exposed to the enemy." He had done what he could.

804 Governor Brown's request was a symptom of the growing dissatisfaction in Georgia. Johnston's retreat may have been masterly, but it abandoned much territory. Was "Retreating Joe" Johnston the man to stop Sherman? Davis wondered, too.

805 **Johnston had little regard for territory—only for armies.** And his remained intact. Still, he should have appreciated the political problems facing the administration. But he kept watching Sherman, and as the Federals got closer to Atlanta, Johnston once more fell back—this time to the Chattahoochee River.

806 General John Schofield's army, one of those in Sherman's command, slipped across the Chattahoochee around Johnston's right flank and forced the Rebels to cross the river.

807 On the night of Saturday, July 9, Johnston's army crossed into the carefully prepared Atlanta defenses. That day, President Davis sent General Braxton Bragg to Georgia for consultation with Johnston—an unlikely messenger, since Bragg wanted Johnston's job and Johnston knew it. Bragg's reports were negative, but Johnston continued his careful planning to hit Sherman while his different corps were separated from one another as they shifted around Atlanta's defenses.

808 President Jefferson Davis's patience thinned, and on July 17, 1864, he replaced Johnston with General John Bell Hood. Although Davis disliked Johnston, the decision was still a difficult one. Changing generals in the middle of a campaign was dangerous—a point made by Lee—but public pressure forced the change. Some questioned whether Hood was the right man to replace Johnston. Sherman greeted the change with jubilation.

809 **Hood understood what Davis wanted and, possibly using one of Johnston's plans, attacked Sherman's divided armies along Peachtree Creek on July 20.** Delays, however, blunted his desperate attacks against General G. H. Thomas's Army of the Cumberland, and when fighting dwindled, about 1800 Federals were casualties, out of 20,000 engaged. Confederates, with about the same number engaged, lost nearly 4800 men. Hood shamefully tried to shift blame to Corps Commander William J. Hardee.

810 On July 22, Hood launched his main battle for Atlanta. This time his purpose was to outflank General James McPherson's Army of the Tennessee between Decatur and Atlanta. But chance had it that Union reinforcements were at the threatened point, and once again desperate fighting accomplished little. Confederate Major General W. H. T. Walker fell, as did Federal Major General McPher-

Federal graves at Peachtree Creek, where Hood's men hit.

son—along with some 3800 Yankees of the 30,000 fighting, and 7000 to 10,000 Rebels of the 40,000 engaged.

811 A vicious fight at Ezra Church, on July 28, ended in another Rebel repulse, with up to 5000 lost against 600 Federals lost. Hood's fights were ruining his army, and Atlanta lay under siege. Sherman slowly extended his lines southwest around Atlanta throughout July and early August as he sought to cut the city's rail communications.

812 Hood tried to cut Sherman's extended supply line by sending General "Fighting Joe" Wheeler's cavalry on a raid into north Georgia and east Tennessee. It lasted from the middle of August to September 9, 1864. Wheeler cut rail lines, damaged bridges, but did not stop Yankee supplies.

813 "That Devil Forrest" also launched

Confederate defenses in Atlanta, the palisades and chevaux-de-frise constructed by Johnston's men at the head of Marietta Street.

a raid on Sherman's communications on September 6, 1864. He struck into north-

ern Alabama and middle Tennessee and kept at it until the middle of October.

814 **"Fairly won," boasted Sherman on September 2, 1864, as he told President Lincoln of Atlanta's capture.** Hood had failed to prevent the loss of his rail lines and, though he sometimes outnumbered Federals on the field, he had failed to defeat Sherman. Nor had he preserved the strength of his army. He began evacuating Atlanta, a huge prize, on September 1. Because of poor planning, the Rebels were forced to destroy vast stores of munitions and other supplies.

815 **Hood pulled his battered army back to Lovejoy's Station, between Atlanta and Macon.** There, he sought to recruit and refit. He also quarreled with

Sherman's men uprooting the railroad before leaving Atlanta.

subordinates who had let him down and—he claimed—brought defeat. **816** President Davis visited Hood's headquarters at Palmetto on September 25, 1864, and approved a plan to recoup Confederate fortunes. On October 1, Hood swung around Atlanta to hit Sherman's supply lines and move into Tennessee. The purpose of the campaign was to lure the Yankees out of Georgia. Worried, Sherman detached forces to counter Hood, but he finally left the Rebel army to the mercies of the Rock of Chickamauga, General George H. Thomas, sent to hold Tennessee.

817 **Trying to sustain the Army of Tennessee,** Jefferson Davis revived his theater command idea and put General P. G. T. Beauregard in overall charge of the Military Division of the West—all the land east of the Mississippi in the western region, including Hood's and General Richard Taylor's forces. The Great Creole took command on October 17 and found himself enmeshed in Hood's logistical arrangements for the Tennessee venture.

818 Although Hood's Tennessee strategy was sound, his estimate of Sherman's reaction was faulty and his tactics terrible. Instead of crossing into Tennessee, Hood dawdled in Alabama for supplies, road repairs, and reinforcements. When, on November 21, 1864, he did at last cross into Tennessee, aided by Forrest's cavalry, he moved in with 30,000 infantry and

Savannah waterfront, 1865.

8000 cavalry. He still hoped to pull Sherman back from Georgia.

819 Hood lost his gamble. On November 16, 1864, Sherman left Atlanta a burned-out shell and began his March to the Sea. Cutting all communications behind him, Sherman determined to have his 60,000 infantry and nearly 6000 artillerymen live off the country—which they did. His "bummers" (zealous foragers) burned, pillaged, and degraded young and old. Sherman's orders: "The army will forage liberally on the country during the march." Any resistance was to be met with "a devastation more or less relentless."

820 On December 22, 1864, the general telegraphed President Lincoln: "I beg to present you, as a Christmas gift, the city of Savannah." Sherman had reached the sea and the Union Navy.

821 President Davis, still hopeful despite Sherman's invasion, tried to shore up the Rebel resistance. To the newly convened second session of the Second Confederate Congress he said that "there are no vital points on the preservation of which the continued existence of the Confederacy depends," and he urged General Hood on that same day, November 7, 1864, to defeat scattered parts of Sherman's army and advance to the Ohio River.

822 Hood pushed on, in growing frustration at bad weather and vexing delays, against Union forces under General John

M. Schofield. Trying to flank Schofield's 30,000-man force, Hood missed an opportunity to cut some of them off at Spring Hill, Tennessee, on the night of November 28–29, 1864. Schofield managed to sneak his whole force past Hood's army and escape toward Franklin. How so large a blunder happened still intrigues historians. Apparently Hood had received some word of Schofield's passage, but did little to stop it.

823 Furious at his own blunder, Hood, in typical behavior, blamed subordinates and conceived the outrageous notion that his army would not fight. He therefore committed the greatest error of his life. On November 30, he foolishly ordered a frontal attack on Schofield's army at Franklin, Tennessee. At about four in the afternoon his army charged heavy Union works at the southern edge of town. So strong were the works, so obvious, that legend says General Patrick Cleburne threatened to kill Hood if he (Cleburne) survived the attack. Cleburne was killed in the bloodbath that cost Hood almost a quarter of his 25,000 men. Schofield lost about 10 percent of his 22,000 men.

824 Six Confederate generals fell during the battle of Franklin. In addition to Cleburne, those killed were John Adams, States Rights Gist, Hiram B. Granbury, and Otho F. Strahl; John C. Carter was fatally wounded.

825 With his desperately depleted army, Hood tried to besiege General G. H.

Hillside spectators watching Hood's Confederates attack the Federals under Thomas's command in Nashville, December 1864.

Thomas's army of nearly 50,000 at Nashville. Fearing that Hood might elude Thomas and somehow reach the Ohio, Grant ordered Thomas to attack. Delays and bad weather held Thomas back, but he did attack on December 15 and 16, 1864. In the Battle of Nashville, Thomas wrecked the Army of Tennessee. Hood lost 4500 prisoners and 1500 casualties out of his thin 30,000. His army was not annihilated, but it never got the reinforcements to rebuild. Nashville marked the last big battle in the Central Theater of War. Hood resigned on January 13, 1865, and a dejected President Davis turned the remnants of the Army of Tennessee over to General Richard Taylor.

826 General Joseph E. Johnston took over the shreds of Hood's army in February 1865 and led it to a small tinge of glory at the Battle of Bentonville, North Carolina, in March. Johnston surrendered the fragments to Sherman on April 26, 1865, at Dunham Station, North Carolina.

THE PRESIDENTS AND THE END

After Richmond's fall, the South began unraveling. Bits and pieces had sloughed away in late 1864. With the capital gone, fragmentation accelerated.

Richmond, fallen capital of the Confederacy, with the ruined armory in the foreground.

827 **It was Sunday, April 2, 1865. Many Richmonders were in church. As President Davis listened that bright morning to the Reverend Dr. Charles Minnegerode's sermon at St. Paul's, a messenger came to him and escorted him outside.** General Lee's lines had been broken; the city had to be evacuated by nightfall. A kind of controlled frenzy took over the city as offices were packed, the small gold reserve put under guard, people win-

nowed for those who were allowed to go, rail cars collected, and eyes cast toward the smoke coming from the Ordnance Works and frothing over Petersburg. The last train left after dark, and the President went toward a temporary capital at Danville.

828 **Davis could not keep the Cabinet together.** Those who wanted to find their families, he allowed to leave. He had a small cavalry guard for himself and the tiny bullion supply, and he refused to give up. A vision came at this, the ruin of his life: a forlorn vision of a renewed struggle in the Trans-Mississippi that would at last bring independence. With the eloquence of anguish, he wrote his last and best state paper:

Danville, Va., April 4, 1865

To the People of the Confederate States of America

The General-in-Chief of our Army has found it necessary to make such movements of the troops as to uncover the Capital, and thus involve the withdrawal of the Government from the city of Richmond.

It would be unwise, even if it were possible, to conceal the great moral, as well as material injury to our cause that must result from the occupation of Richmond by the enemy. It is equally unwise and unworthy of us, as patriots engaged in a most sacred cause, to allow our energies to falter, our spirits to grow faint, or our efforts to become relaxed, under reverses however calamitous . . . Let us not then despond, my countrymen, but, relying on the never-failing mercies and protecting care of our God, let us meet the foe with fresh defiance, with unconquered and unconquerable hearts.

829 Jefferson Davis was captured on May 10, 1865, at Irwinville, Georgia,

Jefferson Davis as Federal prisoner, passing through Macon, Georgia, in an ambulance.

along with his wife, Postmaster General John Reagan, presidential secretary Burton Harrison, and a few others. Apparently he had put one of his wife's shawls over his raincoat and was said to be trying to escape in a woman's dress—a final ignominy. He was to spend two years in Federal solitary confinement, until May 1867, and that would win him, at last, a mite of martyrdom. In Washington, Georgia, the captured President was seen by a young future President, Woodrow Wilson.

830 **On April 10, 1865, with news of Lee's surrender cheering the whole North, President Lincoln asked a band to play "Dixie."** It was "one of the best tunes I have ever heard," he said, and had been fairly won. He had gone to Richmond on April 4, visited Davis's White House, and apparently called at General Pickett's house to inquire about his old friend. Crowds of jubilant blacks followed the President. In response to General Godfrey Weitzel's question about how to handle the conquered Southerners, Lincoln said, "If I were in your place, I'd let 'em up easy—let 'em up easy." Lincoln returned to Washington just as the city erupted with joy at the news of Lee's surrender. He began to think seriously about Reconstruction.

831 **General Dabney H. Maury, after a long and gallant defense,** abandoned Mobile, Alabama, the last major Confederate city, on April 12, 1865. With his garrison reduced to virtually nothing, Maury removed what he could and burned the remaining cotton.

832 **In victory's happy wake, Lincoln met with his Cabinet on Good Friday, April 14, 1865.** Serious issues were discussed, including what to do with Rebel leaders. The President spoke of his old dream about him on a ship sailing "toward a dark and indefinite shore." That evening the Lincolns went to Ford's Theatre to see the highly regarded actor John Wilkes Booth in a light comedy called *Our American Cousin*.

833 Booth had long-standing Southern sympathies and hated Abraham Lincoln. At a moment when he was offstage, Booth slipped into the Lincolns' box and shot the President in the back of the head. Jumping to the stage, he yelled, *"Sic semper tyrannis."* Booth escaped, despite a broken leg, but was found and killed near Port Royal, Virginia, on April 26, 1865.

834 President Lincoln died at 7:22 A.M. on April 15, 1865. Edwin Stanton said, "Now he belongs to the ages." Vice President Andrew Johnson became the seventeenth President of the United States. The North and much of the South went into mourning. Lincoln's body lay in state briefly and on April 21 was put aboard a train for his last trip to Springfield. Thousands lined the rails and wept in an outpouring of grief. In New York City a sobbing Walt Whitman watched and then wrote:

Ford's Theatre, Washington, D.C., where Lincoln was shot.

Catafalque bearing coffin of Abraham Lincoln, sixteenth President of the United States.

*O Captain! My Captain! our fearful trip
is done,
The ship has weathered every rack, the
prize we sought is won,
The port is near, the bells I hear, the
people all exulting,
While follow eyes the steady keel, the
vessel grim and daring;
But O heart! heart! heart!
O the bleeding drops of red,
Where on the deck my Captain lies,
Fallen cold and dead.*

Funeral procession in Washington, D.C., carrying Lincoln's remains to the railway for the trip to his home in Springfield, Illinois.

835 On April 25, 1865, two young boys, nephews of the Confederate European agent James D. Bulloch, watched Lincoln's funeral procession in New York. They were Elliot and Theodore Roosevelt.

836 Scattered Rebel forces soon surrendered. Richard Taylor yielded his forces in the Department of Alabama, Mississippi, and East Louisiana on May 4, 1865; E. Kirby Smith, on the advice of the Trans-Mississippi governors, surrendered his department on May 26. Organized resistance ended.

837 Not every Southerner accepted the end. Some made their way to Mexico and other foreign parts; some former officers served with Emperor Maximilian and with the Army of the Khedive of Egypt.

838 Two important Confederate exile colonies were founded. In Mexico, the Carlota Colony flourished for a time, and there are still descendants in a Confederate colony in Brazil.

839 President Andrew Johnson, on August 20, 1866, proclaimed that the insurrection "is at an end and that peace, order, tranquillity, and civil authority now exist in and throughout the whole of the United States of America."

840 Terrible as the war had been, it brought surprisingly few reprisals. Booth's accomplices, including Mary Surratt, were hanged, as was the hapless Captain Henry Wirz of Andersonville. Beyond that, only civil disabilities plagued certain categories of Rebels, as President Johnson, adopting some of Lincoln's forgiveness, set forth a liberal pardon policy.

WORDS, ODDITIES, AND EXCITEMENTS

841 On July 1, 1863, as the Battle of Gettysburg was shaping up, John Burns, a local citizen who was over seventy years of age and a veteran of the War of 1812 and the Mexican War, joined up again. Ignoring the jibes of his wife, he made himself part of a passing Pennsylvania regiment, picked up a wounded soldier's rifle, and presented himself for duty.

John Burns of Gettysburg, with the gun he used in the battle and the crutches he needed after it.

He proved an excellent shot and won martial admiration. Twice wounded and cared for by a Rebel surgeon, Burns survived to become "the Hero of Gettysburg." When Lincoln came to give his address, he sought out Burns and walked around Gettysburg with him.

842 In one of the first uses of wire entanglements, telegraph wire was wrapped around stumps at Drewry's Bluff, Virginia, on May 15, 1864.

843 On June 17, 1864, about eight-thirty in the morning, an explosion in the cartridge-making building of the Washington Arsenal killed eighteen and wounded fifteen to twenty more.

844 During Lincoln's second visit to Fort Stevens, on July 12, 1864, he stood on the parapet, attracting some of Jubal Early's snipers. Down in the fort, young Captain Oliver Wendell Holmes, Jr., yelled, "Get down, you fool," and an amused President complied.

845 General Joseph E. Johnston, fussy about appearances, lost his hair to illness during the war. He wore a hat almost everywhere, even at the table. Servants and staff stifled their amusement as best they could.

846 During the fighting around Kennesaw Mountain, Georgia, in early October 1864, Union General John M. Corse and

2000 men were cut off near Allatoona. A Rebel 2000-man division attacked. Sherman's signalers on a hill near Kennesaw wig-wagged, "Sherman is moving with force. Hold out." Then, "Hold on. General Sherman says he is working hard for you." Corse took 700 casualties, lost 200 prisoners, and replied to Sherman's question, as to whether he had been wounded, "I am short a cheekbone and one ear, but am able to whip all hell yet." This episode inspired Philip Paul Bliss's hymn, "Hold the Fort, for I am coming."

847 Major Arthur Shoaff's Georgia sharpshooters had a fine cornetist who played in the trenches every evening after supper. Burke Davis quotes a Southern colonel to the effect that when the player shied from heavy fire, the Yanks would shout, "Hey, Johnny! We want that cornet player!"

"He would play, but he's afraid you'll spoil his horn," would come the answer.

"We'll hold fire."

"All right, Yanks."

Solos from operas floated over both lines, and the musician would also sing, in his strong tenor, favorites like "Come Where My Love Lies Dreaming," "Lorena," and "I Dreamt I Dwelt in Marble Halls" to mutual applause. A Union cornetist sometimes alternated with the Rebel. After a concert, war resumed.

848 At 4:45 in the morning of July 30, 1864, the Crater mine exploded under

The Crater resulting from the explosion, on July 30, 1864, of 8000 pounds of powder under Elliott's Salient, in the Petersburg lines.

Rebel Elliott's Salient in the Petersburg lines. The gigantic explosion killed at least 280 Confederates, dug a hole 170 feet long, sixty to eighty feet wide, and thirty feet deep. Yankee miners had been digging the 586-foot tunnel for more than a month—and the Rebels were aware of it. Countermining went on without result.

Right after the explosion, the Confederates rallied quickly and poured concentrated fire into the hole, which was filled with milling men of the Union 9th Corps trying to exploit the breach—many were black soldiers. By early afternoon the attack had failed. Union losses were about 4000; Confederate, 1500. The battle caused

Wharves at City Point, Virginia, August 10, 1864, the day after ordnance stores were exploded by Confederate agents. Union headquarters were hit by fragments and many were wounded, but Grant was unharmed.

strong anger among the Rebels, and when they saw Federal black troops, they screamed, "Kill the niggers!" as they charged among their blown-up dead.

849 About noon on Tuesday, August 9, 1864, an explosion rocked the Union supply base at City Point, Virginia. More than forty were dead, 125 injured, and vast stores were destroyed. Two daring Rebel agents had smuggled a bomb aboard a transport ship that was moored nearby.

850 In August 1864 Grant again refused an exchange of prisoners. He realized that the Confederates needed their men more desperately than the North needed theirs and that the South was sorely strained to feed, clothe, and guard Union prisoners of war.

851 With the loss of Fort Morgan, guarding the entrance to Mobile Bay, on August 23, 1864, Wilmington, North Carolina, became the last Confederate blockade-running port.

852 Reflecting his doubts about the election of 1864, Lincoln, on August 23, asked his Cabinet to sign without reading a memo he had composed. It said: "This morning, as for some days past, it seems exceedingly probable that this Administration will not be re-elected. Then it will be

my duty to so co-operate with the President elect, as to save the Union between the election and his inauguration; as he will have secured his election on such ground that he can not possibly save it afterwards." This gloomy prediction came before he fully understood the Democratic Party's platform problems.

853 Amid various peace rumors, in late August 1864, Lincoln told Henry Raymond, an editor of *The New York Times,* that he could talk to Jefferson Davis. The message: the war would end with a restored Union. But he decided to wait.

854 While most Southern eyes were fixed on the Army of Tennessee's agonies near Atlanta, Lee struggled on at Petersburg. On September 2, 1864, he wrote to President Davis about the manpower shortage. He urged that blacks be "used in every place in the army or connected with it when [they] can be used." Urging stricter rules for exemptions and recruiting, he added that "our ranks are constantly diminishing by battle and disease, and few recruits are received; the consequences are inevitable."

855 President Lincoln proclaimed September 5, 1864, a day of celebration for the victories in Atlanta and Mobile.

856 To the outrage of General John Bell Hood, Sherman ordered civilians out of Atlanta on September 7, 1864. As about 1600 made ready to go, Hood protested, outcries came from others, and Sherman bowed his neck. Facing complaints of "barbarity and cruelty," Sherman said that "war is war and not popularity-seeking."

857 Bitterly disappointed at Atlanta's loss, President Davis sought to reinforce Hood's depleted legions. Davis tried to maintain optimism by telling a congressman, on September 18, 1864, that he believed Atlanta could be retaken and Sherman's army destroyed. Davis went to Georgia in an attempt to brace morale.

858 Speaking in Macon, Georgia, on September 22, 1864, President Davis said, "Let no one despond . . . Our cause is not lost . . . Sherman cannot keep up his long line of communication; and retreat, sooner or later, he must."

859 During a visit to Hood's headquarters near Palmetto, Georgia, Davis heard more complaints against General Hardee; he finally detached him to command the Department of South Carolina, Georgia, and Florida.

860 In Augusta, Georgia, on October 5, 1864, Davis, with Beauregard and Hardee beside him, shared the mood of the cheering citizens. "Never was I so confident," he said, "that energy, harmony, and determination would rid the country of its enemy

. . . We must beat Sherman, we must march into Tennessee."

861 A sobered Jefferson Davis urged General Howell Cobb, on November 18, 1864, to turn out all men in Georgia who could oppose Sherman, even temporarily, and to use blacks to obstruct roads and railroads. Four days later, Davis told officers in Georgia to wreck bridges, cut trees, plant "subterra shells" (land mines), and destroy endangered supplies—the kind of devastation Sherman would soon cause.

862 In Liverpool, England, an important commercial port, Southern sympathizers abounded. On October 18, 1865, a group of pro-Confederate ladies held a large benefit for Rebel soldiers at St. George's Hall.

863 Wade Hampton's cavalry executed a daring "cattle raid" near Coggin's Point, Virginia, on September 11–16, 1864. Rebel horsemen snared 2400 cattle and 300 prisoners at a cost of sixty-one casualties. The cattle were sorely needed by Lee's army.

864 General "Little Phil" Sheridan's ride—done largely by train—toward Cedar Creek, in October 1864, was made somewhat glamorous in a poem by T. Buchanan Read:

Up from the South, at break of day,
Bringing to Winchester fresh dismay,

Railroad cars piled with household goods as refugees leave Atlanta after Sherman's eviction order, September 1864.

The affrighted air with a shudder bore,
Like a herald in haste to the chieftain's
*   door,*
The terrible grumble, and rumble, and
*   roar,*
Telling the battle was on once more,
And Sheridan twenty miles away . . .

But there is a road from Winchester town,
A good, broad highway leading down:
And there, through the flush of the
*   morning light,*
A steed as black as the steeds of night
Was seen to pass, as with eagle flight;
As if he knew the terrible need,
He stretched away with his utmost speed.
Hills rose and fell, but his heart was gay,
With Sheridan fifteen miles away.

The first that the general saw were the
*   groups*
Of stragglers, and then the retreating
*   troops;*
What was done? what to do?—a glance
*   told him both.*
Then striking his spurs with a terrible
*   oath,*
He dashed down the line, 'mid a storm of
*   huzzas,*
And the wave of retreat checked its course
*   there, because*
The sight of the master compelled it to
*   pause.*
With foam and with dust the black
*   charger was gray;*
By the flash of his eye, and his red
*   nostril's play,*

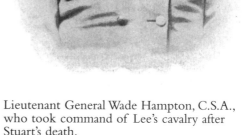

Lieutenant General Wade Hampton, C.S.A., who took command of Lee's cavalry after Stuart's death.

He seemed to the whole great army to
*   say:*
"I have brought you Sheridan all the way
From Winchester down to save the day."

865 On October 19, 1864, some twenty-five Rebel raiders hit St. Albans, Vermont, about fifteen miles south of Canada. Lieutenant Bennett Young and his men planned a series of raids. They snatched over $200,000 from three banks, and a fight erupted. One raider was killed, others wounded. The raiders were pursued across the border and were arrested with about $75,000 of the loot. This was the northernmost land action of the Civil War.

866 The blockade runner *Condor* ran aground while trying to escape a Union warship, near Fort Fisher, North Carolina, on October 1, 1864. The Southern spy Rose O'Neal Greenhow, carrying $2000 in gold, tried to reach the coast in a small boat. The boat was swamped, and Greenhow, weighed down by the gold, was drowned.

867 Another pillar of an earlier period died on October 12, 1864: the former Chief Justice of the United States Roger B. Taney. Despite several of his contentious decisions (notably in the Dred Scott case), Taney had been noted as a shaper of constitutional law.

868 Confederate agents devised a bizarre plot to burn New York City on November 25, 1864. Fires were set in about a dozen hotels and in Barnum's famous museum. Because the materials were faulty, possibly through sabotage, only small damage resulted. The Rebel agent in charge was caught and hanged.

869 Varina Davis worried about morale in the Confederate White House during Christmas 1864. True, "starvation parties" had become fashionable in the depleted Confederacy, but the President's lady tried to find something for the children and the servants. Brandy, a necessity for eggnog,

Confederate spy Rose O'Neal Greenhow, with her daughter, in the Old Capitol Prison, Washington, D.C.

was bought, even at $100 a bottle, because one of the black stablemen had lamented that he did not know how they could get along without eggnog. Currants, raisins, and other ingredients for mince pie yielded to apples and other fruits. Jackets, pieced together from uniform scraps, were given to soldiers' children, and Varina herself supervised the distribution of "rice, flour, molasses, and tiny pieces of meat" to the city's poor. The Episcopal orphan's home, after much effort, displayed a Christmas tree and gave out candy and such weathered toys as could be found. Varina received six cakes of soap "made from the grease of ham boiled for a family . . . a skein of exquisitely fine gray linen thread spun at home, a pincushion of some plain brown cotton material made by some poor woman and stuffed with wool from her pet sheep . . . a few of Swinburne's best songs bound in wall-paper." Davis received a pair of chamois riding gauntlets, a hemstitched linen handkerchief, and loving letters from his children.

870 As the Petersburg siege unfolded in 1865, Confederate rations dwindled, until each of Lee's men was existing on a handful of parched corn and a spoonful of sugar a day.

871 After the fall of Fort Fisher, blockade running almost came to a halt. One out of three runners reached the Confederacy in 1864, one out of two in 1865, compared with the wartime ratio of one out of six.

872 There were several instances of family members meeting during a battle. The most dramatic took place when Confederates reoccupied Galveston on January 1, 1863. Confederate Major A. M. Lea was one of those who captured the U.S.S. *Harriet Lane.* On board, he held in his arms dying Union Lieutenant Lea, his son.

873 When Admiral Franklin Buchanan led the C.S.S. *Virginia* in the battle with the U.S.S. *Monitor,* he attacked the U.S.S. *Congress,* on which his brother was serving as an officer.

874 An Englishman serving the Confederacy led a successful charge that overran a Union battery and took the surrender of the opposing commander, his brother.

875 Rebel Major H. B. McClellan had four brothers in the Union Army as well as his first cousin, General George B. McClellan. The major was Jeb Stuart's chief of staff.

876 Rebel General Patrick Cleburne had one brother in Blue, another in Gray.

877 In an unusual case of serendipity, the 7th Tennessee Confederate Regiment captured the entire 7th Tennessee Union Regiment.

878 In the bitter fighting at Gettysburg, John Culp had a son on each side, both struggling for the family's home at Culp's Hill.

879 Also at Gettysburg, Union General Alexander Schimmelfennig sought refuge in a pigsty as his troops retreated. He stayed for two days; perhaps he was the wisest man on the field.

880 One of the most unusual pieces of Confederate artillery was a double-barreled cannon. It called for putting one shot, attached by a chain, into each barrel. When the cannon was fired, the two shots were to cut a swath in enemy formations. Unfortunately, uneven powder burn caused one shot to come out ahead of the other, whirl around, and do serious damage to those who had fired the gun. The original is in Athens, Georgia.

881 General Lee's last order to his Army

is among the most eloquent messages of the war:

Hdqrs. Army of Northern Virginia
General Order No. 9
                    April 10, 1865

After four years of arduous service, marked by unsurpassed courage and fortitude, the Army of Northern Virginia has been compelled to yield to overwhelming numbers and resources. I need not tell the brave survivors of so many hard-fought battles, who have remained steadfast to the last, that I have consented to the result from no distrust of them. But, feeling that valor and devotion could accomplish nothing that could compensate for the loss that must have attended the continuance of the contest, I determined to avoid the useless sacrifice of those whose past services have endeared them to their countrymen.

By the terms of the agreement officers and men can return to their homes and remain until exchanged. You will take with you the satisfaction that proceeds from the consciousness of duty faithfully performed; and I earnestly pray that a merciful God will extend to you his blessing and protection.

Robert E. Lee in 1865

With an unceasing admiration of your constancy and devotion to your country, and a grateful remembrance of your kind and generous considerations for myself, I bid you all an affectionate farewell.

R. E. Lee,
General

882 The Confederates won the war's last battle. At Palmito Ranch, near Brazos Santiago, Texas, on May 12, 1865, Colonel John S. (Rip) Ford's Texans counterattacked a Union force and drove it from the field, with heavy losses.

OTHER ASPECTS
OF THE WAR

CIVIL WAR WORDS AND MUSIC

883 As President Davis and Vice President Stephens rode to their inauguration, a marching band played "Dixie." It was an old tune, sung by slaves. Properly set to music in 1859 by Dan Emmett of Ohio, "Dixie" became widely popular, not only in the South but, for a time, with Lincoln and the Union Army. After First Manassas (First Bull Run), the song became the Confederacy's unofficial anthem. "Dixie" stood for the area south of Mason and Dixon's Line.

> *I wish I was in the land of cotton,*
> *Old times there are not forgotten;*
> *Look away, look away, look away,*
> *Dixie Land.*
> *In Dixie Land where I was born in,*
> *Early on one frosty morning,*
> *Look away, look away, look away, Dixie*
> *   Land.*

> Chorus:
> *Then I wish I was in Dixie,*
> *Hooray! Hooray!*

> *In Dixie Land I'll take my stand,*
> *To live and die in Dixie:*
> *Away, away, away down South in Dixie*
> *Away, away, away down South in Dixie.*

884 Southerners sang patriotic, defiant, and humorous songs until fate turned against them; then they turned to consoling, sentimental tunes.

885 Yankees marched to martial airs. The most popular song in late 1861 was "John Brown's Body," which boasted endless stanzas and remembered John Brown's body moldering in the grave while his soul marched with the Lord's army. It was the idea of the Lord's army that finally changed Northern music, as the promise of the glory to come when freedom crowned the Union. Lincoln's eloquence lent power to that future as he himself became a legend.

886 Julia Ward Howe (1819–1910), born in New York City, became a famous writer, lecturer, and reformer. She was married to the antislavery leader Samuel Gridley Howe, and more than any-

---

Julia Ward Howe, who helped her husband edit the antislavery journal *Boston Commonwealth* and devoted her later life to women's suffrage.

one else she caught the missionary zeal of the North's freedom crusade. "The Battle Hymn of the Republic" came to her, she said, spontaneously one night. She got up and wrote:

> Mine eyes have seen the glory of the
>   coming of the Lord;
> He is trampling out the vintage where the
>   grapes of wrath are stored;
> He hath loos'd the fateful lightning of His
>   terrible swift sword:
> His truth is marching on.
>
> Chorus:
> Glory! Glory! Hallelujah!
> Glory! Glory! Hallelujah!
> Glory! Glory! Hallelujah!
> His truth is marching on.
>
> I have seen Him in the watch-fires of a
>   hundred circling camps;
> They have builded him an altar in the
>   ev'ning dews and damps;
> I can read His righteous sentence by the
>   dim and flaring lamps.
> His day in marching on.
> (Chorus)
> He has sounded forth the trumpet that
>   shall never call retreat;
> He is sifting out the hearts of men before
>   his judgment seat:
> Oh! Be swift, my soul, to answer Him!
>   Be jubilant, my feet!
> Our God is marching on.
> (Chorus)
> In the beauty of the lilies, Christ was born
>   across the sea,
> With a glory in His bosom that
>   transfigures you and me;
> As He died to make men holy, let us die
>   to make men free,
> While God is marching on.

887 **Almost as popular with the Yankees** was George F. Root's "Battle Cry of Freedom":

> Yes, we'll rally round the flag, boys, we'll
>   rally once again,
> Shouting the battlecry of freedom,
> We will rally from the hillside, we'll gather
> From the plain,
> Shouting the battlecry of freedom

Chorus:

The Union forever, hurrah! boys, hurrah!
Down with the traitor, up with the star,
While we rally round the flag, boys,
Rally once again,
Shouting the battlecry of freedom.

We are springing to the call of our
* brothers gone before,*
Shouting the battlecry of freedom.
And we'll fill the vacant ranks with a
* million freemen more,*
Shouting the battlecry of freedom.

888 Songs often reinforced the North's war needs, especially conscription. Either Stephen Foster (so says Edmund Wilson in *Patriotic Gore* [New York, 1962, p. 96]) or James Sloan Gibbons (so says William Rose Benét in *The Reader's Encyclopedia* [New York, 1948, p. 432]) wrote the popular "We Are Coming, Father Abraham, Three Hundred Thousand More":

We are coming, Father Abraham, three
* hundred thousand more,*
From Mississippi's winding stream and
* from New England's shore;*
We leave our ploughs and workshops, our
* wives and children dear,*
With hearts too full for utterance, with but
* a single tear;*
We dare not look behind us, but
* steadfastly before:*
We are coming, Father Abraham, three
* hundred thousand more!*

Chorus:

We are coming, we are coming, our Union
* to restore*
We are coming, Father Abraham, three
* hundred thousand more.*

889 Another tune that carried a religious theme was "To Canaan":

Where are you going, soldiers,
With your banner, gun, and sword?
We're marching south to Canaan
To battle for the Lord.
What Captain leads your armies
Along the rebel coasts?
The mighty One of Israel,
His name is Lord of Hosts.

Chorus:

To Canaan, to Canaan,
The Lord has led us forth,
To blow before the heathen walls
The trumpets of the North.

890 Sometimes Union songs commemorated great events, as did Henry Clay Work's stirring "Marching Through Georgia":

Bring the good old bugle, boys, we'll sing
* another song—*
Sing it with a spirit that will start the
* world along—*
Sing it as we used to sing it, fifty
* thousand strong,*
While we were marching through
* Georgia.*

Chorus:

"Hurrah! Hurrah! We bring the Jubilee,
Hurrah! Hurrah! The flag that makes you
    free!"
So we sang the chorus from Atlanta to the
    sea,
While we were marching through
    Georgia.

891 Patrick S. Gilmore caught the Yankees' joy at going home:

When Johnny comes marching home
    again,
Hurrah! Hurrah!
We'll give him a hearty welcome, then,
Hurrah! Hurrah!
The men will cheer, the boys will shout,
The ladies they will all turn out.

Chorus:
And we'll all feel gay,
When Johnny comes marching home.

892 The 9th Regiment of U.S. Colored Troops sang "They Look Like Men of War" during the tough winter of 1863–1864.

Hark! Listen to the trumpeters,
They call for volunteers,
On Zion's bright and flowery mount—
Behold the officers!

Chorus:
They look like men,

They look like men,
They look like men of war.

893 Southern songs also reflected moods, hopes, deeds, and fears. In April 1861, James Ryder Randall wrote to fellow Marylanders an enduring battle call:

The despot's heel is on thy shore,
    Maryland!
His torch is at thy temple door, Maryland!
Avenge the patriotic gore
That flecked the streets of Baltimore,
And be the battle-queen of yore,
Maryland, my Maryland! . . .
I hear the distant thunder-hum, Maryland!
The Old Line's bugle, fife, and drum,
    Maryland!
She is not dead, nor deaf, nor dumb;
Huzza! She spurns the Northern scum!
She breathes! She burns! She'll come!
She'll come!
Maryland, my Maryland!

894 Nearly rivaling "Dixie" as the song of the South was Harry Macarthy's "Bonnie Blue Flag":

We are a band of brothers, and native to
    the soil,
Fighting for the property we gained by
    honest toil;
And when our rights were threatened, the
    cry rose near and far,
Hurrah for the Bonnie Blue Flag that
    bears a single star!

Chorus:
Hurrah! Hurrah! for Southern Rights,
* hurrah!*
Hurrah! For the Bonnie Blue Flag that
* bears a single star!*

895 New Orleans ladies in 1861 sent their men to Virginia with the words of the "Volunteer Song":

Go soldiers, arm you for the fight,
God shield the cause of Justice, Right;
May all return with victory crowned,
May every heart with joy abound,
May each deserve the laurel crown,
Nor one to meet his lady's frown.

Your cause is good, 'tis honor bright,
'Tis virtue, country, home, and right;
Then should you die for love of these,
We'll waft your names upon the breeze:
The waves will sing your lullaby,
Your country mourn your latest sigh.

896 Raphael Semmes and the *Alabama* were subjects in many songs. One, by King and Rosier, went like this:

The wind blows off yon rocky shore,
Boys, set your sails all free:
And soon the booming cannon's roar
Shall sing out merrily.
Run up your bunting, caught a-peak,
And swear, lads, to defend her:
'Gainst every foe, where'er we go,
Our motto—"No surrender."

Chorus:
Then sling the bowl, drink every soul
A toast to the Alabama.
Whate'er our lot, through storm or shot,
Here's success to the Alabama.

897 The Civil War was a sentimental war, and music helped express the feelings of love, home, hope, and death. "Lorena" was one of the most popular of the many love lyrics of the war. It was sung by both sides, and at last became a Southern treasure:

The years creep slowly by, Lorena;
The snow is on the grass again;
The sun's low down the sky, Lorena;
The frost gleams where the flowers have
* been.*
But the heart throbs on as warmly now
As when the summer days were nigh;
Oh! the sun can never dip so low
Adown affection's cloudless sky.

A hundred months have passed, Lorena,
Since last I held that hand in mine,
And felt the pulse beat fast, Lorena,
Though mine beat faster far than thine.
A hundred months—'twas flowery
* May,*
When up the hilly slope we climbed,
To watch the dying of the day
And hear the distant church bells chime.

898 Privation became a kind of Confederate boast, as shown in these lines:

The homespun dress is plain, I know,
My hat's palmetto, too;
But then it shows what Southern girls
For Southern rights will do.
We send the bravest of our land
To battle with the foe,
And we will lend a helping hand;
We love the South, you know!

899 Comradeship is the substance that keeps men steady against the worst of war's inhumanities. One song that captures that substance is Charles G. Halpine's "We Have Drunk from the Same Canteen":

There are bonds of all sorts in this world
of ours,
Fetters of friendship and ties of flowers,
And true lovers' knots, I ween;
The boy and the girl are bound by a kiss,
But there's never a bond, old friend, like
this:
We have drunk from the same canteen.

Chorus:
The same canteen, my soldier friend,
The same canteen,
There's never a bond, old friend, like this!
We have drunk from the same canteen.

It was sometimes water, and sometimes
milk,
Sometimes applejack, fine as silk,
But whatever the tipple has been,
We shared it together, in bane or bliss,

And I warm to you, friend, when I think
of this:
We have drunk from the same canteen.

900 The war lasted so long, and so many died. Songs like Walter Kittridge's "Tenting on the Old Camp Ground" brought memories of better times:

We're tenting tonight on the old camp
ground,
Give us a song to cheer
Our weary hearts, a song of home,
And friends we love so dear.

Chorus:
Many are the hearts that are weary
tonight,
Wishing for the war to cease;
Many are the hearts that are looking for
the right,
To see the dawn of peace.
Tenting tonight, tenting tonight,
Tenting on the old camp ground . . .

901 Going home became a dim dream, as George Root's "Just Before the Battle, Mother" shows:

Just before the battle, Mother,
I am thinking most of you,
While, upon the field, we're watching,
With the enemy in view.

Comrades brave are round me lying,
Filled with thoughts of home and God;

For well they know that, on the morrow,
Some will sleep beneath the sod.

Chorus:
Farewell, Mother, you may never,
You may never, Mother,
Press me to your breast again;
But O, you'll not forget me,
Mother, you will not forget me
If I'm number'd with the slain.

902 **Dealing with mass death became the war's most difficult challenge;** never before in American history had decimation threatened the land. As the preceding song shows, soldiers worried about being unknown, being an unmarked corpse thrown into a grave in a forgotten place. Families, too, feared for their lost ones and pledged remembrance. J. H. McNaughton put Northern worries in "The Faded Coat of Blue":

My brave lad he sleeps in his faded coat
of blue;
In a lonely grave unknown lies the heart
that beat so true;
He sank faint and hungry among the
famished brave,
And they laid him sad and lonely within
his nameless grave.

Chorus:
No more the bugle calls the weary
one,
Rest noble spirit, in thy grave unknown!

I'll find you and know you, among the
good and true,
When a robe of white is giv'n for the
faded coat of blue.

903 **"The Southern Soldier Boy" echoed the feeling:**

Young as the youngest who donned the
gray,
True as the truest who wore it,
Brave as the bravest he marched away,
Hot tears on the cheeks of his mother
lay.
Triumphant waved our flag one day,
He fell in the front before it.

Chorus:
A grave in the wood with the grass
o'ergrown,
A grave in the heart of his mother,
His clay in the one, lifeless and lone.
But his memory lives in the other.

904 **How could the South lay the ghosts of the gallant ones who seemed to have died in vain?** Several poets tried to blunt the horror of failed sacrifice—Paul Hayne, Henry Timrod, others of the South—but the best requiem for the Rebel dead is probably Father Ryan's "The Conquered Banner":

Furl that Banner, for 'tis weary;
Round its staff 'tis drooping dreary;
Furl it, fold it—it is best;

For there's not a man to wave it,
And there's not a sword to save it,
And there's not one left to lave it
In the blood which heroes gave it;
And its foes now scorn and brave it;
Furl it, hide it—let it rest!

Take that Banner down! 'tis tattered;
Broken is its staff and shattered;
And the valiant hosts are scattered,
Over whom it floated high.
Oh, 'tis hard for us to fold it,
Hard to think there's none to hold it,
Hard that those who once unrolled it
Now must furl it with a sigh . . .

Furl that Banner, softly, slowly;
Treat it gently—it is holy,
For it droops above the dead;
Touch it not—unfold it never,
Let it droop there, furled forever,
For its people's hopes are fled.

905 **Reconciliation came with time,** especially when Yanks and Rebs joined together in the Spanish-American War. A conversation recorded by John Rooney caught the spirit of a new American destiny:

Says Stonewall Jackson to Little Phil,
"Phil, have you heard the news?
"Why, our 'Joe' Wheeler—'Fighting
Joe'—has gone and joined the blues.
"Ay, no mistake—I saw him come—I
heard the oath he took—

"And you'll find it duly entered up in
yon great Record Book . . .
"The oath 'Joe' swore has done the work
of thrice a score of years—
"Ay, more than oath—he swore away
mistrust and hate and tears!"

"Yes, yes," says Phil, "he was, indeed, a
right good worthy foe,
"And well he knew, in those fierce days,
to give us blow for blow . . .
"Come, Stonewall, put your hand in
mine. 'Joe's' sworn old Samuel's
oath—
"We're never North or South again—he
kissed the Book for both!"

906 **Legend has it that "Taps," the haunting day's-end bugle call of American troops,** originated as a brigade signal for Brigadier General Daniel Butterfield's Union brigade—and that he whistled it for a bugler to play.

907 **War sparked a great deal of writing,** but not much of it was good writing. Northern intellectuals concentrated largely on reform, on political affairs, the religious regeneration caused by war, and on new scientific discoveries. The ferment of ideas that had stimulated prewar writing seems to have been quenched by conflict. A good deal of important writing about the war appeared afterward—after some tempers cooled and perspectives changed.

Daniel Butterfield, chief of staff and corps commander of the Army of the Potomac.

908 Mark Twain's war experience led him to publish a humorous piece, "The Private History of a Campaign That Failed." Fictionalizing something of his experience as a second lieutenant in the informal Marion Rangers, Twain wrote this exaggerated effort in pseudo–autobiography shortly after the publication of *Huckleberry Finn*.

909 The American tradition of humor flourished in the war. One Yankee representative of the tradition was Robert H. Newell. His *Orpheus C. Kerr Papers* ran in different newspapers during the war. Lincoln is reported to have enjoyed the doings of the "office seeker" and the scandals in the "Mackerel Brigade."

910 A few important Northern writers treated the war in poems, novels, essays, and newspaper pieces. Whitman published his war poetry after the war, but his wartime notes preserved themes for such later works as *Drum-Taps* (1865).

911 John Greenleaf Whittier overcame his Quaker antiwar views to become an ardent antislavery and pro-Union man. Aside from his frequent newspaper articles supporting the war, he wrote and published an important war poem. "Barbara Frietchie" celebrated the ninety-year-old lady's alleged defiance of Stonewall Jackson as his men marched through Frederick, Maryland. She hung out an American flag with a challenge:

> *"Shoot, if you must, this old gray head,*
> *But spare your country's flag," she said.*

The poem had a wide following for years.

912 James Russell Lowell, the famous critic and the first editor of the *Atlantic Monthly*, devoted most of his war writings to essays defending Lincoln and the Union. But in 1862 he did revive his New England dialect and "cracker barrel" humor in the second series of his popular *Biglow Papers*. They contained imaginary conversations with Jefferson Davis, caricatures of Copperheads, and support for Lincoln. But this series lacks the freshness of the first, largely because Lowell's humor ebbed. He wrote to a friend in 1863 that "the War and its constant expectation and anxiety depress me."

                                        •

913 **In 1830 Seba Smith created a highly popular cracker barrel character named Major Jack Downing.** Commenting on politics and other affairs in a series of letters, Downing became a kind of dialectical pundit. During the Civil War, Downing's letters appeared in several dailies and took a decided Copperhead stance, with Downing advising his friend Lincoln against emancipation. Downing had Lincoln agreeing but being hamstrung by his Cabinet. Late in the war Downing had Lincoln saying, "I'me in the Abolishin bote, and you can't stop it now eny more than you kin put Lake Superior in a quart bottle." Occasionally banned from the mails, Downing's effusions continued until 1864.

914 **Several Northern novelists wrote about the war.** One of them earned a place as a pioneer of realism in American fiction—John William De Forest. He was later recognized by the important critic Edmund Wilson as "the first of our writers of fiction to deal seriously with the events of the Civil War." His most important novel, *Miss Ravenel's Conversion from Secession to Loyalty,* published in 1868, offered glimpses of the horrors of war and an unveiled view of wartime sexuality. He suffered some censorship from publishers and editors.

915 **Dialect humor amused Confederates, too. Many Rebel soldiers from remote areas spoke a quaint language with traces of almost Old English** measure. Those from the Deep South talked in soft, muffled words; outcountry men, the "po' whites," often spoke in baffling "cracker" tongues—a mixture of words and slurs and dropped letters that was sometimes difficult to understand. At the time, people were products of place, and their place showed in talk. Dialect was important in fixing a speaker's origins.

916 **George W. Harris had won recognition before the war with his character Sut Lovingood,** whose comments first found print in 1854. Lovingood appeared at last in 1867 in a gallimaufry of pieces as *Sut Lovingood: Yarns Spun by a Nat'ral Born Durn'd Fool.* According to Lovingood, he chanced to be traveling with President-elect Lincoln, who made a considerable impression on Sut:

> His mouth, his paw, and his footses am the principal features, and his striking point is the way them-there legs of his'n gets into his body. They goes in at each edge sorta like the prongs goes into a pitchfork. Of all the durned scary-looking, ole cusses for a President ever I seed, he am decidedly the durndest. He looks like a yaller ladder with half the rungs knocked out.

917 **Most camp humor was topical.** One

Southern satire on army life transcended the Confederacy and the times; it rings fresh in every war. Charles H. Smith's *Bill Arp, So Called* has a droll irony that pillories foppish officers and makes comics of regimental rascals. Arp is the protagonist, the "high private's" idol, the pawn of fate. Things go awry as soon as he arrives on the scene. Other times and armies have had Arp's counterpart—the American GIs' Sad Sack, Czechoslovakia's Good Soldier Schweik. All of them discards of fate, they have the one essential of lasting comedy: a touch of pathos.

918 **Most semipermanent Rebel camps spawned army newspapers, often handwritten, one-page sheets specializing in advertisements and jokes.** Butts of jibes were often the great archetypes of armies: bad officers, swindling quartermasters, sutlers in quest of astronomical profits. Egregious though these jokes usually were, they reflected the mood of troops. Nothing brought a quicker laugh from a bivouac than the sarcastic cry, "Mister, here's your mule!" It taunted all visiting contractors and commissaries, who rarely journeyed to the outposts and then always on strong and healthy mounts. Oddly, these mounts tended to wander around the camps, followed by shouted hints as to their whereabouts. So helpful a motto deserved wide popularity, and "Mister, here's your mule" found its way into music and song.

919 **Serious Southern writers felt the** same horror as their Northern colleagues. Prewar Charleston gathered the brightest group of literary lights of the South—such notables as William Gilmore Simms, Paul Hamilton Hayne, and Henry Timrod. They struggled against isolation, apathy, and the amused toleration of sophisticates. Timrod and Hayne gained some attention as wartime poets, but William Gilmore Simms, probably the most luminous of these writers, was strangled by war into silence.

920 **Several Rebel writers wrote about the war.** A popularizer whose work lasted was John Esten Cooke, a successful writer before the war who served on the staff of General Jeb Stuart and saw hard war service. He published a life of Stonewall Jackson shortly after the general's death in 1863, and he drew on his experiences in several successful postwar novels.

921 **Augusta Jane Evans Wilson of Mobile** had won many readers in 1855 with her best-selling *Inez, A Tale of the Alamo.* A fire-eating Confederate nationalist, she worked in army hospitals and, in 1863, published *Macaria: or, Altars of Sacrifice,* a kind of propaganda piece to spur Rebel enthusiasm. It became a pillar of Confederate morale.

922 **One Southern history of the war began appearing during the conflict.** Edward A. Pollard, the editor of the *Daily Richmond Examiner* and a leading critic of the administration, began publishing an anti-Davis history of the war in 1862. He wrote one volume a year and combined them, in 1866, into the large *Southern History of the War.* This first assessment of the conflict lacked perspective, but it accurately reflected much Rebel sentiment.

SEX AND THE WAR

923 **War produced the usual emphasis on prostitution.** Both Washington and Richmond held hordes of "ladies of the town" as the armies gathered; they followed the forces in the field. Complaints about prostitution accumulated as the war continued, and the Young Men's Christian Association, the United States Sanitary Commission, and the Union League were deluged with worries from those behind the lines. Still, verified accounts of sexual outrages against white women in the South were comparatively rare. There were, however, many documented cases of harassment and rape of black women as Federal armies invaded the South. The Confederate troops were not innocent of sexual misconduct, especially the irregulars and deserters who plagued a large part of the Confederacy.

924 **General Joseph Hooker permitted red-light districts in Washington** while he raised his army, and his policy gave rise to the "hookers" who followed the armies.

925 **Venereal disease plagued both armies.** One source suggests that one out of twelve Union soldiers had venereal disease in 1861, and adds that of some 470,000 white Union troops, about 190,000 had VD; of 70,000 black Union troops, 14,000 were infected. Confederate statistics were probably similar although the figures are uncertain. In one case, a Southern artillery battery of forty-five men counted thirteen VD cases.

926 **Probably the most famous case of adultery—out of many—in the war** involved Confederate General Earl Van Dorn. He was shot in the head at Spring Hill, Tennessee, on May 7, 1863, by a Dr. Peters, probably because of a "liaison" with the doctor's wife. An official letter to President Davis said Van Dorn's "great weaknesses in such [sexual] matters must be admitted." Several well-known "skedaddles" involving Union and Confederate officers were recorded.

927 **Sex sometimes became a weapon.** There was the case of two white Union soldiers tried for rape at Petersburg, late in the war. Their loud protestations of having done nothing more than go to a brothel failed to save them, and they were hanged in public view. Years later a Southern woman supposedly confessed that she had accused them "in order to contribute her mite toward the extermination of the Yankee army."

928 There was also a case involving Stonewall Jackson. During his famous Shenandoah Valley Campaign, his men captured a group of prostitutes. They were suspected of being infected, so the general had them sent to the Union lines—an experiment in germ warfare.

SPIES

Spies did yeoman work for both sides. Here are a representative few.

929 The leading Union spy working in the heart of the Confederacy was Mrs. Elizabeth Van Lew. She was born in Richmond of Northern parents, and she was wealthy. She circulated in high Confederate circles and covered her spying by appearing to befriend the prisoners in Libby Prison. Her eccentricities lent her the nickname "Crazy Bet," which excused her doings.

930 Belle Boyd did important service as a Rebel spy. She gave intelligence to Stonewall Jackson during his Valley Campaign and was often arrested, imprisoned, and sentenced to death. She escaped every time and kept up her work. Finally, she married a Federal officer.

931 Some spies were unlucky. One Timothy Weber circulated in Richmond as a passionate defender of the Confederacy, but he was one of Allan Pinkerton's best agents. Exposed at last, he was tried and hanged.

932 In early 1862 a Union scout in the West masqueraded as a Rebel and gained valuable information before the Battle of Elkhorn Tavern. James Butler Hickok was to become famous as Wild Bill Hickok.

933 Various codes were devised for spy

Confederate spy Belle Boyd.

communications. They varied from simple word substitution to sophisticated number/word mixes and even rudimentary machine coding.

ARTISTS

934 Artists on both sides did their bit for morale. Among a large number in the North, Winslow Homer stands out as an accomplished professional whose drawings and paintings caught the mood of Union soldiers. His work, and that of others, was often found in such leading periodicals as *Harper's Weekly.*

935 Southern artists abounded, too, but none achieved the wide audience of Homer. Adalbert Volck of Baltimore did numerous etchings of life behind Rebel lines; among them were *Making Clothes for the Boys in the Army* and *Offering of Bells to Be Cast into Cannon.*

936 Among the most famous Southern paintings was one by William Washington. *The Burial of Latané* offered a soberly sentimental view of women and slaves burying the only casualty of Jeb Stuart's first "Ride Around McClellan" in 1862— Lieutenant William Latané.

937 Works of many of the artists were seen during the war in such popular Northern publications as *Harper's Weekly* and *Frank Leslie's Weekly.* Of these, *Harper's*

boasted the largest circulation and could offer the best illustrators, among them Alfred and William Waud, Thomas Nast, Theodore Davis, and Winslow Homer. But *Frank Leslie's Weekly* was not completely outdone, since its pages included work by Henri Lovie, Frank Schell, J. F. E. Hillen, and Edwin Forbes.

938 Escaping her war-torn home on a blockade runner late in 1863, Mrs. Anna McNeill Whistler headed for England. That visit to her son was memorialized by *Arrangement in Gray and Black,* popularly known as *Whistler's Mother.*

WEAPONS, MUNITIONS, AND UNIFORMS

Often called the first modern war, the Civil War caused myriad innovations in arms and munitions.

939 The rifle, which came into wide use for the first time as a weapon, brought about a drastic change in tactics. The smooth-bore musket, long the standard infantry weapon, lacked range and accuracy. Once the rifling problem had been solved by the ingenuity of France's Captain Claude Minié and America's James H. Burton (who later served the Confederacy) in perfecting what became known as the Minié ball, the range expanded from about 250 yards, effective at only eighty yards, to over a thousand, effective at over 400 yards. This change put the infantry in charge of the battlefield; cavalry and advanced field artillery could be shot to pieces before the infantry closed with the enemy. Defense became much easier, and hand-to-hand combat consequently became rare. Few bayonet wounds were treated in army hospitals. Tactics changed slowly, though, because old lessons died hard. Not until 1864 did both armies abandon the charge by massed infantrymen and settle in behind entrenchments.

940 The Federal infantry was given good Springfield and Enfield rifles early in the war. Domestic production rose, but many rifles were also purchased abroad. By 1863 the Springfield Armory was producing nearly 800,000 rifles; private plants made another 900,000. Amazingly, Northern industry managed to produce over two and a half million small arms during the war.

941 The Confederate infantry started with a baffling collection of small arms—sporting guns, blunderbuses, antique muskets, and shotguns. This, of course, complicated ammunition problems. Chief of Ordnance Josiah Gorgas organized careful scavenging of battlefields and rapidly improvised domestic production. Eventually, captures and importation almost equalized infantry arms. Confederate importation of Enfield rifles often put Rebels ahead on the field. Estimates indicate that about 350,000 rifles were produced in the Confederacy, and almost 700,000 were imported.

942 The Spencer repeating carbine, and other breechloaders, changed the firepower equation by 1864. A seven-cartridge, spring-action clip in the stock made the Spencer an object of Rebel admiration. One Johnny Reb noted that "you could load it on Sunday and shoot it all week!"

943 The Union's pistols came in varying sizes during the war. Samuel Colt's revolvers were the preferred standard and came in two main calibers: the "army" .44 and the "navy" .36. Colt sold nearly 150,000 of the former and 20,000 of the latter to the Union Army. Remington Arms sold almost 150,000 .45's and .36's to the Army, which also bought some 12,000 Whitney revolvers.

944 Rebel pistol makers had numerous problems. The Ordnance Department adopted the "navy" .36-caliber as standard, and, to supplement armories, farmed out production to private manufacturers, some of which got into production. Not only did metal and transportation shortages plague these makers; so did the chronic instability of a skilled labor supply. Often Confederate conscription officials would whisk away workers and halt production at critical moments.

945 The Civil War saw a revolution in artillery types, ranges, production, and usage. In the years before the war, the military's attention had focused on seacoast ordnance, or heavy artillery. The standard light field gun was a six-pound smoothbore that fired solid shot at ranges of 600 to 2000 yards. Quickly, though, the twelve-pounder Napoleon became the favorite field gun on both sides because of its mobility and versatility in the use of ammunition.

946 Confederate material shortages led to the manufacture of iron guns. Some Southern Napoleons were made of iron with reinforced breeches and especially reinforced ("banded") chamber areas in heavy ordnance.

947 Artillery ammunition underwent a Civil War revolution. Since the 1840s the standard gun charge had been solid shot, used against troops at ranges of 600 to 2000 yards and against fortifications. A need for greater killng power led to experiments with spherical case shot, which exploded over the battlefield, and with tin canisters of balls that could be fired at short ranges into massed infantry.

948 Both sides used several types of rifled guns. More ten-pounder Parrott guns were used than any other kind. Heavier than the Napoleon but capable of hurling a shell over 2000 yards, the Parrott could fire canister against massed

An eight-inch Parrott gun, foreground, and a Rodman gun, Yorktown Battery.

infantry and was effective in counterbattery work.

949 Union artillerists used heavier ordnance. Eight-, ten-, thirteen-, fifteen-, and

A ten-inch Columbiad gun, above the James River. With a charge of fifteen pounds of powder, this gun could throw a 123-pound shot over two miles.

twenty-inch Rodman guns comprised part of the siege artillery trains.

950 Rebels used eight-, ten-, and fifteen-inch Columbiads. Seacoast guns were often forty-two-pounders, along with eight- and ten-inch howitzers.

951 Both sides used mortars. These sported short fat tubes, mounted on wooden bases. The Coehorn mortar, a 24-inch behemoth, could move, but usually stayed put. The high arc of the shell made the mortar ideal for antifort work and for some counterbattery action.

952 Lee's army boasted a battery of English twelve-pounder Whitworth breech-loading guns. With a range of 4059 yards (deadly at 2300 yards), they were almost too good for the war; fire control and targeting became difficult problems.

953 Ammunition problems plagued both sides. The varieties of guns confounded logistical arrangements for the first year of the war. Standardization was a goal that the North nearly achieved, but the Confederate Ordnance Department wrestled with the matter until late in the war. Quality control was also a problem. Since the Confederates had to disperse ordnance production more widely than did the North, quality could not always be maintained in such things as fuze production and calibration.

954 Not bound by tradition, Confeder-

Confederate torpedoes (with conical ends), shot, and shell in the yard of the Charleston Arsenal.

ate ordnance officers welcomed innovation. Early in the war "subterra shells," or land mines, were manufactured in Richmond. General McClellan regarded them as inhuman, and he marched Confederate prisoners ahead of his men during the Peninsular Campaign to deter mining. But mines continued to be used, as, of course, were Confederate "torpedoes," or sea mines. The Rebels experimented with "stink bombs" of such noxiousness that they afflicted both sides. Hand grenades came into use, with some efforts devoted to casting them in such a way as to predetermine the explosion pattern.

955 Powder production was a serious Rebel problem, but by the middle of

1863, Colonel George W. Rains of the Confederate Ordnance Department had built one of the world's best powder works. It was in Augusta, Georgia, and managed to supply most of the Rebel needs.

956 **The acute shortage of infantry arms early in the war forced a special Southern innovation.** In early 1862, Governor Joseph E. Brown, of Georgia, ordered 10,000 pikes (bayonet-type blades attached to a wooden staff) made for state troops. An odd kind of pike fever seems to have swept the South for a time. Stonewall Jackson favored pikes; so did Lee, who requested a thousand. Ordnance Chief Gorgas, however, had little confidence in them, and noted that "no excess of enthusiasm could induce our people to rush to the field armed with *pikes.*"

957 **Machine guns made a few appearances in the Civil War.** Confederate Captain R. S. Williams invented a revolving camshaft gun, with bullets fed by a hopper, that would shoot twenty times a minute. It saw some combat in 1862, but fewer than three dozen were built, because of their unreliability. The same problem plagued rapid-fire efforts. A "coffee mill gun" (so-called by Lincoln, because the hopper looked like a coffee grinder) and Richard Gatling's gun (which could shoot 250 times a minute) were both marginal during the war. Gatling's gun became a standard after the war, made him a fortune, and changed the action on battlefields. The name was criminalized later, when gangsters used the "gat."

958 **Although the war was fought between the Blue and the Gray, soldiers were not always easily identified by their uniforms.** Each side had units that wore the color of the enemy. But rank insignia differed. Union officer grades were designated by shoulder insignia; Confederate ranks were marked by swirled gold braid on sleeves or collars. Enlisted insignia, stripes on arms, could be confusing. So could naval rank designations, since the two navies sported much the same uniform. Often, wealthy Confederate officers had uniforms made of fine English blue cloth as well as gray. As the war dragged on, Confederate cloth makers resorted to butternut, a dye made from the oil of white walnuts mixed with copperas.

FOREIGNERS IN THE WAR

Foreigners did vital duty for both warring sides.

959 **The historian Burke Davis, in his stimulating** *The Civil War: Strange & Fascinating Facts* (New York: Random House, 1996, p. 90), cites the high number of foreigners in the war. He notes that there were six foreign-born Union major generals, including George Meade, who was born in Spain of American parents. "Nine

Germans, four Irishmen, two Frenchmen, a Russian, a Hungarian, a Pole and a Spaniard" won commissions as brigadiers. This was not surprising, in view of the 1860 population: four million foreigners in the North to some 230,000 in the South. Germans, perhaps by tradition, perhaps because of their anger at war's pursuing them from Palatinate lands, flocked to the colors. Many regiments were pure Irish, like the famed New York Irish Brigade. Scots often joined with Irish. Probably the most unusual Union outfit was the Garibaldi Guard (the 39th New York Regiment), led by a Hungarian colonel, with an Italian lieutenant colonel and a German surgeon. Its ranks boasted British deserters, Swiss, Bavarians, Cossacks, Sepoys, Algerians of the Foreign Legion, and many other war veterans.

960 Several titled foreigners served the Union. The Count of Paris and the Duc de Chartres were volunteers on General McClellan's staff. Baron von Vegesach of Sweden led a charge by the 20th New York at Antietam. When the man who took Prussian Prince Salm-Salm to see Lincoln announced that the visitor was a prince, Lincoln quipped, "That won't hurt you with us." Burke Davis says that no fewer than fifty-seven titled Germans served the Union cause.

961 Irishmen constituted most of the famous 69th New York Regiment, which, as part of the Irish Brigade, did

Officers of the Irish Brigade, commanded by General Thomas F. Meagher.

some of the heaviest fighting. This Zouave unit's leader, General Thomas Meagher, had been condemned to death in the Irish rebellion and banished to Tasmania. He reached America in 1852 and starred in the war.

962 Gossip had it that a "Major Warrington," who disappeared in action while serving McClellan before Richmond, had royal blood. Florid and gray-haired, he was reputed to be an illegitimate son of King George IV.

963 A good many soldiers of fortune enjoyed the war; several of them fought for both sides. Consider the case of Confederate Captain Peter Kiolbassa, who was captured, joined the Union Army as a private, and reached captain's rank again.

964 Many foreigners served in the Union Navy. The U.S.S. *Hartford,* Admiral Farragut's flagship, had a crew boasting twenty-five nationalities. The U.S.S. *Kearsarge* defeated the *Alabama* with a crew of whom a quarter were foreigners.

The Confederacy had a good share of outside help. 965 Burke Davis points out that five Rebel generals were Irish-born, three hailed from France, two from England.

966 Irish volunteers flocked to the Rebel standard. John Mitchel, Jr., the son of a famous Irish exile, became captain of Charleston's Irish Volunteers. A Confederate newspaper declared, in October 1861, that the Irish were, "everywhere in the Confederate States . . . among the foremost to volunteer, and among the most liberal in contributing to the comfort of the brave soldiers in the field."

967 Among the many prominent Prussians in Gray was Major Heros von Borcke. Attaching himself to Jeb Stuart as an aide, the mustached, six-foot-four-inch von Borcke became the general's chief of staff and earned the thanks of the Confederate Congress. Another Prussian of high rank was Victor von Scheliha, who served General Simon B. Buckner.

968 Baron William Henry von Eberstein, a German, became a sergeant in the 7th North Carolina's Washington Grays.

969 An important aide-de-camp was Britain's St. George Grenfel. A veteran of Turkish, Indian, Moroccan, and South American wars, Grenfel joined the staff of General John H. Morgan.

970 General Joseph B. Kershaw's staff enjoyed the services of Marcus Baum, a German Jew, who earned high distinction for gallantry.

971 Major General Camille Armand

Confederate Major General Camille J. Polignac.

Jules Marie de Polignac, a French prince and a veteran of the Crimean War, had an unusual career. Sent to command in Texas, he proclaimed martial law without permission from President Davis and nearly lost his job. His rough Texas troops objected to his stiff regulations and his upper-class manners, and opined that "no frog-eating Frenchman we can't pronounce will command us." They dubbed him "Polecat." He won their affection by marching them over tough ground in search of polecats.

972 **Another French officer held a brigadier's commission in Texas.** Xavier B. DeBray did outstanding service with a southwestern cavalry unit.

973 **The Irish officer Brigadier General Joseph Finegan commanded the Confederates** in the important victory at the Battle of Olustee in Florida, on February 20, 1864.

974 **The last commission signed by President Davis was for a Scot.** Rising from the rank of private, Peter Alexander Selkirk McGlashan received his brigadier's wreath from Davis while they were both in flight from Richmond.

975 **Louisiana regiments were certainly cosmopolitan.** The 1st Louisiana Regiment had men of thirty-seven nationalities. So many of the Confederate soldiers who served spoke French that General Beauregard coined a word to acknowledge their dual language: *sacredamn.*

976 **Several Louisiana regiments were notorious for violence.** Often recruited from prisons or New Orleans slums, members of some of the Zouave units did damage wherever they were. One group stole a train in Alabama; others wrecked whole settlements. The Avegno Zouaves, made up of French, Chinese, Mexican, Italian, Spanish, and Irish fighters, were nearly uncontrollable.

977 **Probably the most famous Louisiana outfit was the Tigers.** Commanded by an adventurer named Rob Wheat, they were a gang of "pluguglies" collected near the New Orleans levees. Fearsome fighters, the Tigers were tough to handle. At least two were executed, and some of them even killed civilians.

978 **A Rebel European Brigade mustered in New Orleans in February 1862** boasted 2500 Frenchmen, 400 Germans, 500 Italians, 800 Spaniards, Dutchmen, and Scandinavians, in addition to Belgians, Swiss, Britons, and Austrians. The unit did well in policing the Crescent City during the difficult days preceding Union occupation.

979 **Many prisoners switched sides.** Some captured Confederates were offered Union service, and they accepted. Most of these "Galvanized Rebs" chose to serve in

Western operations against Indian tribes. "Galvanized Yankees" served in Rebel ranks, especially in two battalions raised in 1864 by a German, Conrad Nutzel. One of these companies fought gallantly against Grierson's raiders. Another such unit rebelled in Savannah, and the leaders were shot.

980 Texas had an interesting foreign problem. With a white population, at the war's beginning, of some 420,000, a fifth of them German immigrants, the state suffered serious divisions. Many Texas Germans opposed slavery and secession and chose to go North. In August 1862, a group of them were overtaken by Texan riders near Fort Clark, on the Nueces River, and more than half were killed. Many of the wounded survivors were executed. The Nueces Massacre left lingering anger for years.

981 The adventures of blockade running attracted various fans. "Captain Roberts" of the runner *Don,* ranked among the most successful breakers of the blockade.

He was, in fact, the Honorable Augustus Charles Hobart-Hampden, known as Hobart Pasha, a son of the Earl of Buckinghamshire, and once the captain of Victoria's yacht. He gained much wealth from his exploits and went on to further derring-do as commander of Turkey's fleet in its war against Russia.

982 Another Britisher shared the excitement of the blockade. Admiral Hewitt, of the Royal Navy, captained the runner *Condor.* It was he who put the Rebel agent Rose O'Neal Greenhow into the skiff off Wilmington, North Carolina, from which she fell and drowned.

983 Captain Charles Murray, another Briton and a future Lord Dunmore, ran the blockade for three years, and then transferred to General Lee's staff.

984 An Irish civilian worked to save Atlanta. As the city burned, Patrick Lynch collected teams of slaves and saved many buildings as the Union Army arrived.

AFTERWORD

———◆◆◆◆———

What kind of war was the Civil War? Surely it was the costliest in modern memory.

985 The Civil War was the first war of the Industrial Revolution. It became a conflict of machinery and engineering: a cauldron of railroads and iron ships and submarines and stupefying firepower, of telegraphs and the beginnings of air observation, of entrenchments and new tactics, a foretaste of twentieth-century wars.

986 More than 10,500 fights were reported. They ranged from pitched battles to engagements to skirmishes to heavy combat to "affairs." Men died in most of them.

987 Casualty counts are uncertain and have been argued about ever since the war. Carefully adjusted statistics reported by E. B. and Barbara Long in *The Civil War Day by Day* (Garden City, N.Y., 1971, pp. 704, 708–11) show 110,000 Union killed and mortally wounded, 224,580 dead of disease, in addition to 275,175 wounded and 30,218 prisoners of war who died. The total casualties from all causes, army and navy, were 642,427. Confederate numbers are harder to find (no naval figures are available), but the Longs give the Confederate dead or mortally wounded at 94,000, 164,000 dead of disease, in addition to 194,026 wounded. From 26,000 to 31,000 died as prisoners of war. The total casualties were 483,026. Total war-related deaths are conservatively estimated at 1,123,073. More than 25 percent of 1861 Northern and Southern manpower became casualties of some kind.

988 Monetary costs of the war are also in dispute. Careful students estimate that the North spent $13 billion to win, and the losing South spent no less than $6 billion.

989 Numbers do not tell all the wages of the war. Vast areas of the South stood scorched, ravaged, pillaged, wrecked by friendly and hostile armies. In both North and South, the returning veterans were not the men they had been. A scythe had swept the land; whole men of war were hard to find. The lame, broken, and blind lingered as hostages of conflict.

990 **Lincoln and Davis both feared from the start that the war might become an unstoppable agent of change.** And, of course, it did. It generated its own momentum, took on its own image, burst the bounds of "civilized" conflict, and, in the words of the historian Bruce Catton, became a "war against . . ." many old institutions. While Lincoln and Davis sought to contain it within reconcilable bounds, war's anger freed the slaves, reworked the social, economic, and political seams, and left America forever different.

991 **A lingering question about the Civil War can be phrased in two ways,** depending on which side your sympathies lie. How did the North win? Or how did the South lose? Books have been written under each title. Economic determinists may find the questions absurd, since the North's preponderance of everything material surely drove the outcome. But the argument began with the end. Some Northerners saw victory as a triumph of rectitude and of freedom; others, as the wages of sin; some as a judgment by blood and misery; many as not worth what it cost. Southerners, too, were divided. General Lee at Appomattox talked about yielding "to overwhelming numbers and resources." Edward Pollard, a crusty anti-administration Richmond newsman who

chronicled the conflict, blamed the loss on Jefferson Davis's rigidity. As in the North, some crushed Rebels saw the wages of slavery as being paid in ignominy; others, as a direct decision by Providence. Allegedly, the Bishop of New Orleans said at the end of the war, "Oh, Lord, when Thou didst decide to defeat the Confederacy, Thou first had to remove Thy servant Stonewall Jackson."

992 **As social scientists began to form their view,** they raised questions of motivation and speculations about the psychology of Yankees and Rebels. Historians of all outlooks, from Marxist economic determinists to psychological determinists to military determinists to political economists, voiced worries about strategy: Lincoln was a near-genius at grasping high strategy, they argued; Davis was less original, cramped by his personal military experience. They studied leadership: Lincoln, the consummate voice of a cause; Davis, muffled by the zeal congealed in his heart. They studied management and mismanagement of what seemed abundant resources: the logistical efforts of the North were made easy by commercial arteries; Southern efforts were frustrated by the lack of supporting networks of transportation and experience. They studied morale: Northern zeal finally rose to a cause worthy of everything—freedom; Southerners were hampered by the innate guilt of slavery. They even studied patriotism: the Northerners marched to the Lord's word; the Southerners fought for a flawed past amid a welter of corruption.

These arguments will continue as each generation raises more questions.

993 Arguments persist about the strength and depth of Confederate nationalism. Emory Thomas suggests, in *The Confederacy as a Revolutionary Experience* (1971), that the South's try for independence represented an important, well-articulated, conservative revolution. His book *The Confederate State of Richmond: A Biography of the Capital* (1971) indicates the strength of Rebel urban administrative efforts. Thomas's *The Confederate Nation 1861–1865* (1979) makes a strong case for Confederate nationalism and describes its slow erosion as the country fought itself out. I share Thomas's interpretations in *Their Tattered Flags: The Epic of the Confederacy* (1970).

994 Drew Gilpin Faust, in *Creation of Confederate Nationalism: Ideology and Identity in the Civil War South* (1988), supports the case for Rebel identity. Faust, too, concludes that nationalism was unraveled by war.

995 Paul Escott, in *After Secession: Jefferson Davis and the Failure of Confederate Nationalism* (1978), argues against a true Confederate feeling. He believes that President Davis did not project a cause for Southerners to sustain—and that this executive failure was fatal.

996 There are many specialized studies about command confusion on both sides, about lapses in leadership, failures of logistics, military myopia. These were factors in the war, of course, and they hurt the South more than the North. Why? Because the South had only a thin margin for error. It ran its course close to the edge of endurance, sustained by an agrarian system struggling mightily toward modernization, propped by a people yearning for a country they had to make against the odds.

997 I claim the privilege of giving my own views on Southern defeat. The Southerners entered the war with true zeal. Carpers there were, of course, as in all crises, but by and large Southerners wanted to be independent of the colossus in the North that was headed down the path of an impersonal industrialism that would brutalize workers and make automatons of people and destroy a social system. War was better.

998 But war turned out to be more terrible than they had imagined, an engine that sought to change their agricultural oligarchy. And the South changed itself to fight a huge, modern war—changed in ways alien to its history, to its desire to preserve its way of life and achieve its best hope—Independence.

999 In striving to win independence, Southerners became much like their Yankee foes. Political movement toward centralization could be seen from Congress to statehouse, county to village, militia to regular armies as everything changed for the innocents at war.

1000 These innocents learned quickly the odds and the realities of fighting alone. They learned modern methods of mobilization, methods of managing large armies and a Navy, large logistical efforts to sustain the armed forces, even to swallow some of their independent notions as the Confederacy became a nation at war. And they learned to die.

True, the nineteenth century did have a focus on the hereafter, and people trooped to churches for solace against sin, but the war brought death closer than Sunday, closer than fear, until it lurked in the corner of every mind.

1001 The South did not lose because of these lessons, nor did it lose because it abandoned hope. It lost because it learned war too well. It mobilized, organized, built factories and engines and cannon and guns, lived on soft money, on the illusion of King Cotton, until it had sent most of its men, its treasure, to the cold altar of sacrifice—and there was nothing more to send.

The Confederacy was exhausted, then defeated.

INDEX

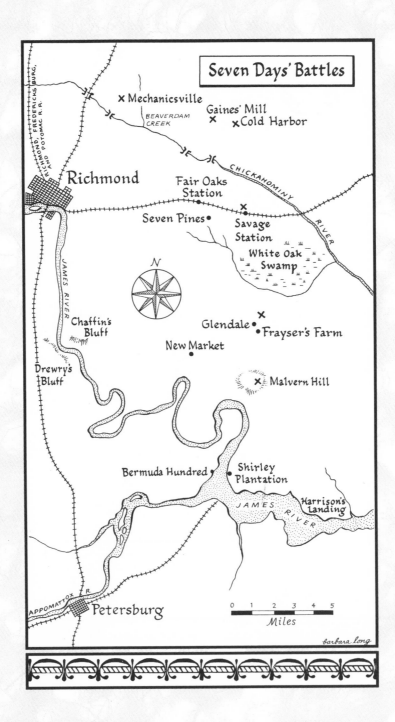

Seven Days' Battles